# Anna Freud

## A view of development, disturbance and therapeutic techniques

## Rose Edgcumbe

London and Philadelphia

First published 2000 by Routledge
11 New Fetter Lane, London EC4P 4EE

Simultaneously published in the USA and Canada
by Taylor & Francis Inc., 325 Chestnut Street, Philadelphia, PA 19106

Routledge is an imprint of the Taylor & Francis Group

Typeset in Times by Mayhew Typesetting
Printed and bound in Great Britain by St Edmundsbury Press,
Bury St Edmunds, Suffolk

British Library Cataloguing in Publication Data
A catalogue record for this book is available from the British Library

Library of Congress Cataloging in Publication Data

Edgcumbe, Rose, 1934–
 Anna Freud : a view of development, disturbance, and therapeutic
techniques / Rose Edgcumbe.
    p.  cm. — (Makers of modern psychotherapy)
 Includes bibliographical references and index.
 ISBN 0-415-10199-9 — ISBN 0-415-10200-6 (pbk.)
 1. Freud, Anna, 1895–  2. Child analysis.  I. Title.  II. Series.
 RC339.52.F73 E34 2000
 618.92'8917—dc21                                     99–056249

ISBN 0–415–10199–9 (hbk)
ISBN 0–415–10200–6 (pbk)

For all the graduates and friends of the
Hampstead Clinic, now the Anna Freud Centre

# Contents

# Acknowledgements

I am indebted to Laurence Spurling who asked me to write this book and was helpful and encouraging as I worked on it. Over the years I have discussed Anna Freud's ideas and work with many colleagues in the Anna Freud Centre (previously The Hampstead Clinic); they are too numerous to list, though some are mentioned in this book; I am grateful to all of you with whom I have enjoyed fruitful discussion. I am especially indebted to Clifford Yorke and Hansi Kennedy who thought over past history with me while I was writing the book, and to Anne Hurry who read a draft and made clarifying suggestions. For the conclusions I have come to, however, nobody is to blame except myself.

I would like to thank the following: Mark Paterson and Associates on behalf of The Estate of Anna Freud for permission to reproduce extracts from *Infants Without Families* by Anna Freud, *Reports on the Hampstead War Nurseries* by Anna Freud and *Normality and Pathology in Childhood* by Anna Freud, Copyright © 1965, 1973 Anna Freud; Extracts from *The Writings of Anna Freud, Vols 1, 4, 5, 7 & 8, Psychoanalytic Study of the Child, Vol. 21*, and *The Analysis of Defence* by Sandler and Freud reproduced by permission of Mark Paterson and Associates on behalf of The Estate of Anna Freud (UK and Commonwealth) and International Universities Press (US); the Institute of Psycho-Analysis and the Hogarth Press for permission to quote from *Instincts and Vicissitudes* (1915) from the *Standard Edition of the Complete Psychological Works of Sigmund Freud*, translated and edited by James Strachey, Sigmund Freud © Copyrights, the Institute of Psycho-Analysis and the Hogarth Press (UK and Commonwealth) and Mark Paterson and Associates (US); Routledge for permission to reproduce quotes from *Journal of Child Psychotherapy* [see http://www.tandf.co.uk], volume 21, 'Memories of a "qualified student"' by Erna Furman; Yale University Press (New Haven and London) for permission to use an extract from *The Psychoanalytic Study of the Child*, volume 39: 1984. Peter Neubauer, 'Anna Freud's Concept of Developmental Lines', p.15; Sheil Land Associates Ltd for material from *Anna Freud* by E. Young Bruehl (© Elizabeth Young Bruehl 1988), London, Macmillan.

# Chapter 1

# Introduction

## Three questions about Anna Freud's work

Anna Freud's work is a mine of information and insight for anyone interested in understanding the vagaries of human development. It is of special value to all who have care of children, whether as parents or professionals. Anna Freud combined a powerful intellect and questioning mind with a keen capacity for observation.

My aim in this book is to describe Anna Freud's innovative and still relevant work in the observation, upbringing and care of children, as well as in child psychoanalysis. I especially want to stress the interaction between her clinical observation and her interest in developing the structural theory of her father. She was an adult analyst who maintained a large practice in addition to her other work throughout her life; and she played an important role in psychoanalytic training for work with adults first in Vienna and then in London. But her earliest papers concerned her work with children, and she was one of the first people to explore the possibilities of psychoanalysing children. It was from children that she gained many of the insights which she incorporated into her contributions to psychoanalytic theory. Her major influence on the theory and technique of clinical work with adults also derives from the understanding of human development which grew out of her immense experience with children. Yet the extent of her influence is not always recognised; and in trying to understand this, I wish to consider three questions.

**Question 1:** *Why did she not accept 'developmental help' – her own innovative approach to deficiency disorders – as a legitimate part of psychoanalytic technique?*

Her developmental theories gave rise to innovations in technique for work with children suffering from developmental deficiencies. She modestly called these techniques 'developmental help', and they were elaborated by generations of her students in the Hampstead Child Psychotherapy Course. Many of us who were her students would now consider this developmental help to be an essential part of child analytic technique in many of the cases we treat today. Further, similar considerations of developmental deficiencies have given rise to modifications of technique in psychoanalytic work with adults suffering from borderline, psychotic and some narcissistic disorders, and Anna Freud's ideas have certainly had some influence in this area. Yet she herself seemed, to many of us who worked with her, doubtful whether these innovations could be considered a legitimate part of the main body of psychoanalytic technique. Instead, she considered them to be a useful extra tool for patients not suited to 'proper' psychoanalysis.

**Question 2:** *Why is she still thought of as a drive theorist only, in spite of her excellent theory of object relations?*

In the debate about what motivates human behaviour, Anna Freud continues to be labelled as a 'drive theorist', although it is evident that she also placed great emphasis on object relations as sources of motivation for development. Her work on development contains a very clear and detailed theory of the development of object relations. It is to be found in her 'developmental lines'; and in many papers her formulations about the development of ego and superego, of impulse control, of thinking, and of the management of emotions, all stress the central importance of the child's relationships, as does her theory of technique. If forced to choose she would no doubt have opted to be counted among those who take drives rather than object relations as the primary motivating force in human behaviour. But she would, I believe, have seen no reason to make such a choice, given that both are important.

I do not claim to have complete answers to these two questions, which are not merely of historical interest, although part of the answer may be historical, and links with the third question.

**Question 3:** *Why is she not better known?*

Her work is not commonly recognised in Britain, and is more widely accepted among analysts in the USA as well as Europe. Yet Anna Freud's work is as relevant today as it ever was, since it offers avenues of approach to understanding and managing the children whose difficult behaviour can create havoc in schools, who become violent, murderous, delinquent or promiscuous, vandalise schools and the areas where they live, or turn to substance abuse. It also offers understanding and ways of treating those who create trouble not for others but for themselves, through crippling anxieties, failure in their schoolwork, inability to cope with social relationships and situations, or incapacity for work. Both groups of children may suffer difficulties in their sexual partnerships and in parenting in later life, because of their anxieties, inadequacies or immaturities, and her work offers ways of helping such individuals as parents, too.

I believe we can go some way towards answering my three questions by examining Anna Freud's relationship with her father's work, and her way of handling controversies within the British Psychoanalytic Society. To put it in a vastly oversimplified way: Anna Freud's loyalty to Sigmund Freud's drive and structural theories, in which instinctual drives are seen as the motivating force for all human behaviour, meant that when writing or speaking theoretically she formulated all her ideas about relationships in terms of drive theory and ego functioning. She believed that those who propounded new theories of object relations were in danger of abandoning drive theory, which she regarded as the bedrock of psychoanalysis. Her own object relationships theory was essentially an attachment theory, similar to Bowlby's in many ways. She recognised this, but also clarified the differences in a discussion of Bowlby's work (Freud, A. 1969a). Her stress is not merely on the importance of the child's external attachments but on the effect of these real external relationships on the child's inner world of self–object relations. She was among those in the analytic community who for many years regarded Bowlby's work with suspicion, feeling that he had abandoned psychoanalysis. Time has softened such extreme positions, and Bowlby's work is now better valued in the psychoanalytic community.

I do not think it was simply fear of appearing to side with those who abandoned drive theory which motivated her. Rather, she genuinely thought that the development of relationships could be adequately explained by taking drives as the primary motivating forces, and aspects of ego and superego functioning as the modifiers of relationships. Her own formulations in these terms are elegant and clear. Moreover, in her later works there does seem to be a gradual shift in the relative importance she accorded to object relations and drives. But her overall adherence to theories which have come to be considered, rightly or wrongly, as outmoded is one reason for her lack of prominence among the psychoanalytic writers of today in this country.

By the time Anna Freud formulated her later theoretical conceptualisations she was doing so very succinctly, often without illustrative material. Her writings are often deceptively simple, but actually so densely packed that they can be difficult to unravel without the experience of observation and clinical work on which she based them. The illustrations of some of this experience are to be found in her early writings, for example, on the war nurseries and on defence, but relatively little in her later writings. Here she differed from Melanie Klein, who continued to publish many case histories. Other reasons include her withdrawal from arguments in the British Psychoanalytic Society, and the fact that she was probably not by nature given to proselytising. Her biographer, Elizabeth Young-Bruehl, also suggests possible political and class differences between Anna Freud and the British Society into which Melanie Klein had become integrated, which would have influenced their scientific style (Young-Bruehl 1988, p. 178).

## Biographical note

This book is not a biography of Anna Freud; it is a book about her work, especially as a child analyst, especially in Britain, and especially those aspects of it which are most innovative. It is my personal attempt to evaluate her work, which spans six decades, and to understand and try to reconcile some of the contradictory elements in it. I became her student at the Hampstead Clinic in 1959, and a member of her staff in 1963, so I know the major part of her work only from reading and being taught by those already familiar with it. But I was more directly involved in the last two decades of her work as it developed. It has been an illuminating and sometimes surprising experience to re-evaluate work I thought I knew well.

For those who wish to read about Anna Freud's life there is a good biography by Elisabeth Young-Bruehl (1988). For those who want more information about her work in Vienna there is a detailed study by Uwe Henrik Peters (1985). Peter Heller (1990) gives an account of his experience as one of her child patients in

Vienna. For those interested in the relationship of her work to that of her father, there is Raymond Dyer's (1983) book. For those wishing to place her pioneering work with children in the historical context of the development of child analysis, there is now an English-language translation of a history by two French analysts, Claudine and Pierre Geissman (1998). There is a short introduction to her work by Clifford Yorke (1997) published only in French. A useful study guide to a selection of some of her main papers, with editorial introductions which help to guide the reader through each paper, has recently been produced by Ekins and Freeman (1998).

Here, I give only enough detail to place Anna Freud in her professional and cultural context. Born in Vienna in 1895, the youngest of Martha and Sigmund Freud's six children, she was the only one to become a psychoanalyst. In clinical discussions she would occasionally joke about the ambitiousness of youngest children. Her first training and work was as a teacher, and she soon became involved in attempts to improve the lives of socially and economically deprived children, especially in the aftermath of the First World War. She began psychoanalytic work in the early 1920s. As well as working with adults she joined the very small band of those developing ways of working with children. Her father's illness with cancer precipitated her into taking unexpected administrative responsibilities in the Vienna Psychoanalytic Institute. Her first book on child analysis was published in German in 1927, but was fiercely attacked by Klein and other British analysts (Peters 1985, pp. 94–100), and rejected for publication in Britain by the International Psycho-analytical Library, where Melanie Klein's influence was great enough to suppress rival theories at that time. Klein, together with other Berlin analysts, had been invited to come to England in the 1920s and had been integrated into the British Society.

The rise of the Nazis made life increasingly difficult for the Viennese analysts. The Freud family fled to England in 1938 following the Nazi *anschluss* into Vienna. Ernest Jones, President of the British Psychoanalytic Society, was instrumental in assisting the escape of the Freuds and other Viennese analysts, who were welcomed into the British Society. When, subsequently, theoretical and clinical disagreements arose between the groups of analysts led by Anna Freud and Melanie Klein, they led to the 'Controversial Discussions' (King and Steiner 1991), a series of meetings in which views were expounded and discussed. But differences were not resolved, and led to the creation of different streams of training to reflect the differing views. Because Anna Freud was grateful to the British Society for helping her family and others to escape and find homes and work in this country, she felt it would have been improper to respond to such kindness with further overt quarrelling (Freud, A. 1979a). So although she remained an important member of the British Society, to some extent she withdrew from it, preferring to become less prominent. She continued to live and work in London until her death in 1982.

## Views on theory and technique

Anna Freud was also extremely aware of the dangers of 'wild analysis': the application of imperfectly understood theory by insufficiently trained people who might misunderstand or misuse classical technique, thereby doing their patients more harm than good. She believed, further, that any departure from classical technique must be based on a careful assessment of the clinical state of the patient, and used only after scrutiny of existing techniques had revealed a gap which needed to be filled by a modified or new technique. She was also aware that throughout the history of psychoanalysis there had been those who found it difficult to accept the full depth of psychoanalytic understanding of unconscious conflict, and were therefore eager to find more superficial ways of understanding and treating emotional disturbances, especially in children. I believe that all these considerations went into her rationale for her careful distinction between the interpretative techniques of psychoanalysis and the more educative techniques of developmental help. The latter seemed to come perilously close to the 'corrective emotional experience' proposed by Alexander (1948) and disapproved of by mainstream psychoanalysts.

In the chapters which follow I will begin by discussing Anna Freud's first major contribution to psychoanalytic theory, her book on defences, which was for years the definitive text on defences, and remains a standard text even today (Freud, A. 1936). This book signalled Anna Freud's focus on Sigmund Freud's structural theory (Freud, S. 1923). Her interest in developing this theory, and in particular her elaboration of the development and structuralisation of the ego can be traced through all her subsequent work, reaching another high point in her diagnostic profile (Freud, A. 1962a), and leading into her work on the developmental lines,

which examined the myriad small strands of intertwining maturation and development which contribute to the growth of the human
personality.

I will then describe her early work as a teacher and director of
nursery schools and residential nurseries. The systematic observations made by all staff became the basis for her first formulations
about the developmental needs of children, including the need for
stable relationships with parents, and for her formulations on the
way in which the effects of relationships become built into the child's
psyche (Freud and Burlingham 1944).

The clarity and power of theoretical conceptualisation and the
careful, detailed and open-minded observation of children are
the two bases on which is founded all Anna Freud's subsequent
work on the internal world of the child.

The early work influenced her ideas on how child analysis could
be conducted, one of the areas which led her into disagreements
with the Kleinian school of thought. One of the issues I particularly
wish to examine is Anna Freud's view of the importance of the
child's experience with his parents, and the importance of involving
them in the child's therapy. This view was based on her awareness
of the complex development of the child's relationships and the
myriad developments in other areas of the child's functioning
which depend on the child's relationships with his parents. This
was one of the areas of contrast with Klein's theory and practice of
child analysis which Anna Freud felt to be insufficiently respectful
of the role of parents, concentrating as it did on the child's internal
world of fantasy to the exclusion of external factors.

Subsequent chapters will describe how these early ideas were
developed largely through the research and study groups of the
Hampstead Child Therapy Course and Clinic, a charitable centre
with the threefold aims of supporting psychoanalytic training for
child psychotherapists, psychoanalytic treatment for children and
adolescents, and research into childhood development and disorders. This institution was founded following Anna Freud's partial
withdrawal from the British Psychoanalytic Society, to meet the
needs of workers in the war nurseries who wished to continue the
training they had begun there. This training has produced therapists
capable of working with children suffering from a wide range of
emotional disorders extending far beyond the neuroses for which
child psychoanalysis was originally deemed appropriate. Anna
Freud encouraged her colleagues and students to devise techniques

for working with children who could not respond to 'classical' psychoanalytic techniques, and needed 'developmental help' in order to progress. For much of her lifetime she doubted that these techniques could be considered truly analytic, seeing them, rather, as 'educational'. Yet she did not think that developmental help, as she envisioned it, could be provided by people without analytic training.

Her developmental profile, a diagnostic tool for the thorough assessment of childhood disturbances (Freud, A. 1962a, 1965a), emerged from the research work of the Hampstead Clinic, as did the developmental lines, which describe the stages a child passes through in a number of key areas of development, and which can be used for assessing the child's readiness for such life events as entry to school or nursery school, separation from parents, or coping with hospitalisation.

Further chapters will cover the later developments in her theories and the results of clinical research, and how these influenced her later views on technique. I will also consider the many ways in which her thinking was applied to professions other than psycho-analysis, since she never lost her more general interest in the well-being of children, or her wish to improve the ways they were looked after by all who had care of them.

After her death, The Hampstead Clinic was renamed the Anna Freud Centre. Her work is continued there. Recent years have seen the drawing together of research work by developmental psycho-logists and paediatricians with psychoanalytic observations. Followers of Melanie Klein and Anna Freud have been able to exchange ideas and work together. Bowlby's work is used in a major study on attachment in progress at the Centre. The wealth of clinical material collected because of Anna Freud's insistence on the importance of thorough recording is the subject of a retrospective study using over eight hundred cases, studying the efficacy of psychoanalytic treatment with different age groups and types of disturbance. Further studies on the technique of child analysis give due weight to what has eventually been renamed 'developmental therapy'. This current work is discussed in a final chapter which considers Anna Freud's legacy to those who work in many capacities with both normal and disturbed children.

# Chapter 2

# The basic theory

The richness of Anna Freud's contributions to psychoanalytic thought derives from the fertile interaction between the clarity of her theoretical conceptualisation and her capacity for penetrating observation. Like her father, she was aware of the extreme complexity of human development and functioning. While apparently simple 'rules of thumb' can be derived from the theories of both Sigmund and Anna Freud, a more complete understanding of theory is required for real clinical competence. Many therapists, however, find it hard to grasp the need for extensive theory, preferring to think of clinical work as somehow separate from theory. This may be another reason for the lack of popularity of Anna Freud's work among those who prefer a simpler approach. But her work makes clear the inadequacies of the simpler approach. Her 1936 book *The Ego and the Mechanisms of Defence* and her 1965 book on *Normality and Pathology in Childhood* in particular demonstrate how important it is to make a careful, all-round assessment of all factors involved in an individual's disturbance.

## ELABORATION OF SIGMUND FREUD'S CONCEPT OF THE EGO

This chapter sets out the early theoretical views which formed one of the two bases for Anna Freud's life work in psychoanalysis. In 1936 she published her first major contribution to psychoanalytic theory, *The Ego and the Mechanisms of Defence*. Some of the ideas it contains had already made an appearance in earlier (and controversial) works on the technique of child analysis, to which I will return in Chapter 4. But this book pulled together all the main strands of her thinking at that time. It set out a general theory of technique which remains a valid approach today, and became a classic text on defence. It also introduced her knowledge of child development derived from direct observation and work with children. This was a valuable addition to psychoanalytic theories of human development which, until the advent of child analysis, had been based on reconstruction from the analyses of adults.

The book served many co-workers as a basis for subsequent elaboration of their thinking about defence. In particular it was used to develop the Manual on Defence in the Hampstead Index. This was a project set up by Dorothy Burlingham and Anna Freud, and chaired for many years by Professor Joseph Sandler. Its aims were to develop headings under which case material could be broken down to facilitate comparative research studies, to assist in finding suitable examples for teaching purposes, and to refine theoretical concepts.

Over thirty-five years later the book was discussed in an Index research group on defences chaired by Professor Joseph Sandler (Sandler and Freud 1985). These discussions further clarified developments in Anna Freud's theories, including the way in which she viewed object relations within her theoretical framework, and the implications for technique.

Extending Sigmund Freud's structural theory (Freud, S. 1923), Anna Freud followed through his line of thought that psycho-analytic attention needed to be extended from the study of the unconscious wishes, impulses and feelings which are the manifestations of instinctual drives to the study of the ego. 'Ego' is the English/Latin translation for the German 'Ich', Freud's term for that part of the personality closest to what the individual recognises as his self. It is also largely unconscious and has the role of mediating between id, superego and external world. 'Id' is another English/Latin translation from the German 'Es' = 'it': a term which also carries childlike or primitive connotations, and which refers to the instinctual drives. 'Superego' is the individual's conscience, which develops out of the ego. The 'external world' is the individual's environment, most especially people who are important to him.

Both Sigmund and Anna Freud emphasised the importance in human functioning of the pleasure principle: the natural tendency to seek pleasure, i.e. gratification and satisfaction of needs, wishes and impulses, and to avoid unpleasure, i.e. frustration, anxiety and pain (Freud, S. 1911, 1915). Conflicts arise the moment seeking pleasure and avoiding pain ceases to be a simple, unidimensional matter, for example, when two pleasurable aims conflict (the child realises he cannot satisfy his greed and get his mother's approval; or he cannot vent his rage on someone who has frustrated him because he also wants to keep that person unharmed); or when unpleasurable happenings he would prefer to avoid (injections, hair washing) are presented as necessities by someone whom the child wants to please; or when pain unexpectedly results from something the child had anticipated as pleasurable (getting bruised in a fall while enjoying climbing over furniture; getting burned by something attractive but hot). In all such situations the child has to come to terms with reality and work at finding compromise solutions between his various wishes and needs; this is the work of the ego.

Anna Freud's interest in the development of the ego linked her with Heinz Hartmann (Freud, A. 1966b; Hartmann 1939, 1950a, 1950b, 1952) and a group of like minded European analysts who emigrated to the US, and became known as 'Ego Psychologists'. This was a misnomer, since they were, like Anna Freud, interested in all aspects of personality development as conceptualised in psychoanalytic theory. But perhaps the misnomer reflects the fear addressed by Anna Freud when she discussed the view held at the time by many analysts that the only proper subject of analysis is the unconscious id (Freud, A. 1936 pp. 3–4), and expected to be criticized for her emphasis on the importance of analysing the ego (Sandler and Freud 1985, pp. 6–7). She, together with Hartmann and his colleagues, were, however, successful in making the analytic community aware of the necessity not only of analysing the ego and superego as well as the id, but also issues of adjustment to the outside world, the social setting in which the individual lives.

## THE TECHNICAL IMPORTANCE OF DEFENCE ANALYSIS

In her book, she made a persuasive case for the technical importance of defence analysis. She described the ego as 'the seat of observation', i.e. that part of the personality which scans the internal world: thoughts, wishes, feelings and impulses arising from the id, as well as the superego's reactions to these. The ego also anticipates reactions from people in the external world, and the likely results of expression of these id manifestations. All this is assessed by the ego which has to decide whether to allow a thought, wish, feeling or impulse to be expressed or acted upon, or whether to institute defence against unacceptable expressions of the id. She described how the structures of the personality work in harmony when there is no conflict, for example, when the superego does not disapprove of an impulse or wish, and the ego finds it safe to allow expression to the impulse. Under such circumstances the divisions of the personality cannot easily be distinguished. They are more obvious when conflict arises, and the person develops anxiety or symptoms (Freud, A. 1936, pp. 5–8). In analysis such conflictual areas are flagged by the appearance of resistance: the patient's free associations dry up, or he ignores or dismisses without consideration the analyst's interpretations. It is, therefore, as important to explore the patient's defences, and other ego and superego reactions, as it is to explore the id impulses which have provoked these reactions.

Anna Freud was well aware that to talk about the ego 'anticipating' and 'deciding', or the superego 'disapproving' and 'forbidding', is to personify what are really simply aspects of a single personality. But she found such formulations useful for clarifying the concept of internal conflict within the mind of the individual (e.g. Sandler and Freud 1985, pp. 33, 284–285, 537). In more technical terms impulses and wishes were described as 'ego-syntonic' when they are acceptable to the ego, and 'ego-dystonic' when they arouse anxiety because they are perceived as unsafe in some way, might be unwelcome to people whom the individual loves, or likely to be disapproved of by the superego.

## NEW DEFENCES

Anna Freud listed and described the defences already uncovered by Sigmund Freud: repression, regression, reaction formation, isolation, undoing, projection, introjection, turning against the self, reversal, and sublimation (Freud, A. 1936, pp. 42–44). She then went on to add several new ones of her own, notably identification with the aggressor (pp. 109–121), and altruism (pp. 122–134), which may be seen as more precise ways of defining certain forms of 'projective identification' – a Kleinian concept which has become so all-embracing as to be more confusing than helpful. She also described denial, a common defence in young children.

## Identification with the aggressor

Anna Freud gives a series of examples of identification with the aggressor ranging in complexity from simple attempts to master anxiety about frightening reality events, to more complex examples in which the use of this defence mechanism has a role in superego development. Among the more simple examples, she describes a 6-year-old boy patient who reacted to painful dental treatment by cutting up and breaking various items in the analytic treatment room. The same child arrived very distressed one day after an accident at games in which he bumped into the games master and cut his lip. The following session he came dressed and armed as a soldier. In both episodes the boy finds an active way of become the aggressor to deal with the anxiety and narcissistic mortification caused by painful incidents which felt to him like being attacked. These were examples from analysis, but Anna Freud notes that children's play commonly includes similar attempts at active mastery of passive experiences: playing at doctors, dentists, angry schoolteachers telling off stupid pupils, or parents scolding bad children (1936, pp. 111–114).

She goes on to describe a stage in the development of the superego when the child criticises or attacks other people in order to forestall criticism or punishment he expects for his own activities: for example, a child who became aggressive in his play when he was anxious about masturbation, for which he anticipated punishment. He was behaving in the punitive way he expected from adults (ibid., pp. 114–116). This indicates a stage in superego development when the child has not yet developed fully internalised self-criticism, but is still looking for someone else to blame. Here, identification with the aggressor is supplemented by projection of guilt. Anna Freud notes that 'true morality' begins when the ego accepts its own fault, i.e. becomes self-critical instead of finding fault in others (ibid., p. 119).

## Denial

She also elaborated several forms of denial: in fantasy, word and act (ibid., pp. 69–92). This defence, very common in children, is directed not against the child's instinctual wishes and feelings but against painful realities, such as the child's small size, relative helplessness, incompetence or impotence. Anna Freud cited 'Little Hans' (Freud, S. 1909) as well as cases of her own. For example, a 7-year-old boy who denied his Oedipal fear of his father by elaborating a day-dream in which he owned a tame lion, harmless as long as he kept it under control, but which would terrify other people if they knew about it. Anna Freud notes that this kind of fantasy is common in fairy-tales about young men who are helped by wild animals to overcome a powerful king or other father figure. This means of dealing with the unwelcome reality of not being big, powerful or strong enough is common in early childhood, but if not superseded in later development can lead to disturbance in reality-testing (Freud, A., pp. 74–80).

Denial in word and act is also common in children's games, in which they play at being various admired grown-ups, for example, wearing father's hat or mother's shoes, pretending to drive a car or go shopping; or more adventurously commanding a space ship or running an office. These games may also be understood as the child's way of learning about and practising becoming grown-up. Adults often support these efforts of the child to feel big, but also expect the child to be able to step out of the fantasy role and back into reality: stopping the game when it is time for tea or bed. A child who cannot make that transition is on the way to pathological rather than normal development (ibid., pp. 83–92).

Anna Freud recognised such defensive denials of reality as manifestations of the small child's subservience to the pleasure principle. Normally this search for pleasure is gradually modified by the reality principle as the ego develops the capacity for reality-testing. The individual comes to understand why some things are not safe and others are disapproved of. He also develops frustration tolerance: the ability to wait in the knowledge that the pleasure or success will come in the future. The child comes to recognise the inadequacy of denial and adds other defences and adaptations to his repertoire.

In the years following the publication of Anna Freud's book, more and more forms of defence were recognised. In the Hampstead Index an attempt was made to differentiate between the basic defence mechanisms she delineated, and 'defensive measures' which came to include almost any form of behaviour which has a defensive purpose (unpublished Index Manual on Defence). Following this line of exploration to its logical conclusion, Charles Brenner (1982) deduced that there are no separate defence mechanisms, only ego functions which can serve defensive, as well as other purposes. Numerous alternative theories of defence have been put forward according to whether they are set in the context of instinct/structural theory, object relations theory or self-psychology (for a survey see Cooper 1989).

In the 1972/1973 discussions Anna Freud and Joseph Sandler took the view that any existing capacities and abilities can all be used defensively, i.e. as further defensive measures in addition to the main mechanisms (Sandler and Freud 1985, p. 134f.). She thought that some defences are more primitive than others. Sigmund Freud had already described how instinctual vicissitudes, such as turning around on the self and reversal of aim, can develop into defences; also how primitive id processes such as projection and introjection, which initially contribute to the recognition of boundaries between self and other, can come to be used defensively (Freud, S. 1915; Freud, A. 1936, pp. 43–44; Sandler and Freud 1985, pp. 111f., 138, 537). Later defences may be built on abilities of the ego. For example, mastery, originally a normal, pleasurable way the child exercises various developing physical and intellectual capacities, may also be used defensively to ward off feelings of helplessness or incompetence (Sandler and Freud 1985, pp. 134f.).

## SOURCES OF ANXIETY: INTERNAL AND EXTERNAL

A particularly important section of the book is her clarification of the sources of anxiety which lead to defence, based on Sigmund Freud's distinctions (Freud, S. 1926). Anna Freud distinguished between fear of impulses, wishes and feelings in one's own inner world, and what she called 'objective anxiety': fear of the real anger or disapproval of parents, dislike of unpleasant things in the external world (Freud, A. 1936, pp. 54–65; Sandler and Freud 1985, pp. 263–265, 270–272, 317–320). This distinction leads into a developmental view of defence, in which children frequently defend against recognition of unpleasant external realities in ways which are normal for certain stages of childhood, but pathological if continued into adulthood, for example, denial in phantasy (Freud, A. 1936, pp. 69–82) and identification with the aggressor (pp. 109–

121). In the 1972/1973 discussions Anna Freud spoke of her wish to formulate a developmental line for defence (1985, p. 525). These discussions show that most of the elements for such a line were already present in her thinking (Sandler and Freud 1985, pp. 111f., 233f., 237f., 248–255, 340-347; see also Chapter 6).

## INTERNALISATION AND OBJECT RELATIONSHIPS

This distinction between sources of anxiety also allowed her to examine the way in which conflicts which originate between child and parent are gradually transformed into internalised conflicts between the child's own id, ego and superego (Freud, A. 1936, pp. 56–58; Sandler and Freud, pp. 317–318). Internalisation is an extremely important concept in Anna Freud's thinking. It refers to the process by which the child 'takes in' or identifies with and learns from other people. It also marks major differences between Anna Freud's conceptualisation of object relations and those of Melanie Klein and Fairbairn.

The psychoanalytic term 'object' has been criticised as a dehumanising way of referring to a person. The term derives from Sigmund Freud's discussion of the four main characteristics of instinctual drives: the *pressure*, which is the force of the drive, or the measure of the demand for mental work; the *aim*, which is to achieve satisfaction; the *source*, which lies in unknown somatic processes; and the *object*, which is the thing through which the instinct can achieve its aim. Freud said that the object 'is what is the most variable about an instinct and is not originally connected with it, but becomes assigned to it only in consequence of being peculiarly fitted to make satisfaction possible' (Freud, S. 1915, p. 122). The object may be frequently changed. Or the instinct may become 'fixated', i.e. become closely attached to a particular object early in development. Freud used the term 'object' because his emphasis was on whatever served to satisfy the drive, and he did not envisage exclusively other human beings, but also parts of the subject's own body, or of the object's body, or even inanimate objects, as in fetishism (Freud, S. 1915, pp. 122f.). His further discussion makes it clear, however, that human objects were what he mostly had in mind when discussing the vicissitudes and development of instincts (ibid., pp. 127–140).

In one way or another most subsequent analysts became interested in the role of the object in its own right, not merely as an
adjunct to the drives. Anna Freud retained the link between drive
satisfaction and the finding of an external object, unlike Fairbairn,
who disagreed with Freud's emphasis on drives as motivators of
behaviour, and substituted the pressures of relationships as the
principal motivators. Anna Freud's conceptualisation also differed
from that of Melanie Klein who also retained drive theory, but
linked it more closely with internal fantasy objects than with real,
external people.

Anna Freud was interested in the role played by parents and
other important people in the shaping of the child's developing ego
and superego, and the way in which a child gradually builds the
wishes, prohibitions and attitudes of these external objects into his
own internal world, so that it becomes part of his own personality.
Thus she extended the conceptualisation of the object by giving it a
role in ego and superego building, consequent upon its necessity
for drive satisfaction. The child needs the parent to look after him,
and out of that need grows love.

Thus a child may initially curb impulses such as greed, aggression
or sexual excitement because he wishes to please a parent who
disapproves of such behaviour, or because he fears punishment. But
gradually these object-related reactions become built into the child's
own moral code, or superego, and develop into feelings of guilt. The
child then begins to experience as conflict within himself what was
initially a conflict with someone in the external world. Anna Freud
differentiates such 'internalised' conflicts from the fears and conflicts which occur within the individual's own mind from his earliest
days, i.e. which have always been 'internal'. These include the
primitive anxiety aroused by the strength of instincts and needs
which threaten to become overwhelming and unmanageable to an
immature ego, as well as the conflicts which may arise between
incompatible instincts (Freud, S. 1926; Freud, A. 1965a, p. 145).

Other important forms of internalisation influence ego development as the child learns from his parents and other adults, sometimes consciously, sometimes unconsciously. He not only imitates
the way his parents go about their everyday work and play, their
mannerisms and speech; he also identifies with their ways of
relating to others, their preferred modes of defence, and their ways
of coping with problems and traumatic events; and he tunes into
their emotional reactions.

Anna Freud's awareness of the minutiae of processes of internal-isation derived from her work with babies and small children (see Chapter 3). Internalisation is a concept which places object rela-tions at the centre of development, but not as a substitute for instinct theory or structural theory. Anna Freud used the develop-ment of object relations as an additional dimension in under-standing structural development. The effects of relationships have to be understood as they influence the internal world, especially the development of identifications which strengthen the ego, and introjections which help to build up the superego.

In the 1972/1973 discussions her views on the importance of the child's relationships were clarified, as she stated her view that we have not neglected object relations, which are 'almost the most basic subject for us' (Sandler and Freud 1985, pp. 190f.). She particularly discussed the role of objects in superego development, as well as in ego development (pp. 146–156, 510–513).

These discussions also clarified how her drive/structural frame-work can be linked with the self–object representation theory of Sandler, who described the building up of successive mental rep-resentations of objects and self into an internal 'representational world' as a crucial function of the ego (ibid., pp. 57–59).

Her discussion of the child's experiences of helplessness in the face of overwhelming inner experiences as well as external events stressed the role of the object in protecting the child from these experiences. This is particularly relevant for her thinking on developmental help (ibid., pp. 469f.), as is the discussion of defence against narcissistic hurt (ibid., p. 529) and against the disruption of feeling states, where the individual may use defences which change the feeling state, or may use defences aimed at avoiding whatever produced the feelings (ibid., pp. 532–535).

## FORMS OF TRANSFERENCE

She also contributed several clarifications to the understanding of different forms of transference, for example, distinguishing between transference and other initial reactions in therapy such as ordinary caution about a stranger, or anxiety about a new situation (ibid., p. 64). Another distinction is that between the externalisation on to the analyst of an aspect of internal conflict (e.g. assigning a super-ego role to the analyst, who is then perceived as being the one who opposes the patient's wishes, so that the patient need not acknowledge his own conscience), and the transference of a past object relationship (e.g. one in which the parent might, in reality, have opposed the patient's wishes) (ibid., p. 137). Perhaps most importantly she distinguished between the transference of defence and resistance. Patients transfer on to the analyst not only impulses, wishes and feelings towards objects, but also the defences they normally use against them; in the transference these defences inhibit the full expression of the unconscious as they do in real life. This differs from the resistance to free association which is specific to the therapeutic situation in which the analyst encourages the patient to reveal things he normally does not allow himself or other people to know about (Freud, A. 1936, pp. 13–23; Sandler and Freud 1985, p. 41; see also Chapter 6).

## EGO RESTRICTION

An extremely important contribution is her distinction between inhibition of an impulse (a neurotic defence) and ego restriction: a more drastic reaction to anxiety in which the individual gives up whole areas of ego functioning such as perceiving, thinking, learning or remembering. This outcome had already been adumbrated in an earlier discussion of the loss of curiosity and imagination in latency children (Freud, A. 1930, pp. 112–113). In 1936 she discussed it in greater detail (Freud, A. 1936, pp. 93–105; Sandler and Freud 1985, pp. 358–364). The concept of ego restriction, introduced as early as 1936, was to be elaborated in her later work on developmental deficit, in which ego functioning may become stunted. There is here an important consequence for technique: inhibitions may be lifted by interpretation of the underlying conflict and the functioning thereby restored; but ego restriction results in there being no functioning to restore; it is a developmental distortion such that developmental help is required to set the functioning going again before the original conflicts can be meaningfully addressed (Edgcumbe 1995; Fonagy et al. 1993). The nub of developmental help is the distinction between 'making conscious' in the sense of lifting repression, and 'making conscious' in the sense of helping the patient acquire a previously non-existent representation (Sandler and Freud 1985, pp. 70–72). Ego restriction is another example of a normal process whose defensive use may become pathological. In normal development people have to make choices between activities and occupations. Any child may choose to avoid some things he is not good at but develop his capacities in other areas. The process only becomes damaging to personality development when too many possibilities are ruled out (ibid., pp. 364–374).

## TRANSFORMATION OF AFFECT

A further important contribution was her discussion of the transformation of affects, especially important in child analysis where the observation of changes in feelings, inappropriate or absent feelings can give clues to the motives and development of the child's disturbance. This helps to fill in the gaps left by the child's failure to free associate, or sometimes even to play or talk in any way that may reveal the dynamics of his underlying difficulties. Nowadays most therapists take for granted the importance of exploring a patient's feelings. But at the time Anna Freud wrote her book, 'defence against affect was not really talked about . . . affect was considered as an accompaniment to the drive or as a drive derivative, and it was more or less taken for granted that the defence was directed against the drive and not the affect'. In the later discussion it was also clarified that not all feelings and emotions are derived from drives; they arise for many reasons (Freud, A. 1936, pp. 31–41, 61–64; Sandler and Freud 1985, pp. 81–84).

There are a number of other issues raised in her 1936 book which will be discussed in later chapters, such as her views on the development of aggression, and her impressive early contribution to the psychology of adolescence, in particular the new defences such as intellectualisation and asceticism which arise in response to the renewed battle with the instincts, and the changes in superego and ego ideals as a result of the struggle to relinquish the infantile objects (Freud, A. 1936, pp. 152–172).

It was Anna Freud's early interest in the functioning and development of the ego which was to lead her into the areas of major importance in her later work: the study of the interacting factors involved in development, the delineation of psychopathology based on deficit rather than conflict, and the different therapeutic techniques required for such pathology.

# Chapter 3

# Observation

The observational material discussed in this chapter is a *sine qua non* for full understanding of Anna Freud's theories. It merits thorough study because here we can see the buildup of understanding which went into her later theoretical formulations in the developmental profile and the developmental lines (see Chapters 5 and 6), her final formulations about types of psychopathology and her theory of technique (see Chapter 7). Without these observations, or one's own equivalent experience, it can be difficult to understand the intricacies of her theories or why they are so important.

Anna Freud was a teacher by profession before she became a psychoanalyst, and the two interests are combined in her work. In the introduction to the first volume of her collected works she speaks of Vienna as 'a fertile ground for the analytic study of normal child development and for the application of these new findings to education' (Freud, A. 1974a, p. viii). She was inspired by Siegfried Bernfeld, and valued colleagues such as August Aichhorn, Editha Sterba and Willie Hoffer. Though not politically involved herself, she was interested in the views of social activists who believed that altering the environment is crucial to improving the psychic condition of children (Young-Bruehl 1988, pp. 177–178). Her awareness of social deprivation in Vienna in the 1920s and 1930s led to her involvement in setting up the Jackson nursery in 1937. As a Jew in 1930s Vienna, Anna Freud was not permitted to be in charge of any institution, so the nursery was set up with the assistance of influential American friends, Edith Jackson and Dorothy Burlingham. The venture ended with the rise of the Nazis, and the enforced emigration to Britain. Here the interest continued during the Second World War, when Anna Freud and her companion, Dorothy Burlingham, set up the war nurseries for children separated from their families by the death, illness, absence in the armed forces or on war work of their parents. They were among the pioneers who sought not merely to provide for the physical and educational needs of young children, but also for their emotional and psychological needs.

What makes this work unique is the collection and scrutiny of literally hundreds of detailed written observations by all the nursery workers, as part of their in-service training. These observations could be placed within an overall theoretical framework which was itself being modified and developed by the information gained from new observations. In Vienna Anna Freud had already given lectures to teachers and parents on the psychoanalytic view of development, education and upbringing. These had focused on infantile sexuality, the problems of bringing drives under control, and the development of a 'reasonable ego' and superego. They stressed the child's dependence on and love for his parents as motives for curbing instinctual behaviour (Freud, A. 1930, 1934). The papers on the war nursery material elaborated on more details of the development of attachments to parents and the results for all areas of ego and superego development. The observations facilitated the formulation of extremely detailed descriptions of the many intertwining constitutional, maturational and environmental factors which contribute to a child's development. This was at a time when little was written about the emotional needs of a child. Some mothers and teachers understood these intuitively, or had learned from close experience, but to many institutions, ideas which today seem commonplace then seemed revolutionary. For example, mothers who refused to let their children be evacuated alone were not being negligent of their children's safety, but mindful of their emotional health. Or parents should be encouraged to visit their children in residential placements and hospitals even if the children became upset and 'difficult' when the parents left. Or a child who ignores the arrival of a parent is not showing lack of concern, but deep hurt and mistrust. One of the pioneers in creating the post-war changes in hospital practice and later in foster care was James Robertson, who became the social worker in the war nurseries. He and his wife Joyce both helped in the early stages of setting up the nurseries.

The conclusions which may be drawn from the observations made in the 1940s are still insufficiently understood by many professionals who have to deal with children and adolescents suffering from a variety of personality defects and behaviour disorders resulting from the disruption or inadequacy of their early family relationships. As Anna Freud and Dorothy Burlingham wrote in 1974 (p. xviii):

> Infants are orphaned or torn away from their families for a variety of reasons such as death, illness, accident, divorce, financial disaster, i.e. through circumstances which occur at all times and in all strata of society. Wars merely favour and multiply the dissolution of family units and thereby bring into greater prominence the harmful effects of such breakdowns on the individual child.

The monthly reports on the war nurseries covering the period from February 1941 to December 1945 (Freud and Burlingham 1974) gave the initial summaries of observations on various themes as well as examples. These are then used in later papers which present more general conclusions. Most of these monthly reports were published for the first time in 1974. The only exception was report 12, published in 1942. The first major summary to be made from the reports was published as *Infants without Families* in 1944. A number of follow-up studies followed later (Kennedy 1950; Bennett and Hellman 1951; Burlingham 1952; Hellman 1962; Burlingham and Barron 1963). These were directly concerned with the children of the war nurseries. But apart from this, the work done during these years informed all the later developments in Anna Freud's thinking.

## THE EFFECTS ON DEVELOPMENT OF SEPARATION FROM PARENTS

*Infants without Families* compared the development of children raised in residential institutions with those raised in families. Both this book and the detailed monthly reports on which it was based focused on the children's reactions to separation from their parents, not only their directly expressed distress and longing, but the effects on many other areas of their behaviour and abilities. The very first report stressed that parents should visit as often as possible even though such visits ended in crying and upset, as these repeated shorter separations gave children more chance to overcome the shock and loss than being suddenly separated for the first time and not seeing mother again for weeks or months (Freud and Burlingham 1974, pp. 9–10). The reports gave many examples of reactions to separation, both the immediate distress and the longer term disruption of development. From these negative reactions the authors increased their understanding of the child's requirements for normal development. Over the years these increments in understanding built up into a detailed theory of the development of the child's attachment to objects, and the vital role of this attachment in the development of personality as well as in the areas of cognitive and emotional development. They also described the practical measures taken to minimise the damage to the children. But in 1974 they concluded: 'when we consider the case for or against residential upbringing as a whole, our verdict today is less favorable even than that pronounced 30 years ago' (ibid., p. xix).

## EXAMPLES OF REACTIONS TO SEPARATION

Many examples were given of initial reactions to separation. Monthly report 7, for example, stated that out of twenty-two toddlers there were only two who showed little overt sign of distress. Most children reacted with shock to the separation (ibid., pp. 81–86).

### Maggie

Maggie, aged 2 years 8 months, enjoyed the experience of the nursery for a few hours until she understood that it meant separation from her mother. She then broke down and cried incessantly. Visits from her mother aggravated her distress. She made violent but frequently changing attachments to teachers, and wanted to hold someone's hand all the time. After about two weeks she could let her favourite teacher leave the room for a time, and she began to enjoy her mother's visits without bursting into tears at every parting. After six weeks she seemed more settled (ibid., pp. 82–86).

### Derrick

Derrick, aged 2 years 6 months, became inseparable from a toy dog, Pat, he had brought from home, insisting that it should be cared for like another child. He seemed relatively happy for the first two days. He threw his first tantrum when his mother visited, alternately kissing, clinging, scolding and hitting her. He made her kiss and hug Pat. From then on he reacted angrily to any imaginary hurt to Pat and would throw himself on to the floor in despair if he accidentally dropped Pat. Anna Freud comments that Pat is a symbol of Derrick himself (ibid., pp. 82–83).

## Evelyn

A child whose development had already been seriously harmed was Evelyn, aged 3 years 3 months, who had been evacuated and had to change her billet six times for various reasons of maltreatment, illness in the foster-mother, etc. She was so bewildered or angry that she no longer recognised her own mother at first, although she recognised her father. She remained easily upset, with fits of crying alternating with laughing (ibid., pp. 85–86). Later reports mentioned her many changing fears and phobias, as well as compulsive behaviour. She tended to restrict her activities, and referred to herself in the third person. She would return from visits home with fantastic tales of frightening or aggressive happenings, but seemed withdrawn from interest in the real world (ibid., pp. 98–99, 206–207).

## Tony's developmental difficulties from age 2 years 9 months to 5 years

Longer descriptions were also given of a number of children whose progress was followed over many months or years, and whose developmental difficulties were especially instructive. Tony, for example, was admitted to New Barn, the country house, at age 2 years 9 months, in September 1941, following five or six changes of foster home because of his bedwetting – a symptom which disappeared as soon as he entered the nursery (ibid., pp. 240–243). He was delicate, charming and superficially friendly, but also frightened and lost, making no emotional contact with anybody. His father had left for the army when he was 8 months old, and he then lived alone with his mother until he was 2. She described him as a happy and carefree little boy during that time. But she fell ill with tuberculosis and had to enter a sanatorium. She made efforts to find him a good foster home but the arrangements broke down. She was distressed to find him becoming cowed and inhibited. Her letter to the nursery about him demonstrated her strong attachment to him and her efforts to do the right thing (ibid., pp. 113–116).

When Tony first entered the nursery he did everything he was told, and was no trouble to anybody. But he remained devoid of emotion, and for several weeks it was difficult to get near him. He then fell ill and a nurse cuddled him on her lap while taking his temperature. This position seemed to revive some pleasant experience and he became attached to her, asking frequently for his 'temperchure' (ibid., pp. 205–206). This attachment passed, but in December he contracted scarlet fever and was isolated with another nurse, Mary, in the sick-room for some weeks. This time the attachment deepened. He began to love Nurse Mary, lost his impersonal behaviour, and passionate character traits began to appear. He became clinging, jealous of other children, demanding her sole attention, continually afraid of losing her, frequently angry and resentful, accusing her of misdeeds. Bedtime was especially fraught: he would cry, tell Mary he did not like her, send her away, then want her back. He changed from an obedient child to one 'quite able to upset a whole bedroomful of children'. With the support of Anna Freud and Dorothy Burlingham, Nurse Mary weathered the storms and Tony gradually became more secure and intimate with her. He could allow her to do her work while he played elsewhere, needing only to know where she was and that he was free to run to her when he wanted (ibid., pp. 242–244). He began to tell her such memories as he had of home, for example, 'my daddy carried my mummy in his arms' (ibid., p. 244), possibly a memory of his mother's collapse with a haemorrhage while she and Tony were visiting father (ibid., p. 114). He helped Mary with her work, accepted that she had 'time off', and even helped her pack when she went away for a few days. Inevitably there were times of troubled moods when he slept badly and became more clinging and weepy. Bedwetting reappeared at such times. But he remained open, affectionate and in good contact. He enjoyed the postcards his father sent him (ibid., pp. 240–246).

Tony's mother was too ill ever to visit. The nursery sent her letters and reports about him, his father visited when on leave, and various uncles and aunts came (ibid., p. 242). In November, two months after Tony arrived, the outbreak of scarlet fever put the house in quarantine and visiting was stopped for three months (ibid., p. 121). During this time efforts were made to keep contact between parents and children via letters, parcels and messages. In February 1942, the arrival of the 'parents' bus' after a three-month break was a great event. Most children seemed 'to have managed the difficult task of maintaining a double relationship, to the parents on one hand and to the staff on the other', and soon became familiar again with their parents. Tony was visited by a sister of his mother, but he had met her rarely and was deeply distressed and upset. He lost the gains he had made and his face resumed its 'half-empty and wholly tragic expression' (ibid., p. 214). Tony's mother died in May 1942 (ibid., p. 240). He had not seen her for eighteen months. It was left to Tony's father to tell him (ibid., p. 246).

The father visited in July, when Tony was 3 years 6 months. Tony was friendly, but quiet and undemonstrative. It was several days before he told Mary: 'I have not got a mummy anymore.' He also explained that he had not wanted to talk to his father. He produced a fantasy which probably expressed his blaming father for mother's death, or his sense of being attacked by the news his father brought: 'I came here with my daddy and my daddy chucked a big stone at me and I cried, and I do not like my daddy anymore and I will never like him again.' This hostility persisted for several weeks, though he liked to hear Mary's stories about daddy. He developed a tendency to lose his precious possessions, including father's postcards. This is a common symptom in children who feel themselves 'lost'. He expected Mary to find these things for him. Otherwise his development seemed normal (ibid., pp. 296–300).

Tony did not see his father again for four months. Other relatives visited, with whom he was friendly but not affectionate. He seemed to prefer uncles to aunts and proudly showed them off to other children. The father had been invited to spend at least two nights with Tony in the country house when he had leave after three months. Tony's hostility had by now abated; he helped prepare father's room with great pleasure and excitement, and talked incessantly of the anticipated visit. But it was cancelled at the last minute as father had a fall and was admitted to hospital. Tony now began to talk about his father to other people as well as to Sister Mary. Two days in the sick-room brought back many (accurate) memories of a time nine months earlier when father had visited him in the sick-room.

Father finally visited when Tony was 3 years 11 months, and was greeted by Tony rushing towards him and jumping into his arms, very happy and affectionate. Father was accompanied by a young woman, introduced as his future wife. She tactfully removed herself after making friends with Tony. He talked freely, telling his father, 'I have not got any mummy, I have only you first and then my Mary'. He also asked many questions about father's life in the army. He slept in father's room and spent the days with him. He did not seem overtly jealous of the new woman, saying to Mary: 'The lady is coming to see me, Mary. She is nice, isn't she? My daddy says so.' He seemed able to be pleased for his father's happiness, but the lady meant nothing to him as a mother substitute. He told Mary: 'No, I don't want a lady, I want a mummy.' He continued to talk about real and imaginary activities and qualities of his father, and was especially impressed that his father had called him 'son' (ibid., pp. 296–305).

It seemed that Tony did come to like the idea of his prospective new mother, and he talked of going home to father and her after the war. He continued to improve, including being less clinging and demanding with Sister Mary, for example, sending her away more quickly to have her own supper after she had put him to bed. He made good friendships with other boys, and enjoyed all the occupations offered by the nursery school, workshop and garden. He was eager to enter primary school.

Then in April 1943, when Tony was aged 4 and 3 months, his father visited unexpectedly, bringing with him a different woman whom he had recently married, with no prior warning or explanation to Tony. Father told Tony to kiss his new mummy and both adults were astounded when Tony burst into tears. He managed to control himself and appear cheerful on this and subsequent visits; but with Mary he became regressed and clinging again, saying such things as: 'Mary, I don't want this mummy, I want my daddy to myself.'

During the Summer Tony digested his experiences. He went on a visit 'home', but on his return was unable to communicate anything about his experience there. With Mary he spoke of a worry: 'somebody told me that lots of soldiers will be dead when the war is over and then my daddy will be dead too and where shall I go home then?'

In the Autumn he began school a few months before he was 5 years old, and at first his development seemed to progress again.

But then once again he became clinging and demanding with Mary, with disturbances around bathing and bedtime, unable to be satisfied and settled whatever Mary did. His difficulty leaving Mary eventually extended to going to school.

Six months after the visit home he was finally able to explain to Mary: 'I have a baby in my home. . . . My daddy says I have to share my daddy with my baby and, Mary, is daddy still my very own daddy?' This was the first the nursery had known of this baby, but Tony's accounts of its behaviour 'seemed precise and real'. The authors comment: 'It would mean that he kept this, for him overwhelming, experience secret for all this time, unable to communicate it and forced to express it instead through highly disturbing behaviour' (ibid., pp. 368–373). In *Infants without Families* this is given as an example of behaviour which has to be tolerated as part of the painful process by which the child learns to deal with emotions (Freud and Burlingham 1944, p. 594).

## SUMMARY OF WARTIME EXPERIENCES

Report 49 summarised the experiences of the war years with older children and babies. Most of the older ones presented problems of behaviour in reaction to experiences which had made them bewildered and insecure: loss of one or both parents, experiences of severe bombing, being moved from billet to billet; all had experienced the complete breakup of family life. They needed a prolonged period (often as long as three or four years) of rehabilitation to help them re-establish emotional contact, to understand their disturbed behaviour and to get them back on to the path of normal development. The babies had never experienced home life at all. With these the problem was to develop the ties to their parents 'to give them at least the remnants of a family attachment' and to assist their development along normal lines within the nursery (Freud and Burlingham 1974, pp. 472–475).

Monthly report 10 contained one of the earliest papers arising from the war nurseries experience, 'The need of the small child to be mothered', given in October 1941 at a Conference on war time nurseries (ibid., pp. 125–131). Anna Freud pointed out that in peacetime nurseries play a role complementary to that of home, and are simply one link in a chain of welfare services for the child.

But in wartime they may find themselves trying to fill the gaps left by the disruption of home, education and children's clinics. They have to act as convalescent homes for children weakened by shelter life and the shock of bombing. She stressed:

> It is perhaps not widely enough recognised that the most difficult of these various tasks is to lessen the shock of the breaking up of family life and to find – during absence from the mother–a really good substitute for the mother relationship.
>
> (Ibid., p. 127)

She pointed out that nursery workers have to have time off, whereas mothers attend to the child's needs twenty-four hours a day. She also voiced her astonishment that more attempts were not made to include mothers in the life of the nursery, regarding love from a parent not as a luxury even in time of war, but as an essential. Her own nurseries made great efforts to encourage parents to visit and 'gladly suffer every disturbance of routine to make the parents take their share in the life of the nursery' (ibid., p. 128).

The comments on the difficulties of lessening the shock of the breakup of family life are, of course, equally relevant for other situations such as divorce, parental illness and working away from home. This report also contained one of the earliest summaries of the development of relationships: during the first year of life, out of the initial 'stomach love' of the baby, there develops a real attachment to the mother which is 'personal, exclusive, violent, is accompanied by jealousies and disappointments, can turn into hate, and is capable of sacrifice'. This relationship extends to include father and siblings. It is important in two ways for the child's development. First, it is the pattern for later relationships. 'The ability to love – like other human faculties – has to be learned and practised. Absence or interruption of early relationships means that later relationships will be weak and shallow. Second, education makes use of this first love of the child when it demands sacrifices:

> to become clean, to lessen his aggression, to restrict his greed, to renounce his first sexual wishes. He is ready to pay this price if he gets his parents' love in return. If such love is not available, education either has to threaten or to drill or to bribe – all methods unsatisfactory in their results.
>
> (Ibid., pp. 130–131)

A much more elaborated view of development was given in report 12, which summarised findings in the first year of the nurseries' existence. Physically, most of the children were better off in the residential nursery where they were better fed even on wartime rations than those from poor homes had been before the war. They slept better than in the underground shelters and tube stations. They were protected from the worst of the bombing and lived in safer and more hygienic conditions than in their own bomb-damaged houses. When ill, they had a paediatrician and nurses to look after them in a comfortable sick-room. But psychologically they felt more secure with their own mother, however bad the material conditions, than with strangers, however good the conditions. For these children, sleeping in underground shelters next to their mothers 'is the state of bliss to which they all desire to return' (ibid., pp. 177–178). This applies even when the mothers are not 'good'.

> The attachment of the small child to his mother seems to a large degree independent of her personal qualities and certainly of her educational ability. This statement is not based on any sentimental conception of the sacredness of the tie between mother and child. It is the outcome of detailed knowledge of the growth and structure of his mind in which the figure of the mother is for a certain time the sole important representative of the whole outer world.
>
> (Ibid., pp. 178–179)

## REACTIONS TO SEPARATION LINKED WITH THE GROWTH OF ATTACHMENT

The report describes the growth of this attachment, and its importance as the basis for the development of later love relationships. In the first phase (approximately the first six months) the baby's relationship to his mother is governed by need, and the mother brings satisfaction and removes discomfort. The 'special atmosphere of affection' with the mother is important. But at this time of life the baby is so helpless that he must accept food and care from a mother substitute. Babies left in the war nurseries suffered a short period of upset: crying, difficulty in sleeping and irregularity in digestion. 'We still have to learn how much of this upset is due to the disturbance of routine and how much to the change away from the individual handling and from the particular atmosphere of intimacy created by the mother.' The upset is more serious where the mother has been breast-feeding (ibid., pp. 179–180).

In the second half of the first year the baby also begins to pay attention to his mother when there is no urgent need.

> He likes his mother's company . . . the mother is already appreciated or missed for her own sake. . . . His need for her affection becomes as urgent for his pychological satisfaction as the need to be fed and taken care of is for his bodily comfort.

At this stage disturbances after parting from the mother last longer, including not only physical upsets but withdrawal from contact with the outside world. Smiling, friendliness and playfulness reappear only as the child establishes a new relationship with a mother substitute (ibid., p. 181).

## REACTIONS TO SEPARATION LINKED WITH THE GROWTH OF OBJECT LOVE

In the second year of life this personal attachment to the mother reaches its full development: 'it can now safely be said that he loves her.' His feelings 'acquire the strength and variety of adult human love' and 'the child's instinctual wishes are now centred on the mother'. But the child is virtually insatiable; brothers and sisters are recognised as rivals for mother's affection, as is the father even though the child also loves him. 'With this conflict of feelings he enters into the whole complicated entanglement of feelings which characterises the emotional life of human beings' (ibid., pp. 181–182).

> Reactions to parting at this time of life are particularly violent. The child feels suddenly deserted by all the known persons in his world to whom he has learned to attach importance. . . . His longing for his mother becomes intolerable and throws him into states of despair. . . . Observers seldom appreciate the depth and seriousness of this grief of a small child.
>
> (Ibid., pp. 182–183)

This is because it is relatively short-lived. Unlike the adult, the child cannot use his memories of the past and outlook into the future to maintain an inner relationship to loved ones. His needs are so urgent that he must turn away from the mother image in his mind and unwillingly accept comfort from another person. The seriousness of the shock of parting is seen in the number of children who fail to recognise their own mothers when they visit. This is not due to lack of memory, but to the child's disappointment and unsatisfied longing; 'so he turns against her with resentment and rejects the memory of her person from consciousness' (ibid., p. 185). Fathers are more likely to be recognised because the children have been more used to their coming and going, and less dependent on them for satisfaction of needs (ibid., pp. 183–185).

## REACTIONS TO SEPARATION WITH FURTHER DEVELOPMENT OF EGO AND SUPEREGO

From the third year on, the child's growing intelligence gradually permits better understanding of real situations, such as being sent away, which helps to lessen the shock (ibid., pp. 186–190). Relationships between the child and his parents are, however, complicated by Oedipal rivalry and hostility, and by the role of the parents in curbing and criticising the child's aggressive, destructive and cruel impulses as well as his sexual ones. In this education the parents make use of the child's love for them and his fear of losing their love. He adapts to their demands in order to preserve the relationship. In fantasy he may vent his anger and resentment by momentarily wishing the parents dead or gone, but at the same time fears to lose them. As long as the parents do not disappear in reality, the child can gradually resolve all these conflicts within himself and develop his own morality. But separation seems like confirmation of his fears and wishes.

> Father and mother are now really gone. The child is frightened by their absence and suspects that their desertion may be another punishment or even the consequences of his own bad wishes. To overcome this guilt he overstresses all the love which he has ever felt for his parents. This turns the natural pain of separation into an intense longing which is hard to bear.
>
> (Ibid., p. 189)

In the war nurseries visits from parents were often difficult because 'The children acted as if they could feel love only toward the absent mother; toward the present mother resentment was uppermost' (ibid., pp. 186–190).

After the age of about 3 children do not normally forget their parents. But often:

> In fantasy life the absent parents seem better, bigger, richer, more generous, and more tolerant than they have ever been. It is the negative feelings . . . which undergo repression and create all sorts of moods and problems of behaviour, the origin of which remains unknown to child and teacher alike.
>
> (Ibid., p. 191)

Yet even at this age new ties are formed and the child may slowly become estranged from his parents. It is the fear of this development which prompts many parents to take their children home (ibid., pp. 191–193). Before forming new attachments, children who are abruptly separated from their parents may pass through 'the no-man's land of affection' in which they retreat into themselves. During such a state a 5-year-old said: 'I am nobody's nothing.' A child aged 3 years and 9 months said: 'I don't like you, I don't like anybody, I only like myself' (ibid., p. 209). This report ends by recommending a gradual handover process when children have to be separated from their parents so as to avoid creating 'artifical war orphans' (ibid., pp. 208–211).

## THE DEVELOPMENT OF AGGRESSION AND ANXIETY

Report 12 also contained a discussion of the development of aggression and anxiety in the context of a consideration of the way children's reactions to bombing and destruction of houses differs from that of adults (ibid., pp. 160–163). They are less likely to be traumatised by being bombed if they are with their mothers, and if the mothers remain calm. Young children may be unconcerned, even excited by the sight of destroyed buildings. The authors pointed out that children only overcome their natural destructive and aggressive wishes with the guidance and support of adults who help them develop controls over their behaviour and wishes, reaction formations such as pity and caution, and a general moral tendency to 'do good' rather than bad.

> The real danger is not that the child, caught up all innocently in the whirlpool of the war, will be shocked into illness. The danger lies in the fact that the destruction raging in the outer world may meet the very real aggressiveness which rages in the inside of the child. At the age when education should start to deal with these impulses, confirmation should not be given from the outside world that the same impulses are uppermost in other people. Children will play joyfully on bombed sites and around bomb craters with blasted bits of furniture, and throw bricks from crumbled walls at each other. But it becomes impossible to educate them toward a repression of, or a reaction against destruction while they are doing so. After their first years of life they fight against their own wishes to do away with people of whom they are jealous, who disturb or disappoint them, or who offend their childish feelings in some other way. It must be very difficult for them to accomplish this task of fighting their own death wishes when, at the same time, people are killed and hurt every day around them. Children have to be safeguarded against the primitive horrors of the war, not because horrors and atrocities are so strange to them, but because we want them at this decisive stage of their development to overcome and estrange themselves from the primitive and atrocious wishes of their own nature.
>
> (Ibid., pp. 160–163)

In a similar way the authors linked the five types of anxiety a child may feel about air raids with stages of development and the reactions of adults.

1   Children can feel 'real anxiety' insofar as they are able to understand what is happening. But small children quickly turn away from unpleasant things and will ignore them if possible. For example, the children were at first mildly interested and afraid of an unexploded bomb in a neighbour's garden, and learned to keep away from glass windows. 'By keeping up continual talk about the possible explosion we could have frightened them into continuation of that attitude.' But they were more concerned about being unable to play in their own garden

because of the danger, and after a week declared: 'The bomb is gone and we shall go into the garden' (ibid., pp. 164–165).

2    Slightly older chidren who have only recently learned to curb their own aggressive impulses may become anxious about their own impulses which are re-aroused by the external destruction (ibid., p. 166).

3    Children who are in the throes of developing their own conscience, i.e. internalising the prohibitions of the adults they love, often suffer for a while from bad dreams and night-time fears of various sorts of ghosts and bogymen. The form taken by the specific fears depends on their own experience (ibid., pp. 166–169). 'For children in this stage of development of their inner conscience air raids are simply a new symbol for old fears' (ibid., p. 168).

4    Young children may share their mother's anxiety because of the primitive emotional tie between mother and child, and irrespective of their own stage of development in understanding reality, development of conscience, or inhibition of their own destructiveness. Children do not develop this type of anxiety if their mothers are able to remain calm and optimistic (ibid., pp. 169–171).

5    Children whose fathers have actually been killed by bombs may try to counteract their experiences by manic gaiety in quiet times, but air raids may provoke them into remembering and re-enacting their experiences. This often involves the mother's emotion and reactions which the child shared (ibid., pp. 171–172).

## REACTIONS TO EVACUATION

### The children

The greatest emphasis, however, is placed on the children's reactions to evacuation.

> The war acquires comparatively little significance for children so long as it only threatens their lives, disturbs their material comfort, or cuts their food rations. It becomes enormously significant the moment it breaks up family life and uproots the first emotional attachments of the child within the family group. London children, therefore, were on the whole much

less upset by bombing than by evacuation to the country as a protection against it.

(Ibid., pp. 172–173)

The monthly reports demonstrate the gradual learning that took place among the workers in the nurseries. For example, reports 7 and 8 describe the move from London to the country house which went smoothly, and the children adapted quickly because they went with familiar staff (ibid., pp. 79–81, 90–94). At first, however, Anna Freud and her co-workers had assumed that the children in the London nursery whose mothers could visit frequently would not need to be assigned to specific substitute mothers, but report 14 describes how they were persuaded to change to family grouping by two observations. First, some children developed strong preferences for particular workers, followed them about and wanted to be cared for by that particular person, thereby laying themselves open to disappointments. Second, some children were slow to take expected developmental steps, or to overcome reverses such as wetting and soiling provoked by their separation from home. These difficulties were attributed to lack of a stable mother relationship. Therefore the large nursery group was subdivided into six family groups of about four children each, keeping real families together but otherwise following the prefences shown by the children and the workers. Each 'mother' became responsible for all the physical care and basic needs of the child.

Hansi Kennedy was one of the nursery workers who subsequently trained as a child analyst, became an important member of Hampstead Clinic's staff and eventually one of its directors. She recalled the initial dismay of the substitute mothers and how they wondered if they would be able to cope with the uprush of new demands and difficult behaviour from the children. But before long the children did settle better than before. The personal and training needs of the staff meant that some of these substitute relationships were also disrupted, but others were maintained for several years. Duty rotations also interfered, though to a lesser extent as contact between child and housemother could be maintained (personal communication).

Anna Freud described how the immediate result of the change for two or three weeks was an uprush of possessiveness, anxiety about being left, jealousy and fights as the children transferred to the workers their attachments to their own families. Subsequently, as they became more sure that their 'mother' would not desert them but would return after absences, a quieter and more comforting attachment developed.

Simultaneously the children's development speeded up. Toilet training was rapidly achieved by children who had previously seemed 'hopeless' about it. Bathing became a time of special intimacy and interchange. This in turn aided children who were backward in speech development to catch up.

Anna Freud attributed all these happenings to the children's transference on to the workers of their early relationships to their families. Both the stormy and conflicting nature of the attachment, and the resumption of progress in development follow from the 'full return to the type of attachment which had been interrupted by the separation from the family' (ibid., pp. 219–222). Later, when the children from the London house were sent to the country house for a Summer holiday, they went with their substitute mothers (ibid., p. 239).

So great was the importance given to the child's attachments that when children in the London nursery had to be evacuated to the country house because of renewed air raids, enormous efforts were made to preserve both their relationships to their own parents and those to their substitute mothers in the nursery. Report 42 describes how, rather than separate children from their housemothers, the staff accepted overcrowding and poor accommodation for themselves, together with the inconvenience of transforming a day nursery into a dormitory for the children each night and back again each morning by moving furniture in and out of the room (ibid., pp. 419–421).

Report 43 discussed why difficulties of space should not be solved by placing children elsewhere: children who had been 'billeting failures' until they settled into Anna Freud's nursery would again become 'problem children' because of the renewed experience of loss of the substitute mothers to whom they had formed attachments (ibid., pp. 437–451).

In the London nurseries visiting by parents was unrestricted. In practice this meant weekends for the majority of parents who were working and did not live nearby (ibid., pp. 9–10), but in the country house difficulties of travelling drastically reduced the possibilities of visiting. Report 44 notes that to overcome the difficulties of travelling and shortage of fuel a bus was provided to bring parents and other relatives to 'Parent Sundays' once a month in the country house. Meals were provided for them, and in general the staff tried to make these days as enjoyable as possible (ibid., pp. 455–456).

## The mothers

The emotional strain on mothers who were separated from their children was also recognised, and some of the monthly reports attempted to counter newspaper criticisms of mothers who were accused of wanting to get rid of their children in order to earn more and have a good time. The authors described the efforts most parents were making for their children (ibid., pp. 9–10) and pointed out that few of them were having a good time, but were coping with trying circumstances (ibid., pp. 250–251).

Report 4 pointed out that mothers, as well as children, need time to get used to the idea of separation, to discuss it, to achieve it in slow stages, and to be kept informed in detail about their children's new surroundings, behaviour and development (ibid., pp. 49–50).

In report 15 there was a fuller discussion of the unconscious emotional factors influencing mothers' behaviour. Conscious conflicts were described, for example, between the wish to send the child away from danger and the belief that no one will care for him as well as herself; or, when visiting, between the wish to find the child well and happy, and the tendency to be critical of others who care for him. A sensitive child tunes in to these emotions in the mother, and they add to the difficulties of parting at the end of the visit (ibid., pp. 226–227). The report went on to discuss some unconscious factors underlying the conscious conflicts, for example, that every mother at times also finds the baby a burden, a disturbance in the relationship to her husband, a threat to her own body, or a hindrance to enjoying herself. Such feelings are usually repressed, but enforced separation may arouse the mother's anxiety or guilt about the unconscious wish to get rid of the child (ibid., pp. 234–235).

Several of the later reports described how the nursery social worker, James Robertson, gave much time to working with parents in order to maintain contact between parents and children, and the careful planning that went into finally reuniting children with their parents at the end of the war (ibid., pp. 459–460, 505–510, 512, 519–520, 532–536). This was the forerunner of his and Joyce Robertson's later work as one of the pioneers in reforming hospital and fostering services for children (Bowlby *et al.* 1952; Robertson 1952; Robertson and Robertson 1971).

## PRINCIPLES OF UPBRINGING AND EDUCATION

Some of the later reports discussed the principles of early upbringing underlying the staff's dealings with the children. Report 49 discussed the general aim of education: 'to rid the child of his antisocial behaviour, and to redirect his wishes according to the norms of morality which exist in the adult society' (Freud and Burlingham 1974, p. 475).

'Old-fashioned' methods were repressive, expecting the children not merely to refrain from giving active expression to forbidden wishes, but to eradicate such wishes from their minds. Punishments and rewards seem to produce quick results, but may leave the children unduly restricted, not able to exercise sensible control over instincts and wishes, or to change with growing maturity. 'The same children who have, to the satisfaction of their parents, become "good", and socially adapted, develop in many cases, to the disappointment or to the despair of the same parents, into inhibited, stunted, and impoverished personalities' (ibid., pp. 476–477).

'Modern' methods may make mistakes in the opposite direction, not wishing to distress the child by too much frustration of his wishes, or criticism. They therefore leave the child to 'grow out of' his undesirable behaviour, failing to give the help and guidance he needs to transform and redirect his instinctual forces. Without this help the child may become afraid of his own instinctual forces, sensing the unexpressed attitudes of the society around him, but unable to adapt, and becoming anxious, disatisfied and unhappy (ibid., pp. 477–479).

In the war nurseries gradual methods were used to help the child gain mastery over time, without sudden emotional upheavals or changes in behaviour. 'In his instinctual life, as in his bodily and intellectual achievements, the child learns through battling with the difficulties of the task, and through his failures' (ibid., pp. 479–480).

### Feeding methods

Reports 53 and 54 discussed feeding methods. They pointed out that the feeding methods adopted by mother or nurse constitute the first interference by the outside world with the child's desires. Hence they are supremely important for the child's future adaptation to the demands of his environment (ibid., p. 513). The authors stressed the importance of preserving the child's pleasure in eating so as to avoid eating disturbances. This involves minimising the imposition of adult regulation of diet, timing of meals, table manners, etc.; for example, only introducing new foods gradually, neither forcing a child to eat nor making a hungry child wait longer than he is capable of at his particular age and stage of development, allowing him to feed himself with fingers or implements even if this is messy at first (ibid., pp. 514–518, 522–524). In the war nurseries toddlers were allowed as much choice of foods as rationing permitted, and it was found that they chose a balanced diet, for example, making up one day for what they had left out the previous day, finishing the first course if they were allowed to put it aside and come back to it after their pudding. They developed a good sense of their own needs and put on weight satisfactorily (ibid., pp. 524–526).

## Toilet training

In report 50 Ilse Hellman discussed toilet training, which differs from feeding in that the child has to be discouraged from retaining his instinctual pleasure (ibid., pp. 482–483). She stressed that timing should depend on the child's physical capacity to sit comfortably, his intellectual capacity to understand the adult's demands, and his being in a good, steady relationship with one adult, usually at about the age of 1 year. The child is then motivated by wishes to please the adult, gain love and avoid criticism (ibid., pp. 485–486). Even then, it takes a long time, as the child goes through various stages: understanding what is wanted of him; fighting his mother (or her substitute) for the right to instinctual pleasure; struggling to give up his overvaluation of his excreta; developing disgust at dirtiness and pleasure in cleanliness; coping with his own anxiety and distress at failures of control. The adult can help this process best by praising success and only gently indicating disappointment in the early stages when the battle is still between the child and the adult. Once the child begins to develop his own inner conflict between wishes to be clean and wishes to enjoy being wet and dirty the adult needs to be sympathetic about accidents, not adding her criticism to the child's own self-criticism. The child is helped by opportunities to find substitutes for his original impulses: to play with sand and water, clay, paint, etc., and by being free to talk about the subject (ibid., pp. 486–494).

## COMPARISON OF DEVELOPMENT IN CHILDREN RAISED AT HOME AND IN RESIDENTIAL INSTITUTIONS

*Infants without Families*, first published in 1944, is a comparison of the development of children brought up in residential institutions with that of children brought up in families. Except in very few areas, institutional children were found to be at a disadvantage. The 1974 Foreword commented that today's verdict on residential upbringing is even less favourable.

> Our advances in knowledge of child development, whether gained in the field of education, of child care, or of child analysis, all point towards three needs of the growing child which override all others: the need for intimate interchange of affection with a maternal figure; the need for ample and constant external stimulation of innate potentialities; and the need for unbroken continuity of care. Experience shows that even the most strenuous efforts of the organisers of residential institutions inevitably fail in providing even for any one of these needs in full measure, let alone for all three of them.
>
> (Freud and Burlingham 1974, pp. xix–xx)

Essentially, this book made the case for the importance of living within a stable environment and in loving relationships. The disadvantages resulting from disruption of family life apply to many other common situations as well as to the dramatic one of war. The various areas of development described here were later to be elaborated in Anna Freud's (1963a) paper, 'The concept of developmental lines' (see Chapter 6).

### Areas in which residential care was advantageous

This book began by pointing out what was already known about the differences between children raised in institutions and families. Institution children can acquire the superficially well-adapted behaviour of middle-class children, but their character development is often more like that of destitute or neglected children (Aichhorn 1925). Anna Freud and Dorothy Burlingham described a few areas in which the war nursery children developed better than children in

low income families, because of the better hygiene, carefully prepared food, balanced diet, skilled handling by staff, better provision
of toys and equipment, less cramped conditions, and more time
spent in the fresh air. Babies up to about 5 months old looked
healthier, gained weight more regularly and had fewer digestive
upsets than bottle-fed family babies. Breast-fed babies, however, are
better off wherever they are. Babies who could be breast fed by their
own mothers within the nursery setting did best of all. In the second
year, motility and muscular control developed better in the nursery,
because the children had more carefully supervised opportunities
for movement and exploration, handling toys and other objects
without danger to themselves or the things they handled. Toddlers
became more competent in helping themselves, for example, in
dressing and undressing, setting out the table and chairs for meals,
and self-feeding. They generally had good appetites, with fewer
eating difficulties than children at home, because their pleasure in
eating suffered minimum interference. They were given as much
choice as possible in regard to what and how they ate. More
importantly, feeding did not become an area for battles with
mother. (Freud and Burlingham 1944, pp. 543–558).

## Areas in which the home environment was advantageous

However, in all areas which need the context of a close relationship
with mother or with the family to provide motivation or stimulation, the nursery children developed more slowly. Thus in the
second half of the first year home babies were much more lively
and socially responsive, actively interested in the comings and
goings of the few people who concerned them. At home, emotional
interplay between mother and child can spread over the whole day,
whereas in the nursery it is largely confined to bathing, changing
and feeding times. Speech development during the first year was
fairly even, because babies initially enjoy the actual production of
sounds and practising different kinds of babbling. But nursery
children fell behind in the second year, when language learning
depends on the urge to communicate with mother and to understand what the family talk about. Similarly, toilet training was
slower, because it, too, depends on a wish to please mother (ibid.,
pp. 545–554).

## Qualitative differences in peer relationships

In the area of relationships, the nursery children were not simply slower in development. Instead, there were actual qualitative differences. Toddlers in the nursery had to learn much earlier to fend for themselves, being in the company of other children of the same age and stage of development, rather than in the more protective environment of the family where allowances are made for the younger child even by older siblings (ibid., pp. 559–561). In the nursery, relationships with other children were precociously stimulated and developed. The authors described a range of reactions to and interactions with other children (ibid., pp. 559–585). (These form the basis of Anna Freud's (1963a) developmental line, from egocentricity to companionship.)

Initially, infants have little conception of other children's feelings, so they are indifferent to them, and treat others in the same way as toys or lifeless objects

> Freda (20 months) pushed four children over in succession and tried to sit and rock on them. Each of them cried in turn and had to be rescued from her. When Freda was defeated in her aims, she collected five soft toys, piled them up, and rocked on them.
>
> (Freud and Burlingham 1974, p. 563)

Other children may be treated aggressively because they are experienced as a disturbance, for example, in a relationship with an adult, arousing jealousy, or in envious fear of losing a wanted toy.

> Agnes (19 months) sat on the nurse's lap; Edith (16 months) tried to push her off, but was not successful. Edith hit Agnes; Agnes pulled Edith's hair; Edith pulled Agnes's hair. The nurse moved Agnes to her other side to protect her against Edith who was the stronger one. Edith, suddenly thwarted, looked at the nurse with fury, hit her, pulled her hair, then suddenly petted her and gave her a kiss.
>
> (Ibid., pp. 564–565)

> Terry (2 years 2 months) loved the big push dog, and all the other children somehow accepted the assumption that he had

the first right to play with it. When he was away at home for two and a half days, Agnes (19 months) got a chance to play with the dog. When Terry returned he wanted to resume ownership, but Agnes did not feel inclined to surrender the dog. Terry pulled and shook the dog; Agnes screamed but held tight. Terry threw the dog over, and Agnes went down with it. She clung to it with one hand and grabbed hold of Terry's leg with the other. Terry scratched Agnes. Agnes got up, still holding on to the dog, and pulled Terry's hair.

(Ibid., pp. 565–566)

At first the child does not realise what harm he can do to another child; for example, 'Larry (16 months) often took a toy away from another child. When that child cried he was very surprised, and did not know what he had done' (ibid., p. 567).

Next he realises that the other child is harmed, but this does not bother him, and he may even enjoy it. Eventually he can begin to feel sorry (ibid., pp. 567–568).

Dick (2 years 3 months) was in a phase of special aggressiveness toward other children. The expression on his face left no doubt about his enjoyment of every kind of hurt which he was able to inflict on others. This reaction changed slowly when he grew attached to a particular nurse. Once again he had attacked Ida (22 months) and was found with a tuft of her hair between his fingers. The nurse reproached him for his conduct. He was repentant, went back to Ida, held his clenched fist over her head, opened out his fingers and carefully returned the tuft of hair to the place where it belonged.

(Ibid., p. 568)

At first small children may be unable to defend themselves against the menace of other children. They may be surprised by an attack, even though they do the same thing themselves; for example, 'Sam (21 months) was playing peacefully, when suddenly Larry (19 months) took his ball away. Sam looked at his empty hands helplessly and began to cry' (ibid., p. 570).

Children gradually find ways of defending themselves.

Sophie (19 months) had a rusk in her hand which Larry (19 months) wanted badly. She began to scream as soon as Larry approached her, evidently guessing his evil intentions. When she screamed, Larry withdrew his hand. . . . He tried repeatedly for an opportunity to snatch the rusk; but Sophie did not give him a chance. Finally, he walked away disappointed.

(Ibid., p. 571)

Small children are capable of pity when they can identify with the feelings of the victim, and may attempt to console or comfort another child; for example, 'Violet (2 years 4 months) sat in a corner crying. Agnes (19 months) suddenly rushed to the next toy box, took out two toys, gave them quickly to Violet, and ran away again' (ibid., p. 572).

They may also help each other, on the basis of identifying with the other's need.

> Rose, (19 months) sat at a table and drank her cocoa. Edith (17 months) climbed up and tried to take the mug from Rose's mouth. Rose looked at her in surprise, then turned the mug and held it for Edith so that she could drink the cocoa.
>
> (Ibid., p. 574)

Peers may also exert an 'educational' influence on each other on the basis of superior strength or achievement.

> Freda (21 months) pulled Sam's hair. Sam (21 months) cried but did not defend himself. Jeffrey (2 years 4 months) crossed the nursery quickly, hit Freda twice, and then comforted Sam. When Sam stopped crying, Jeffrey once more turned to Freda and looked at her with indignation, whereupon Freda immediately shrank back into a corner. Then Jeffrey walked away, obviously pleased with himself.
>
> (Ibid., pp. 576–577)

> Bridget (2 years 6 months) joined the dinner of the bigger children for the first time and did not know how to handle a fork. Her friend Dick (3 years 2 months) watched her at first and then said: 'Not like that, Bridget, look at me.' Bridget looked at him and copied him carefully right through the meal.
>
> (Ibid., p. 580)

Under residential conditions young children are more likely to form long-lasting friendships than family-raised children (ibid., pp. 581–583).

> Reggie (18 to 20 months) and Jeffrey (15 to 17 months) had become great friends. They always played with each other and hardly ever took notice of another child. This friendship had lasted about two months when Reggie went home. Jeffrey missed him very much; he hardly played during the following days and sucked his thumb more than usual.
>
> (Ibid., p. 581)

They also show affection to one another.

> The nurse who entered the rest room during the children's afternoon nap found Paul (2 years) and Sophie (19 months) standing at one end of their cots kissing each other. She was amused and laughed. Paul turned around and smiled at her for a moment, then again held Sophie's head between both his hands and kissed her over and over again. Sophie smiled and was obviously pleased.
>
> (Ibid., p. 583)

The strength of attachment to peers, in children separated from their parents, was demonstrated even more dramatically by a group of six concentration camp children who were sent to England after the Second World War. All their parents had been sent to the gas chambers within the children's first year of life. By various routes the children arrived at Terezin, where they became a group. The adults who tried to care for them were able to do little other than care for their basic needs for food and shelter. The children were hostile, aggressive and unmanageable at first with their new carers in Britain, but very clinging with each other. They refused to be separated and looked after each other as best they could. They shared willingly, and could not even accept individual treats, or travel separately on the same outing without worrying about the others. They were sensitive to each others' attitudes and feelings, and there was remarkably little rivalry, jealousy or competition between them. After some weeks they did begin to make individual attachments to adults, but these ties did not reach the strength of their ties to each other (Freud, A. 1951a).

## Relationships with adults: mothers

In less extreme situations the emotions a child feels towards his peers cannot make up for those he would feel towards his parents. These 'remain undeveloped and unsatisfied' in institutional settings, but 'ready to leap into action the moment the slightest opportunity for attachment is offered' (Freud and Burlingham 1944, p. 586). When children were placed in artificial family groups within the nursery (as desribed in report 14) they quickly developed the emotional reactions of children in a natural family setting. Their strong, possessive attachment to their particular nurse made them more exacting but also more willing to make sacrifices for her (such as toilet training). Towards other children in their group they developed the mixture of jealousy and toleration characteristic of siblings, but this tolerance did not extend outside the family. They showed understanding of other families and the rights of particular children to particular adults (ibid., pp. 586–587).

> Bridget (2 1/2 years) belonged to the family of nurse Jean, of whom she was extremely fond. When Jean had been ill for a few days and returned to the nursery, Bridget constantly repeated: 'My Jean, my Jean'. Lillian (2 1/2 years) once said, 'My Jean,' too, but Bridget objected and explained, 'It's my Jean, it's Lillian's Ruth, and Keith's very own Ilse.'
>
> (Ibid., p. 588)

Children who develop this kind of relationship become more amenable to educational influence, more expressive, and their personality development unfolds more fully. But they also become more demanding, possessive and jealous, and often more clinging, especially those who have already experienced the loss of a loved person. Differences in behaviour towards the foster-mother and the group teacher often mirror those between home and school, due to the difference in emotional response to mother and teacher (ibid., pp. 590–591).

The authors stated that the first love relationship with the mother enriches the child by laying the foundations for future relationships. 'Like all love, it entails a wealth of complications, conflicts, disappointments, and frustrations' (ibid., p. 592). Often the child cannot clearly express all he feels.

Jim was separated from a very nice and affectionate mother at 17 months and developed well in our nursery. During his stay he formed two strong attachments to two young nurses who successively took care of him. Although he was otherwise a well-adjusted, active, and companionable child, his behaviour became impossible where these attachments were concerned. He was clinging, overpossessive, unwilling to be left for a minute, and continually demanded something without being able to define in any way what it was he wanted. It was no unusual sight to see Jim lie on the floor sobbing and despairing. These reactions ceased when his favorite nurse was absent even for short periods. He was then quiet and impersonal. Love on the one hand, and intense feelings of frustration on the other, seemed inextricably bound up with each other in his case.

(Ibid., pp. 590–593)

To the question whether the child might not be better off without the disturbing complications of such a relationship, the authors answered:

only in the sense in which we would all be better off, i.e., more sensible, without emotions. In reality it is not the absence of irrational emotional attachments which helps a child to grow up normally but the painful and often disturbing process of learning how to deal with such emotions.

(Ibid., p. 594)

When choosing between the two evils of broken and interrupted attachments and an existence of emotional barrenness, the latter is the more harmful solution because . . . it offers less prospect for normal character development.

(Ibid., p. 596)

An almost passing comment refers to issues that analysts would today refer to as 'countertransference'. Children often appear to 'choose' their foster-mother from among available adults. But they are usually responding to some 'answering spark' in the adult which makes her especially attracted to a particular child. The authors note the importance for those who work with children of recognising and gaining control over these emotional trends in themselves.

Although the adult in the nursery serves as object and outlet for the emotions which lie ready in the child, the children should on no account serve as outlets for the uncontrolled and therefore unrestrained emotions of the adults, irrespective of whether these emotions are of a positive or negative kind.

(Ibid., pp. 597–598; see also Freud, A. 1930, p. 131)

The authors went on to discuss ways in which parent-substitute relationships could satisfy the child's instinctual needs, and ways in which they must inevitably fail. The infant gains pleasure from playing with his mother's body as well as from his own, and to some extent this can be satisfied by playing with the nurse's hands or fingers, putting food in her mouth as well as his own, etc. But natural mothers normally handle their child's body far more frequently than can a nurse who has other small children to care for and other duties (Freud and Burlingham 1944, pp. 599–605). Consequently, autoerotic and autoaggressive behaviour is more preponderant in institution children than in family babies. Thumb sucking, rocking and masturbation are common as means of self-comforting and as regressive reactions to separation. Head knocking is also common as a reaction to frustration and impotent anger (ibid., pp. 605–612).

Exhibitionistic wishes, whether it be to show off the child's own body or his possessions or achievements, are important for gaining admiration and encouragement from parents. There is much less scope for this form of gratification in the nursery, and the child may show off indiscriminately to strangers if the exhibitionistic wishes cannot become focused within an attachment to one person (ibid., pp. 612–620).

The child's natural curiosity can be exploited in the nursery, as in good schools, to promote the child's pleasure in learning. Some of the more destructive manifestions of curiosity, such as taking things to pieces to see how they work, may be unwelcome in a family home or dangerous to the child, resulting in restriction by adults of the child's spirit of adventure and discovery. Residential nurseries can often satisfy this form of curiosity more easily than can an ordinary family since they have the facilities and skilled staff who can redirect the curiosity into constructive channels. Sexual curiosity, however, is less easily satisfied in a residential nursery, apart from the plentiful opportunities to see other children's naked bodies. Children have little opportunity to observe aspects of the staff's private lives. They might never even see an adult sleeping or eating. Nor do they encounter the ordinary family concerns about money or buying food. In the war nurseries the children instead became very curious about staff meetings, details of duty rotas, etc. The authors expressed misgivings about the picture of the world the children may build from the set and artificial routine of institutional existence (ibid., pp. 624–633).

In summary, they suggested that through the sharing of bodily pleasures the infant first learns to love. Lack of such gratification leads to withdrawal into autoerotic activities and possibly withdrawal into a psychological and emotional world of his own. Admiration in response to the child's exhibitionistic wishes serves to develop his abilities, gifts and talents; lack of admiration may stunt such development. Partial satisfaction of curiosity drives the child towards learning and developing. Refusal of knowledge or the opportunity to acquire it may set up intellectual inhibitions (ibid., p. 634).

## Relationships with adults: fathers

The authors pointed out that although a young child's most immediate needs are for his mother, and she is the person whom children call for when hurt, frightened or unhappy, children also need their fathers, who play a different role than the mother in maintaining the family and supporting the child's development. It was already known that absence of the father played a part in the development of pre-adolescent and adolescent delinquency. In a normal family of this time, the father would be admired and emulated by the small child for his size and strength, and for the various things he could do. He would gradually be recognised as the provider of material things, and as the power behind the mother, reinforcing her criticisms, praise and guidance in moral development. He would therefore attract his share of the child's anger and frustration. He would also be a rival for the mother's attentions, and during the child's Oedipal phase would play his role of rival or love object in the stormy emotional development of children of either sex (ibid., pp. 635–641).

In the war nurseries mother substitutes were provided but not father substitutes. Although the children superficially seemed to accept the separation from father better than from mother, they clung to an inner image of him. The children whose fathers had actually been killed could not accept his death, and produced many fantasies as a defence against the inner feelings of loss and deprivation (ibid., pp. 641–643).

> Bertie (5 1/2 years), whose father was killed in the raids, said: 'Why can't all killed daddies come back and be little babies and come to the mummies again?'
>
> 'God can make my daddy alive, can't he? Why cannot God put people together again if they have been killed and send them down from heaven? I know why: because He hasn't got the things together, all the stuff. After the war God will have everything again. We have to wait till after the war, then God can put people together again.'
>
> (Ibid., pp. 641–643)

Absent fathers were equally the subject of fantasy; for example, Tony, described at greater length on pp. 25–29, whose mother died of tuberculosis, saw his father only rarely when he was on leave. But as the sole surviving parent this father was especially over-valued by his son. Tony talked and imagined a great deal about his father.

> When he was about 4 years old, his father was seldom absent from his thoughts . . . he mentioned his name continuously in every conversation. When he picked blackberries, flowers, leaves, he wanted to keep them all safe for his father. . . . When he disliked having his hair washed, he asked: 'Does my daddy cry when his hair is washed?' When bathed he would say: 'My daddy can dive in the water.' He would eat greens though he disliked them, so as to 'get strong like my daddy'.
>
> (Ibid., pp. 643–645)

Perhaps the most striking example of a child's need for a father is Bob, an illegitimate child who never knew his father at all (ibid., pp. 645–649). He nevertheless created one in fantasy, possibly initially based on the foster-father in the last of several foster homes before joining the nursery. He cried when this man left after a visit at 2 years 8 months. He had seen his mother only rarely during his early life, but she began to visit daily when he joined the nursery, as she worked nearby. He became involved with her as well as with his substitute mother in the nursery, and mention of

his father ceased. But from 3 years 2 months he began speaking of
visits and presents from his father, convincingly enough to make
people think at first that this might be a friend of his mother. A toy
car he claimed his father gave him actually belonged to another
child. When he felt disbelieved he insisted his father was real. From
about 3 years 5 months Bob was in a rather naughty and destructive phase, unable to curb his greed or his excessive exhibitionistic
masturbation. He would then explain, 'My daddy told me to'. In
trouble after inciting other children to throw soft toys into the
lavatory he was upset, and admitted: 'I did it. But my daddy told
me to' (ibid., p. 647).

At 3 years 6 months his mother introduced him to an 'uncle',
who subsequently never reappeared. But Bob used him as evidence
for his father's existence, recalling the details of his visit. At 3 years
10 months, a 9-year-old boy whom his mother knew and called 'big
Bobby' became used as an ideal, who could do and possess everything Bob wished for himself, and who served as his conscience:
'Big Bobby does not like it when me naughty.'

At the age of 4 the father fantasy gave evidence of Bob's own
violent feelings and wishes: 'The uncle killed my daddy and my new
daddy came and killed my uncle.' Or his father had 'fallen out of
an airplane. He was a bomb and he fell down and he went all to
pieces' (ibid., p. 648). At this time he began to use swear-words
towards his substitute mother.

Eventually, at around 4 years 6 months the father and big Bobby
fantasies fused into a father who never did anything wrong, and
indeed put right everything that went wrong. For example, seeing a
bombed house he said: 'My daddy has lots of bombs which don't
break houses' (ibid., pp. 648–649). Or, when the canary died: 'My
daddy has lots of dicky birds which never die' (ibid., p. 649).

This kind of material demonstrated the way children identify
with and use fathers in the development of their self-esteem, ideals
and conscience, and search for a suitable person if none exists.

The authors described how children imitate and identify with both
parents and other important adults in the process of growing and
learning how to manage themselves and negotiate with others in
their daily lives. This influences the way they behave. Some developmental steps occur spontaneously; for example, boys between the
ages of 3 and 5 develop 'masculine' attributes without the presence
of a real man, and may adopt a pitying attitude towards women.
Other steps, notably the development of conscience, require a real

and lasting attachment to real, stable parent figures, and it is in this area that the nursery children are most at risk. They acquire the 'rough and ready methods of social adaptation' induced by living in groups of peers, but may not build into themselves the moral values which depend on the influence of long-term loving family relationships (ibid., pp. 650–662).

The authors end this book with the comment that where residential care is inevitable, it offers the opportunity for detailed and unbroken observation of child development. This valuable material about the emotional and educational responses at early ages could be applied to the upbringing of children in more normal circumstances (ibid., p. 664). This is exactly what Anna Freud herself went on to do in subsequent years.

# Chapter 4

# Theories and techniques

## Controversies and repercussions

Arguments about ways of understanding clinical material and other observations and the construction of explanatory theories are part of the life-blood of psychoanalysis as of any science. Such arguments help to move knowledge forward when the debate is constructive, and sometimes, though more slowly, even when it is not. Anna Freud was involved in many such debates. There are two areas which I particularly wish to consider here. The first is the so-called 'Controversial discussions' conducted in the British Psychoanalytic Society during the early 1940s, familiar to all British analysts as well as to many in other countries. These had been preceded in 1927 by a symposium in London criticising Anna Freud's book on child analysis (Peters 1985, pp. 94–97).

Neither Anna Freud nor Melanie Klein were the first to attempt child analysis. Among the pioneers the most widely acknowledged is Hermine Hug-Hellmuth (Geissman and Geissman 1988, pp. 40–71), whose work was known to both women. But Anna Freud and Melanie Klein were the first to gather schools of followers around themselves in Vienna and London. The British Society had early become interested in child analysis and had invited Melanie Klein to give some lectures in 1925 (Grosskurth 1986, p. 137). In 1926 Klein moved permanently to Britain. She was well established by the time the Freuds arrived in 1938.

The differences of opinion between Anna Freud and Melanie Klein about technique in child analysis and the related theories, especially of early development, were of great interest and importance. But for many years the exchange of thinking was made difficult by the entrenched positions taken up, because the scientific issues became enmeshed with the political and economic ones about which group controlled the training and running of the society and the allocation of referrals. It was also confused by the personal battles between Melanie Klein and her daughter, Melitta Schmideberg, backed by Edward Glover, as well as by transference allegiances of members to their training analysts (Grosskurth 1986; King 1994; King and Steiner 1991; Young-Bruehl 1988).

The issues of theory and technique subsequently received lively and somewhat more productive discussion in the Association of Child Psychotherapists (ACP) where rival training schools carried on the debate. Many of the same problems of transference allegiance arose, since all child therapists were in personal analysis with members of the British Society. But members of the Association were also held together by a common need to assert their competence. The International Psychoanalytic Association held that only those who had also trained as psychoanalysts of adults could call themselves child analysts. Those whose first and often only training was in child analysis were not recognised as psychoanalysts. The title 'child psychotherapist' was a compromise adopted to secure tolerance if not active support from the British Psychoanalytic Society, but exclusion from the British Society served to enhance the need for unity within the ACP. Thus although entrenched positions were taken up at times, at others there was less timidity in exploring each other's ideas.

The other area of debate I want to consider here is that between Anna Freud and John Bowlby, a less notorious argument but in some ways a more interesting one, because the two seem to me to have been much closer in their thinking than Anna Freud and Melanie Klein could ever have been. But their points of disagreement seem to have become exaggerated.

## ANNA FREUD AND MELANIE KLEIN

The two women shared the belief that psychoanalysis could benefit children as well as adults, and both thought that child analysis could add to the knowledge of development already gained from reconstruction in adult analysis (Freud, A. 1928). Both had to contend with fears, even among the psychoanalytic community, that children's innocence might be destroyed by talk of sexual and aggressive wishes, or that a child's impulses might be let loose by the analytic process (Freud, A. 1945). But they differed in the way they thought psychoanalysis could be used with children. The

Kleinians believed that a child's development could be safeguarded by early analysis of psychotic residues from early infancy, and initially recommended analysis as part of the normal upbringing of every child. Anna Freud took the view that in many cases the application of psychoanalytic knowledge to educational handling is sufficient to protect development and that analysis should be reserved for cases of severe disturbance (1928, 1945).

It is not surprising that Anna Freud's theory of technique in child analysis differed markedly from that of Melanie Klein. Anna Freud's detailed understanding of the many interacting strands in a child's development, and her awareness of the crucial importance of the child's real relationships in facilitating all areas of psychological development, stand in marked contrast to Klein's emphasis on the fantasy life of the child. Further, whereas Klein increasingly focused on the early months of life for the origins of psychopathology, Anna Freud took into account developments extending throughout the years of childhood. Her focus on the Oedipus complex in the 3- to 5-year-old as the period during which the infantile neurosis is consolidated is often taken to mean that she discounted the importance of earlier disturbances. This is far from true, as has been demonstrated (Chapter 3) by the views deriving from the war nursery observations.

I do not wish here to go into detail of all the arguments about the nature and timing of the development of fantasy; nor whether it is appropriate to equate all unconscious processes with fantasy. These and many other issues have been more than adequately discussed elsewhere (see e.g. Hayman 1994; King 1994; King and Steiner 1991; Sandler and Nagera 1963; Sandler and Sandler 1994; Segal 1994). Suffice it to say that Klein and her followers extended the concept of fantasy to cover all forms of early thinking, as well as to describe unconscious mechanisms. Anna Freud's work was moving in the opposite direction of distinguishing different forms of thought and fantasy, as well as defence mechanisms and other unconscious processes from the content and processes of fantasying.

What is of importance here is that Klein's emphasis on the fantasy life of the child as centring on innate instinctual conflicts focused on internal objects led to a technique which emphasised early interpretation of primitive sexual and destructive wishes (Klein 1932). Melanie Klein and Anna Freud responded in radically different ways to Sigmund Freud's (1920) theory of the life and death instincts. Melanie Klein used the death instinct as a clinical concept, and took it as the main cause of anxiety in infants who fear destroying themselves or their objects. Anna Freud regarded it as a theory on the biological level. She developed a psychological theory of aggression more consonant with Freud's later ideas. She pursued the role of aggression within the context of the structural theory, whereas Klein moved to a theory of conflict between instincts. Klein thus used Freud's concept of the death (or destructive) instinct in a more directly clinical way than did Anna Freud, seeing it as a major, early cause of primitive anxiety; later in her work she also introduced the concept of envy as a manifestation of this destructive instinct (Klein 1957). Klein gradually moved away from describing development in terms of the libidinal stages postulated by Freud (1905) and Abraham (1924), and substituted the paranoid-schizoid and depressive positions for Freud's structural theory of ego and superego development (Klein 1935, 1946; see also Segal 1964, 1979). Klein also developed the view that the superego was formed in the early months of life rather than in the 3- to 5-year-old period where Freud had placed it. All these modifications led her to a very condensed view of development, in which similar interpretations could be made to children and adults of all ages, because relatively little allowance needed to be made for cognitive development. She saw the child's experience of real people as serving to correct the frightening internal fantasies, rather than as having primary importance in the development of patterns of relationships. Further, her view that what had to be addressed were the innately given internal relationships between self and objects meant that she expected the transference of these relationships on to the analyst to be much the same in children as in adults, leading to an emphasis on transference interpretation in child analysis as in adult analysis.

Anna Freud differed from Klein on all these issues, and her arguments derived from her experience of children in situations which interfered with their real relationships to parents (See Chapter 3).

## The 'introductory phase'

In Anna Freud's view, because the young child is dependent on his parents for his very existence, he is reluctant to allow others to take care of him except in extreme necessity. She therefore did not expect normal children to involve themselves willingly with a stranger. Children do not refer themselves for treatment. They are brought, often unwillingly, by their parents. It is often the parents, not the child, who are troubled by the child's symptoms. Whether or not the child enters analysis may depend rather on the understanding and willingness of the parents than on the severity of the child's disturbance. These were the issues which gave rise to Anna Freud's original belief in the necessity for an introductory phase of analysis in which the therapist builds a relationship with the child. The aim of the introductory phase was to produce the missing insight and active wish for help which adults usually come with but children do not (Freud, A. 1927, 1945), or, as she later put it, 'to alert the child to his own inner disharmonies by inducing an ego state favourable for their perception' (Freud, A. 1965a, p. 225).

Anna Freud believed that the analyst needed to gain the child's trust by allying herself with the child, showing understanding of his needs, fears and wishes, and demonstrating her ability to help him, in order to establish 'the necessary conditions for beginning a real analysis – the sense of suffering, confidence in the analysis, and the decision to undertake it' (Freud, A. 1927, p. 11). In later years she moved away from her belief in the necessity of an introductory phase, as she recognised that analysis of defensive mechanisms and manoeuvres could achieve the same end (Freud, A. 1974a, p. xii). Nevertheless, it is instructive to examine what techniques she used when introducing children to the idea of analysis. When she wrote of 'allying' herself with the child, she was actually describing a range of approaches which demonstrated sensitivity to the individual child's needs and capabilities.

In some instances the 'introductory phase' may be no more than an initial meeting, as in the case of a 6-year-old girl who already knew something about analysis because two of her friends were in analysis. One of them accompanied her to her first meeting with Anna Freud. In the second session, upon being asked why she thought her parents sent her, she replied: 'I have a devil in me. Can it be taken out?' Anna Freud explained that the work would be long, hard and not always agreeable. After some thought the child agreed: 'If you tell me that this is the only way to do it . . . then I shall do it that way.' This child was ready to acknowledge that the trouble lay in herself (Freud, A. 1927, pp. 8–9).

Few children reach agreement with the analyst so easily. Anna Freud cites another case in which she followed Aichhorn's (1925) recommendation for work with delinquent children: in order to start work *with* the child instead of *against* him, the worker must begin by assuming that the child's attitude towards the environment is justified. An 11-year-old girl was coming into conflict with her stepmother in various ways, including stealing and lying. To her, Anna Freud said: 'Your parents cannot do anything with you . . . with their help alone you will never get out of these constant scenes and conflicts. Perhaps you had better try the help of a stranger.' This child accepted Anna Freud as an ally against her parents, but after a few weeks the parents terminated the analysis (Freud, A. 1927, pp. 10–11). This was doubtless one of the cases that caused Anna Freud to emphasise that analysis can only work if the parents can co-operate with the analyst.

A much longer period of work was required with a 10-year-old boy suffering from an 'obscure' mixture of anxieties, nervous states, 'insincerities' and perverse infantile habits. He was aware neither of divisions within himself nor of conflicts with his parents. He was rejecting and mistrustful of Anna Freud, intent on concealing his secrets. Anna Freud described herself as winning his confidence by 'devious methods' and 'forcing' herself on a person who felt he could do without her (ibid., pp. 11–13). Her choice of words indicates her belief that these 'devious' methods were not truly analytic. In fact she used methods that all child therapists now recognise as indispensable techniques with reluctant patients in whose psychopathology there is a large element of developmental distortion or delay. She followed his moods, joined in his activities, discussed with him any subject he chose to introduce from geography to love stories. 'My attitude was like that of a film or novel meant to attract the audience or reader by catering to their baser interests. My first aim was in fact merely to make myself interesting to the boy.' Next she began making herself 'useful' by writing down his day-dreams and stories, and making things for him during the hours. She learned a great deal about him, of course, during this period. Next she demonstrated the 'practical advantages' of analysis, acting as mediator between the boy and his parents over his 'punishable deeds'. She became someone who could protect him from punishment and help him repair the consequences of his rash acts; i.e. someone powerful whose help he needed. Only at this point did she begin to ask him to give up his secrets, 'with which the real analysis could finally begin'. She comments that in this introductory phase she was not establishing insight, merely creating 'a tie strong enough to sustain the later analysis' (ibid., pp. 11–14). She distinguishes this from attempting to maintain a positive transference. Her own comments also make it clear that she did not view these initial techniques as real analysis.

Another 10-year-old boy was willing to come for analysis because he envied his sister's analysis. But he was not willing to part with his symptom: outbursts of rage and defiance which were at odds with his otherwise timid personality. Indeed, he was proud of these outbursts because they distinguished him from others, and he enjoyed the worry they caused his parents; i.e. the symptom was 'ego-syntonic'. In this case Anna Freud had to induce the split in his personality which would turn the symptom from a 'treasured possession' into a 'disturbing foreign body'. This time, the 'devious and not very honest' device she used to create conflict in the child's mind was to enquire repeatedly how far he was in control of himself, and to compare his fits of rage to those of a madman. The child began trying to master the outbreaks, and realised he was unable to do so. This made him aware of suffering which then led him to claim the analyst's help (ibid., pp. 14–15). Later, with recognition of the alternative possibility of analysing defence, Anna Freud would probably have approached the symptom via interpreting the defensive denial of his fear of being mad, or the defensive exaggeration of pride in his strength to protect himself against shame about his lack of control.

Another case in which Anna Freud promoted a split was that of a 7-year-old girl. After a long preparatory period, Anna Freud personified the child's 'badness', giving it a name of its own. The child could then begin to complain about this person who caused her suffering (ibid., p. 15). Most child therapists will recognise this as a device many children invent for themselves: the imaginary companion, or sometimes another real child on to whom they project their own badness. This displacement allows the child to feel more comfortable with examining the problems until a point is reached when the child can reclaim this split-off part of herself.

In another case Anna Freud had to cope with loyalty conflicts which interfered with the analysis. An 8-year-old girl with a symptom of frequent outbursts of crying was eager for help, but proved resistant to probing the depths of what lay behind her symptom. This turned out to be due to her attachment to her nanny who resented the analysis. This loyalty conflict between analyst and nanny repeated the child's having had to choose between her parents when they had separated. The understanding of this transference was not enough to overcome the resistance. Anna

Freud had to work on getting the child to question her uncritical loyalty to her nanny. In this case Anna Freud felt that the nanny's influence was undesirable for the child's whole development, but she pointed out the need to consider whether it is worth risking depriving the child of the support of someone whose influence is otherwise favourable. It may be impossible when the opponent to analysis is one of the child's own parents (ibid., pp. 16–17).

We can see that in these cases the techniqes do not consist simply of forming an alliance with the child against the parents, or with one part of the child against another split-off part. They also include many ways of engaging the child in the analytic process, creating age-appropriate conflicts where none had yet developed, making the child aware of suffering and of his own role in perpetuating it. Overall they tend towards the development of a treatment alliance, which can be distinguished from a positive transference (see Chapter 7).

This, of course, is a very different view from that derived from the analysis of adults at that time, which regarded all disturbances as based on conflict, and the technique required was to uncover the unconscious conflict and help the patient to find a different way of resolving it. Inteperations aimed at uncovering and resolving conflict are inappropriate for children who lack internalised conflicts, or who are still battling with their real parents, or who lack parental figures able to provide suitable guidance and models for development. If, in addition, a child does not yet trust the analyst sufficiently to accept that he might hear something useful, he will be unable to make use of interpretations, except for those about the child's expectable anxiety with a stranger in an unfamiliar situation, or work on the defences which underpin the reluctance to become involved in the analytic process.

Anna Freud believed that such elements of preparation also occurred in adult analysis, without the analyst necessarily being aware of it. The analyst's initial questions, comments and interpretations help the patient to see how and why he needs to look into himself, as well as engaging his interest and co-operation in the analytic work (1927, pp. 19–35).

## The child's participation in analysis

Anna Freud was also aware that the child lacks many of the cognitive and emotional capacities required for understanding the need for therapy and willingness to participate actively in the process of analysis. A very young child, or an older one whose development has been delayed or distorted, may not have developed boundaries between self and object and may need active intervention to build such boundaries. Or he may have a defective superego, and will require a model for identification in order to develop an adequate moral sense. This differs from the Kleinian technique of intepreting projection or projective identification, which assumes that boundaries do exist, that the child can understand he is disclaiming something that belongs to himself, and that even the youngest child has a superego deriving from early infancy.

Anna Freud was aware that the child expects external not internal solutions to his problems: he wants his parents to remove him from whatever troubles him, or to do something to make him feel better. He is not given to introspection and cannot readily understand the need to consider what is going on in his own mind. Young children are not yet able to use speech as a substitute for action, and do not free associate, so child analysis cannot be conducted as a verbal interplay between patient and analyst; nor does the child lie on the couch or even sit still on a chair (ibid., pp. 36–49).

She was hesitant to accept play as a full substitute for free association, which was Melanie Klein's solution to the problem. Klein believed that the child's play could be used as a substitute for the verbal free association regarded by analysts as the patient's essential contribution to the analysis. She also believed that the child's primitive anxieties could provide the motivation for engaging in the psychoanalytic process. Anna Freud believed that the Kleinian technique of interpreting the symbolic aspects of the child's play directly in terms of unconscious sexual and aggressive fantasy ran the danger of missing the individual nuances of the child's experience, or even of being wrong altogether.

Anna Freud also emphasised that it is wrong to assume that everything the child does in analysis is dominated by the aim to further the analytic process. He does not agree to tell the analyst all his thoughts. He usually does not even wish to be helped by the analyst in any way. The child plays in order to enjoy himself, to distract himself from anxiety-provoking aspects of a strange situation by doing something familiar, or to draw the analyst into an activity the child can control. The analyst attempts to draw the child's play into a communicative role. Anna Freud believed that

while the child's play could certainly be useful in providing information about the child's interests, fears and fantasies, how he views
the world, it cannot be taken as a communication equivalent to the
free association of the adult (ibid., pp. 37–45).

Instead she believed that the gap left by the lack of free association is better filled by examining transformations of affects (Freud,
A. 1936, pp. 38–41). Children's feelings are normally 'less complicated and more transparent' than those of adults, and it is easier to
see what evokes them (ibid., p. 38). They can thus be used to see
what makes the child happy, disappointed, jealous, fearful, etc. If
the child's feeling reactions are missing, or seem inappropriate, this
indicates the type of defence he is using, and hence how he is likely
to handle instinctual urges. She gives examples, of a boy who
regularly reacted to any event arousing castration anxiety by
becoming aggressive: wearing a soldier's uniform and equipping
himself with a sword and other weapons, thus avoiding having to
experience the anxiety. A little girl, whenever she might have been
envious or jealous of her brother, pretended to be a powerful
magician, thus avoiding insight into her penis envy. Such observations give the analyst 'a kind of technique for the translation of
the defensive utterances of the ego' similar to the analysis of resistance in free association (ibid., pp. 38–41). The ultimate success of
the analysis depends on the child developing an attachment to the
analyst which can allow an identification with the analyst's analytic
aims.

## The role of education

Anna Freud also believed that child analyses need to be accompanied by education, or re-education, in the sense that the parents
or their substitutes might need to add to or alter their educative
measures with the child. It is essential to understand that Anna
Freud was speaking of 'education' in its widest sense: upbringing
which facilitates psychological and emotional development, by
offering moral guidance as well as models for understanding and
coping with life tasks and social interactions; helping the child to
subdue and channel instincts in constructive ways, to find socially
acceptable ways of expressing or defending against strong feelings,
to manage rivalries and jealousies, to develop the strength needed
to cope with fears and anxieties (Freud, A. 1930, 1934). Throughout her work she emphasised that what motivates the child to

participate actively in this 'educative' process is attachment to the person of the 'educator'.

I think it may be that her frequent emphasis on the role of 'education' made it possible for those with only a superficial acquaintance with her work to dismiss her as a teacher rather than an analyst. But all her writings make it abundantly clear both that she distinguished this educative role from psychoanalytic treatment, and that her view of education encompasses all the inner developmental processes which can be influenced by the attitudes and demands of important people in the child's life, and is therefore truly psychoanalytic.

This view led her to believe that during analysis the analyst may also need to influence the parents because their impact is so important (Freud, A.1928). Initially she thought that the work of re-education needed to be done by the parents, if they were able; or if they were too disturbed or indadequate themselves, by other workers such as remedial teachers. In other words, this would be additional work undertaken by others outside the analysis, but guided by psychoanalytic understanding. It was later, during her work at the Hampstead Clinic that she came to believe that much 're-educative' work could and should be done by analysts because it required their skills and not those of teachers or parents (see Chapter 7).

## Transference

Because of her conviction that young children would naturally prefer to keep their positive feelings for their parents, and transfer only the negative feelings on to strangers, including the analyst, she believed most child analyses would inevitably begin with a negative transference which would prevent analytic work unless and until the child developed a positive attachment to the therapist strong enough to build up and preserve the treatment alliance. The distinction between transference and treatment alliance was not clearly spelled out in these early years of child analysis, but much thought was given to it by Anna Freud and colleagues in later years (see Chapter 7). The child's real dependence on his parents also reduces the possibility of his developing a transference to the analyst: the child seeks to work out his difficulties with the people who are still involved in those difficulties.

Very importantly, Anna Freud did not believe that most conflicts were present in the child's mind from soon after birth. She believed that the child, dominated initially by the pleasure principle, experiences his first conflicts not within himself but with the people who oppose his wishes or fail to provide the gratification he seeks. It is only through learning within important relationships that the child develops conflicting wishes within himself: wishes to please and preserve the object conflict with various other wishes for pleasure and gratification. It follows from this that it is not appropriate to make interpretations in terms of internal conflicts to small children who have not yet developed that far. Nor is it appropriate to make such interpretations to children who have lacked the close relationships within which such conflicts develop, or whose parents have provided inadequate models for development. Such children are not suffering from conflict-based disorders but from deficit disorders.

Anna Freud's later work explored in greater detail the important role played in ego development by the child's relationships. But even in these earlier days she thought that while the fear of analysis letting loose children's instincts was not justified in the case of neurotics who have a strong ego and superego, it might be justified in the analysis of dissocial, delinquent or 'otherwise deficient' characters (Freud, A. 1945 pp. 5–6). In the early days Anna Freud thought that such children were not appropriately treated by analysis but required educational help and the provision of an appropriate relationship. Later she and the therapists of the Hampstead Clinic developed the techniques known as 'developmental help' which could precede or be combined with 'classical analysis' of children, and which required analytic training to be correctly used (see Chapter 7).

She believed re-educational work within an appropriate relationship to be particularly important in disorders of aggression, since she viewed aggression as being modified by regard for the object's wishes and the need to preserve the object. But for this to happen, children have to feel loved and have learned to love in return. Without this there can be no wish to please or preserve the object (see Chapter 6). In drive theory terms she phrased this modification of aggression as due to its fusion with libido.

## Drive/structural theory

It is relevant here that Anna Freud did not believe that the young child had a sufficiently well-formed and well-functioning superego to assume conflict between it and the child's instinctual wishes. Her view was that the superego develops gradually, and is initially unreliable and dependent on external reinforcement from the object. When it does function it may be overly punitive and vicious. This is because it contains too much aggression unfused with libido and turned against the self. So the therapist may sometimes have to interpret superego conflict, and try to help the child modify its superego to become less punitive, but at others may actually have to help the child build superego and develop conflicts so as to resolve them in the direction of more socially acceptable behaviour.

This was one reason why Anna Freud believed that the analyst could not avoid being a 'real' or 'new' object for the child, which contributed to her scepticism about the child's capacity to form a transference which could override the real relationship.

She believed, too, that the analyst needed a position of authority, sufficient for the child to use the analyst as an alternative to the parents. The child's ego is too immature, and his superego still too dependent on the parents who provide the models for it, for the child to be able to take responsibility for his future development after he has been made conscious of his id impulses and his conflicts about them. He needs the support of the analyst as an external ego ideal in controlling his own behaviour. This, of course, makes it vital for analyst and parents to be in agreement about the aims of the analysis. The child cannot be expected to work with the analyst if the parents oppose the changes in the child, or do not agree with the analyst's views on what would constitute 'health' for the child. The parents themselves may need re-education in their approach to the child's upbringing. All this adds to the difficulties of child analysis. These problems also led Anna Freud to believe that Melanie Klein was insufficiently respectful of the role of the parents.

On the other hand, the advantages of treating young children are: that there is less distorted or disturbed development to undo; the natural developmental push assists the child in moving away from bad solutions; the analyst can influence the environment to make it more favourable to the child's development, and she can influence the development of the child' superego (Freud, A. 1927). Later, Anna Freud was to include more specifically the analyst's ability to influence ego development also (see Chapter 7).

Anna Freud's views on both the need for an introductory phase and the need for 'educative', or what we might now call 'remedial' measures, derive from her recognition that immaturity, whether age-adequate in a young child or due to developmental delay or deficit in an older person, renders the individual unsuited to psychoanalytic techniques based on interpretation of unconscious conflict.

Both Anna Freud and Melanie Klein took adult analysis as the model for technique. But whereas Klein thought there was little difference between adult and child analysis provided one accepted play as the substitute for free association, Anna Freud thought there were major differences because of the child's ego and super-ego immaturity. Because child analysis was being judged against the conflict interpretation model of adult psychoanalysis with neurotic patients, Anna Freud concluded that the technical para-meters required to prepare the child for the analytic process could not be considered part of psychoanalytic technique as it was understood at that time. In her later writings, however, she moved to the opinion that child analysis would be better viewed as a discipline in its own right, rather than as a subspeciality of adult psychoanalysis. In this view it has its own technique which may include the introductory and educative work she called develop-mental help (see Chapter 7).

## ANNA FREUD AND JOHN BOWLBY

The controversies with the Kleinians were followed by further controversies with Bowlby in which Anna Freud spelled out her own view of the development of attachment, and the points of agreement and disagreement with Bowlby.

In 1958 Bowlby read an early version of his paper on separation anxiety to the British Society (Bowlby 1960a), which took further the arguments in his paper on the nature of the child's tie to his mother (1958). Two years later his paper on grief and mourning in infancy and early childhood was published (1960b) together with discussions by Anna Freud (1960a), Max Schur (1960) and Rene Spitz (1960), and a further reply by Bowlby the following year (1961). Anna Freud's reply to the 1958 paper remained unpublished for some years, until Volume 5 of her *Writings* came out (1969). The two discussions together summarise well her view of the points of agreement and disagreement between herself and Bowlby.

Bowlby thought he was appropriately interpreting and legiti-mately developing Sigmund Freud's theories of anxiety and mourning as reactions to loss of object. Many other analysts thought he was departing from these views. This was at a time when almost everyone in the British Society found it necessary to assert their basis in Sigmund Freud's work (Fairbairn (1952) was a rare exception), and more energy seemed devoted to claiming to be the true descendants of Freud than to the scientific evaluation of each others' theories. Jeremy Holmes (1993) notes that all this was going on in the aftermath of Freud's death when everone was trying to find a new direction for psychoanalysis.

Bowlby had compared the observations from the war nurseries published in 1942 and 1944 (Freud and Burlingham 1974), with his own and James Robertson's observations of the sequence of protest, despair and detachment in young children separated from their mothers in hospital (Bowlby *et al.* 1952). Anna Freud agreed that their observations were similar. They were also in agreement about the importance of the child's tie to the mother and the major psychopathological results in later life if the child failed to remake his attachment to the mother, or to find a substitute attachment. Their differences came over the theoretical explanation of the observations. Some of these seem to be genuine differences, but others seem to be more attributable to misunderstanding. Bowlby objected to what he saw as Anna Freud squeezing the observations into a theory of narcissism which denies the existence of an object relationship to the mother. She replied that by narcissism she means a state in which the infant uses the mother for his own psychological as well as physical needs in a way which does not yet recognise her separate existence in her own right, but which certainly acknowledges the biological tie out of which the pychological tie is developing. She elaborated the early narcissistic phase as a type of relationship to mother which is still focused on the infant's needs, and which precedes a true object relationship and object constancy. Anna Freud used Hoffer's concept of the 'narcissistic milieu' in which each partner treats the other as an extension of self; but she also regarded this as consonant with Sigmund Freud's view (Freud, S. 1914).

Anna Freud saw Bowlby as failing to distinguish biologically programmed attachment behaviours from the underlying mental representations which are the internal essence of psychological attachment.

She also thought he failed to distinguish sufficiently between different levels of ego development. In the first four to five years of life changes are rapid and vast, which means that children of different ages bring quite different equipment (reality testing and many other ego functions) to the task of coping with separation and loss. Their ego development influences both the way in which they can understand separation, as well as how they are able to react to it (see Chapter 3).

She does not seem to have objected to Bowlby's interpretation of Sigmund Freud's theory of anxiety as much as some analysts (e.g. Schur). But she did believe that the child's ego capacities greatly influenced how he could understand and cope with separation and longing for mother.

Perhaps Bowlby equated Anna Freud's interest in ego development with an emphasis on narcissism (possibly a confusion between the concepts of ego and self which was common at that time).

Bowlby thought that Anna Freud saw object relationships as secondary to the gaining of pleasure, and seemed to include her among those whom he thought used a secondary drive theory to account for attachment to mother. She responded that all mental functioning is governed by the pleasure-pain principle, which is not an instinctual drive but a tendency of the whole mental apparatus. The notion of an anaclitic object relationship does not, in her view, refer to anything secondary about the relationship. The libidinal drive is inherently object seeking; the term 'anaclitic' merely refers to the way in which the libidinal drive 'leans on' or is guided by the path of the self-preservative one; the mother who cares for the child offers herself as the first love object.

## REPERCUSSIONS

The fact that this argument happened within the already existing tensions between Kleinians and Freudians probably influenced Anna Freud's reactions. Perhaps she wished to distance herself from those criticised as non-analytic. The tensions in the British Society at that time were highly charged and often personal, and distasteful to Anna Freud. Her American colleagues were less involved in the disputes with Klein, but some were involved in the discussions with Bowlby, which at times became equally polemical. Reading the papers and discussions of that time, one gets the impression that the protagonists were not really listening to one another, not really trying to understand the other's point of view, simply defending their own with increasing attention to minutiae of theoretical positions. Some of the arguments sound more like religious discussions of heresies than scientific exchanges of views. Anna Freud perhaps comes close to being an honourable exception to this in her discussions of Bowlby's early papers, where she clarifies points of agreement and disagreement with Bowlby. She does not engage in detailed discussions of minor points, but simply spells out a few major differences which, once understood, make it easier to sort out minor differences; and in her later works she continues to use Bowlby's evidence about separation and delinquency.

Holmes describes the atmosphere in which Bowlby's work was received mainly in terms of his disagreements with the Kleinians, and their 'indifference' to him. I wonder if this indifference was that of a Society so involved with Melanie Klein and her theories that no one else could arouse interest. The early Kleinians were among those who thought that analysis of the ego was not a proper subject for psychoanalysis (Freud, A. 1936, pp. 3–4), and claimed as evidence of being true analysts their emphasis on unconscious fantasy. In fact, many analysts were becoming interested in the early development of mental functioning, but most were linking it with interaction between child and environment. At that time the Kleinians had less interest in the role of the external world in the child's development, and were perhaps reluctant to contemplate any observational evidence or theoretical view which challenged the primacy of inborn fantasy, whether these challenges came from Bowlby, Anna Freud, Fairbairn (1952), Winnicott (1949, 1960), Balint (1968), or any other analyst who found the influence of the environment important in patterning development. The consolidation of the independent group in the Society led to its becoming the home for those who espoused non-Kleinian theories of object relations, except for Anna Freud who remained, of course, in the Freudian group, and continued to be labelled as a drive theorist, or sometimes as an ego psychologist, as if these were mutually exclusive.

Anna Freud's dissatisfaction with the British Psychoanalytic Society led her to keep her distance from it, and was an important factor in her decision to found the Hampstead Clinic to provide her own training in child analysis. (The other factor was the wish of people who had worked in the war nurseries to continue their training. There was also considerable demand at that time from professionals working in child guidance clinics for a more thorough training in child development and child psychotherapy.)

Outside the British Psychoanalytic Society Bowlby became well known for his stress on the importance of environment, and was influential in the development of care and therapeutic services for children. He played a major role in the establishment of the Association of Child Psychotherapists, and was keenly involved in the National Health Service. Why has Anna Freud achieved less impact? She chose to keep the Hampstead Clinic outside the Health Service, fearing (possibly correctly) that involvement would mean a loss of freedom to provide the kind of psychoanalytic treatment, training for child therapists and opportunities for research that she believed were important. She kept herself marginal to the ACP without being actively hostile. Her students became members of the ACP and went to work in the Health Service. Yet we were all aware of some tension in this: there was a kind of disapproval which was sensed by us, though only occasionally overtly expressed by her, and which had to do with her fears of analytic treatment becoming less effective or superficial where only non-intensive therapy was possible, and of analytic theory being diluted by admixture with other theories. This latter was probably one of her main concerns about Bowlby: she feared that ethology was not an adequate substitute for psychoanalytic theory. Perhaps she, like many other analysts at that time, could not see how ethology might be integrated with psychoanalysis to the benefit of both.

This seems a pity, as she would have been the person best equipped to work with him on integrating their observations and theories about them. Attachment theory might have become a subject for research much sooner in this country. As it was, it was received more eagerly in America, and has only returned to this country via the work of Mary Main, taken up in research projects by Fonagy and the Steeles (Fonagy *et al.* 1993; see Chapter 8).

Implicit in report 12 from the war nurseries is a view of attachment as the necessary precursor of object love, where she described the growth of attachment during the first year of life, and its development into love for the mother in the second year of life (Freud and Burlingham 1974, pp. 179–82; see also Chapter 3, pp. 31–33). Thus she may have intended to reserve the concept of attachment for the earliest form of relationship to the mother.

Anna Freud was not averse to the development of object relations theory as long as she could see how to encompass it within the drive/structural theory. She encouraged Joseph Sandler to pursue his elaboration of the notion of the representational world and the self–object relationships within it, in the index research groups of the Clinic (see Chapters 2 and 5). This was not always easy for her or for him, but I have often heard her translating his formulations back into the libidinal and structural ones which she found more comfortable, and which enabled her to accept and support his work.

She even attempted to encompass some of Melanie Klein's ideas within her own way of thinking. As part of her interest in developing a chronology of defence mechanisms in 1936 she was already considering whether introjection and projection are to be viewed as processes which assist differentiation of self from the outside world, or as defences which can only become effective after the establishment of boundaries between self and object world (Freud, A. 1936, pp. 52–53). Later she was to clarify the view that they are both early processes which serve differentiation between external and internal world, self and object, and later, once boundaries between self and object are established, they also come to be used as defences (Sandler and Freud, pp. 111-112; 138–139).

Following Sigmund Freud's death in 1939 the whole psychoanalytic society was struggling to come to terms with it and to find new directions. Young-Bruehl points out that in the early 1940s Anna Freud was still in mourning for her father, and that at this stage she found it intolerable to contemplate rearranging his theory (Young-Bruehl 1988, p. 265). This reaction passed, according to Young-Bruehl, in the late 1940s, but it actually seems to have been earlier than that. Grosskurth describes an attempt in 1942 by Melanie Klein to ease the tension in the Society by suggesting to Anna Freud some private discussions of their ideas. Anna Freud reacted positively, inviting Klein to her home and suggesting that each bring a few colleagues. This might have developed into a series of seminars in which more measured debate about psychoanalytic ideas could have taken place. But it was cancelled due to the intervention of Marjorie Brierley, who thought such discussions should not take place without the knowledge and consent of the Society (Grosskurth 1986, pp. 299–301). We can only regret this lost chance to speed up the process of understanding and exchange of ideas.

In the calm of her own papers, Anna Freud continued her attempts to integrate some of Klein's ideas with her own. For example in 1950, surveying the development of psychoanalytic child psychology, she discussed how Sigmund Freud's own later modifications of theory served as starting points for new schools of psychoanalytic thought, especially concerning early development. She includes some of the ways Melanie Klein made use of these changes. For example, she again considered the nature of defence before the division between ego and id is fully established, and noted Klein's view that special pathogenic significance should be attached to the defensive mechanisms of projection and introjection, leading to new theories about psychotic disorders (Freud, A. 1950, p. 619).

Concerning Klein's use of Freud's concept of the life and death instincts, Anna Freud stated that Klein had applied this biological hypothesis to a theory of basic pathogenic states, or positions, in the first year of life, which Klein ascribed to mental conflict between the infant's love for mother and destructive wishes towards her (ibid., pp. 617–618). Anna Freud questioned whether opposing instinctual urges can cause conflict before a central ego has come into being, powerful enough to integrate the mental processes, and therefore to recognise the incompatibility of the instinctual urges. But she regarded such controversies as capable of resolution by further investigation (ibid., pp. 622–623; 1949c pp. 69–70).

In a study of infantile feeding disturbances she considered the relevance of Klein's thinking on very early oral-aggressive fantasies for eating inhibitions (1946b, pp. 53–54). In 1958 in a memorial lecture in honour of Ernst Kris, she discussed among other things the uses of a double approach (direct observation and analytic reconstruction) to investigation of sequences in child development, especially in the early mother–child relationship. She mentioned Klein's concept of the 'good' and 'bad' mother used to describe the infant's experience at the breast, and Klein's demonstration of how actual experience may become complicated and overlaid by processes of introjection and projection which intensify the bad image by adding to experienced frustration the projection of the child's own aggressive and destructive impulses. Anna Freud commented that she herself was more familiar not with a concept of a double internal image, but with a double trend of impulses, love and hate, directed at the same object, i.e. ambivalence (Freud, A. 1958a, p. 119). This is typical of the way Anna Freud could translate other people's conceptualisations into her own concepts in order to understand them and examine their fit with her own theory. Later she even found a place for Klein's 'part objects' in an early stage of her own developmental line of object relationships (see Chapter 6). She thought that Klein's distinction between part and whole objects might correspond to her own distinction between the relationship to the need-satisfying object and object constancy (1952c, pp. 233–234). Klein may not have agreed with Anna Freud's interpretation of her work, but a proper scientific debate would have been enlightening.

Young-Bruehl noted that Anna Freud's conception of the stages of development and their timing loosened over the years of her controversies with Klein, and that the Kleinians tried to present this as a victory for their camp, which was certainly not the case (Young-Bruehl 1988, p. 268). It is clear from reading Anna Freud's own work that her views changed as the result of further research and observation by herself and many other colleagues, and that her ideas had in any case been misunderstood by many Kleinians. In particular her stress on the importance of distinguishing between early (pre-Oedipal) disturbances and the later Oedipal neuroses seems to have been misinterpreted as discounting the importance of early disorders. It also seems clear that her ideas were developing along a very different line from those of Klein.

Young-Bruehl thought that the personality differences between the two women were refracted through their groups, and she described the group psychology involved. Klein and her followers believed in 'direct and aggressive attack and defence', while Anna Freud 'put her efforts into research' and waited for truth to prevail. Anna Freud 'exerted control in her group by being . . . lucid, iron-willed and conscientiously devoted', while Melanie Klein inspired her group with 'imaginative verve . . . ambition . . . and . . . startlingly uninhibited egoism'. Anna Freud was a 'cautious and circumspect leader' but known to her group as 'an adventurer in her plans and fantasies'. Melanie Klein presented herself as an adventurer but relied on the support of others to avoid becoming too cautious. The Kleinians thought of themselves as 'crusaders' and the Anna Freudians as 'authoritarians' unwilling to be challenged. The Anna Freudians regarded themselves as 'bastions of reasoned science' and the Kleinians as subversive power seekers and manipulaters (Young-Bruehl 1988, pp. 268–269).

It is clear that the theoretical differences were not merely exaggerated by the political and personal battles going on in the British Society (as they are described by Young-Bruehl, Grosskurth and King and Steiner), but their resolution was actively interfered with.

Under happier circumstances Anna Freud's attempts to understand Melanie Klein's views might have developed into a more fruitful exchange. As it was, the potentially interesting and exciting views expressed in the 'controversial discussions' have emerged only slowly from the political and personal context to a point where a more genuine exchange of scientific views could begin to take place, with the different schools of thought beginning to absorb some elements of each others' views. Meira Likierman, in a contribution to a special issue of the *Journal of Child Psychotherapy* marking the centenary of the birth of Anna Freud, suggests that she and Klein each highlighted different but valuable aspects of children's mental life, and together laid the foundation for a comprehensive mental health service for children. She suggests that the failure of the two women to collaborate represents a loss that is both scientific and professional (Likierman 1995).

It seems that part of the answer to my question (see Chapter 1) why Anna Freud is not as well known in Britain as in the US lies in her quieter and more reasoned approach both to argument and to making known her findings; also her willingness to wait for the results of further study before deciding between opposing points of view or modifying hitherto satisfactory theory. Another part of the answer may lie in her insistence that only a rigorous understanding of theory could permit thorough clinical understanding, and only a thorough knowledge of all areas and stages of a child's development could permit an accurate assessment of the child's difficulties and needs, and of appropriate treatment techniques: points which I will take up in Chapter 5. Melanie Klein's theory was in some ways simpler, her innovations often used as substitutes for the more complex conceptualisations of Sigmund and Anna Freud. It was a theory more attractive to those who sought simplicity.

# Frameworks, institutional, informational and theoretical

## The developmental point of view

Undoubtedly the most positive result of the controversial discussions was that Anna Freud's dissatisfaction with the British Psychoanalytic Society reinforced her move towards setting up the Hampstead Clinic. She had already organised a training in child psychoanalysis in 1947, in response to the needs of former war nursery workers who had moved on to work in child guidance clinics. Initially seminars took place in Anna Freud's own home and those of other participating teachers; and students treated their training cases in child guidance clinics (Freud, A. 1957). But the purchase of 12 Maresfield Gardens in 1952, followed by the acquisition of numbers 21 and 14 in 1956 and 1967 respectively, provided a base for the training as well as the development of services and research. In the 1970s an arrangement was reached with the British Psychoanalytic Society whereby adult analysts could choose to do their training in child analysis at the Hampstead Clinic.

Anna Freud's organisational skills had already been demonstrated a number of times in setting up institutions: the school for children in analysis and the Jackson nurseries in Vienna, as well as the war nurseries in Britain. Her lectures on child psychoanalysis in 1926/1927 had stimulated interest among many analysts. They formed a seminar in which case material, technical innovations and theoretical conclusions were discussed. Many participants went on to become very well known, for example, Berta Bornstein, Edith Buxbaum, Erik Erikson, Elizabeth Geleerd, Willie Hoffer, Edith Jacobson, Anny Katan, Marianne Kris, Anna Maenchen, Margeret Mahler, Marian Putnam, Helen Ross, Edith Sterba and Jenny Waelder Hall (Freud, A. 1966c). In addition, Anna Freud had been secretary and then a vice-chairman of the Vienna Psychoanalytic

Society, and general secretary of the International Psychoanalytic Association, during a time of growing difficulty and danger in Vienna before the *anschluss* (Peters 1985, pp. 122–126). Her ability to engage the interest and co-operation of others in creating, funding and running institutions was based on her clear thinking about what was needed and her enthusiasm about providing it, but above all on her conviction that psychoanalytic theory and understanding of human development was the best basis for getting it right. Her capacity to organise and facilitate the work of others must surely rank as second in importance only to her own creative thinking. Hampstead was the last and most enduring of her organisational feats. Hansi Kennedy made the point that colleagues from the Jackson nursery in Vienna remained loyal to Anna Freud, and those who went to the United States supported her in raising funds for the war nurseries and the Hampstead Clinic (personal communication). People she trained or worked with carried her ideas around the world.

The Hampstead Child Therapy Course and Clinic, to give it its full title, was founded as a charity with the threefold aim of providing psychoanalytic training, treatment and research. In this enterprise Anna Freud provided invaluable frameworks of three kinds: institutional, informational and theoretical.

## THE INSTITUTIONAL FRAMEWORK: TRAINING, SERVICE AND RESEARCH

Within the institutional framework she organised three overlapping areas. The *first* was the *training* in psychoanalytic theory, normal child development, child psychopathology and psychoanalytic technique with children, which produced not merely psychotherapists, but 'child experts' (Freud, A. 1965a, p. 9). Some scholarships eventually became available for students who could not afford the very expensive training. The training fed workers into the *second* area: the *services* provided by the Clinic (Freud, A. 1957). The initial treatment service was soon supplemented by a day nursery, a well baby clinic, a day nursery for young blind children, mother-toddler groups, and from time to time other groups for children with handicaps of various kinds. In pursuance of Anna Freud's belief that such services should be available to all, there were no charges, only contributions from those who could afford it. These services were also sources of observation for students in training, and for the *research* groups. The research groups made up the *third* area within the institutional framework, and secured most of the funding which kept the whole enterprise going (Freud, A. 1957–1960).

These were not academic research groups. There were no randomly selected samples, control groups, rating scales, tests for reliability and validity, or statistical analysis of results. These groups existed at a time when it was thought unethical not to match the treatment given to the assessed needs of the patient, and when it also seemed impossible to quantify the complexities of psychoanalytic data. They were more in the nature of clinical study groups, where colleagues could meet regularly to pool observations, ideas and theories. In this way they could do collectively what individual analysts had been doing ever since Sigmund Freud first began to develop psychoanalytic ideas: using clinical material as a basis for tentative theory to be confirmed, discarded or modified in the light of further clinical experience. It is a model taken from clinical medicine. New clinical observations throw up new problems which require modification of existing theory or the development of new theoretical explanations. New theories in turn influence clinical understanding and technique. This interaction between clinical experience and theory building can proceed more effectively when larger amounts of clinical material can be pooled for many people to think about. The Hampstead groups were initially chaired by senior analysts, then also by senior graduates of the Hampstead training. Their membership included analysts from the British Society, long-term visitors from other countries and sometimes people from related professions. Students joined them as part of their training. Some of the groups were long running, like the diagnostic study group, the study group on adolescence, the study group on borderline children, and the study group on blindness. Others had a shorter existence, designed to focus on more specific issues such as psychosomatic illness in children, language development, or the role of play in analysis.

Because annual reports had to be sent to the funding bodies, a steady stream of papers was produced, many of which went on to publication. Consequently, many people who did not initially think of themselves as writers found themselves in print because of the facilitation provided by working in a group. Thus, on a

practical level Anna Freud provided the physical and organisational framework to accommodate a huge and varied amount of
research work, training and service.

On a less overt level many people experienced the clinic as a
matriarchal framework, sometimes even as a 'nunnery', with Anna
Freud as the mother authority. Women did outnumber men, but it
was probably the dedication to psychoanalysis that Anna Freud
expected and usually got from us that made us feel totally absorbed
and secluded from life outside the clinic. Nor perhaps was it surprising that inexperienced students often felt like children; but this
seemed, at times, to apply to staff members as well. As a (male)
colleague once remarked: 'We are all Anna Freud's girls – of both
sexes.' The matriarchy had its uses, the most obvious being that it
created a sense of family into which visitors were welcomed for
their contributions to our work (Edgcumbe 1983). More dubious
perhaps was the ease with which Anna Freud could be used as an
object for projection when someone needed authority to back up
some idea of their own, whether it was the sacrosanct nature of
Sigmund Freud's drive theory, or the impropriety of wearing a
low-cut blouse when working with excitable children. This was
Anna Freud's less voluntary contribution to the Clinic's frameworks.

She also played a part in starting the annual publication *The
Psychoanalytic Study of the Child*. This journal was based in the
US, where it had a wider readership than in the UK. The research
funding which sustained the Clinic came almost entirely from
American foundations, because it was in the United States that
Anna Freud had influential colleagues who were able to support
her efforts to find financial backing for the Clinic (and she did most
of the fund-raising personally). The majority of the papers from the
Clinic were published in the *Psychoanalytic Study of the Child*. All
these positive links with America rather than Britain are doubtless
further reasons for Anna Freud's work being better known in the
US than in the UK.

In 1979 she instituted a series of international colloquia. These
occurred annually and were attended by colleagues from the
United States and Europe as well as Britain. A core group attended
regularly and others occasionally. Over the years a way of working
together has developed which is fruitful in developing common
ideas, and these international weekends have continued since Anna
Freud's death.

## THE INFORMATION FRAMEWORK: REPORTING

The information framework developed from Anna Freud's requirement for regular written reporting of case material, observations
and discussions. Short weekly reports on treatment cases to indicate the most important developments of the week, longer termly
summaries which included tentative theoretical formulations, and
occasional more formal case presentations at clinical conferences
were supplemented by diagnostic profiles and sometimes indexing.
This was in addition to the process notes which students kept on
their cases for supervision and clinical seminars. As in the war
nurseries, observation cards were made on children in the nursery,
baby clinic and toddler groups, noting interesting or puzzling
behaviour. All clinical and research discussions were minuted,
often in some detail so that they sometimes formed the basis for
subsequent papers. This meant that over the years a wealth of
recorded clinical and observational material accumulated which
was available for scrutiny by study groups, and by Anna Freud
herself. In turn, ideas and findings emanating from each study
group were available for use by other groups.

## THE THEORETICAL FRAMEWORK

The most important framework, however, was the theoretical
one. These days the word 'metapsychology' tends to send people
running for cover. It has unfortunately become associated with the
notion of boringly convoluted theory irrelevant for clinical practice.
This seems to be due to contributions from both authors and
readers. On the one hand some theoretical papers are densely
written without clinical examples. These require a background of
clinical experience that many beginning readers do not have. Even
the most conceptually elegant theory is hard for the uninitiated to
follow. Other papers are difficult to follow because the theory is in
fact muddled. The reader's contribution on the other hand is sometimes an intellectual laziness that leads to a preference for simple
uncomplicated theories or rules of thumb that may seem an
adequate answer to clinical and technical problems, but which prove
limited in scope. Anna Freud had no patience with people who
wanted quick fixes. She believed that it was only possible to do a

good job if one had a thorough understanding of all that was involved. In her hands metapsychology was an enlightening framework that allowed one to order and make sense of apparently contradicatory, chaotic or unwieldy amounts of information derived from treatments or observations so as to arrive at good decisions. It proved well worth the trouble of learning it.

I well remember my own delight and excitement when In 1959 I first attended seminars and meetings as a student. I came from academic psychology which had failed to give me satisfactory answers about human functioning, and from working as a clinical psychologist in a child psychiatric clinic where psychologists, social workers and psychiatrists alike were struggling to learn how to help disturbed children since none of us was trained in psychotherapy. It was a revelation to sit in discussions with people who could explain what was going on in the minds of the children we saw, what inner and environmental factors had interacted in producing their state of mind, and what, in consequence, needed to be done to help them. It all made such wonderful sense after the confusion in which I had been working. I have never quite lost this sense of wonder in spite of subsequent discoveries of doubts and unclarities – at least I can now formulate the difficulties and find a place for them in the context of possible ways of resolving them.

All the research groups were influenced to a greater or lesser degree by Anna Freud's theoretical thinking, as well as by Sigmund Freud's metapsychology. In return, the ideas and formulations emanating from the groups stimulated Anna Freud's own thinking, as did the clinical material of the cases in treatment and the observations in the other departments of the Clinic.

Dr Clifford Yorke, for many years medical director and subsequently joint director with Anna Freud and Hansi Kennedy, is of the opinion that the most important thing Anna Freud ever did was to gather together in the Hampstead Clinic so many good people and to facilitate their work in the research groups and clinical departments (Yorke 1996). Her own thinking was fed by colleagues and she inspired the start of many groups. She did not necessarily agree with the ideas emanating from the groups but she nevertheless encouraged the continuation of discussion as long as she thought that people were seriously struggling with the issues.

Two forms of metapsychological framework were particularly important in the research work of the Clinic: the index and the diagnostic profile (together with the developmental lines: see below and Chapter 6). Both were ways of ordering clinical material within theoretical categories which facilitated the assessment of its significance.

## The index

The index was the brainchild of Dorothy Burlingham who saw that the staff needed a means of finding comparative material in the growing number of cases treated in the clinic. It resembled a book index: cards were made for each case giving brief clinical examples and page references to further material in treatment reports for topics broken down according to metapsychological categories (see e.g. Bolland and Sandler 1965). The examples and theoretical discussion given on the cards could be used for teaching and research purposes. Joseph Sandler became chairman of the index research group which continued for many years. One of its projects on defences resulted in the discussions with Anna Freud already reported in Chapter 2 (Sandler and Freud 1985). Another series of discussions with Anna Freud resulted in a book on technique (Sandler et al. 1980). The index research group worked its way through a series of problems and spawned numerous sub-groups (Berger and Kennedy 1975; Burgner and Edgcumbe 1973; Edgcumbe and Burgner 1973, 1975; Edgcumbe et al. 1976; Holder 1975; Joffe and Sandler 1965; Novick and Novick 1972; Sandler 1960; Sandler and Joffe 1963, 1965; Sandler and Nagera 1963; Sandler and Rosenblatt 1962; Sandler et al. 1962; Sandler et al. 1963).

## The diagnostic profile: psychopathology viewed developmentally

Thirty years on from *The Ego and the Mechanisms of Defence*, Anna Freud wrote her second book, *Normality and Pathology in Childhood* (1965a). This latter book was organised to show the theoretical thinking that had resulted in Anna Freud's diagnostic profile and her developmental lines, and which influenced her views on technique. Clifford Yorke, in his introduction to the 1989 reprint, says that this would be his choice if he could have only one book on psychoanalytic child psychology, because of its comprehensive, clinically based discussion of normal and disturbed development (ibid., pp. xiii–xiv). It is true that it is simple and elegant in style, and for psychoanalysts it is undoubtedly an excellent summary of Anna Freud's thinking as it had developed up to that point. In many places she also summarised the main points of Sigmund Freud's theory within which she was placing her own work. But its deceptive simplicity and compactness can make it hard to follow for those previously unacquainted with her (and her father's) work, or who do not yet have the clinical experience to flesh out her statements with their own examples. The book gave some examples from Clinic cases, but not the lengthy examples from her own work that were found in *The Ego and the Mechanisms of Defence*. It needs to be read in conjunction with the clinical and observational material in her earlier works (see Chapters 2, 3 and 4) as well as with the shorter papers from the 1950s and 1960s in which she went into greater detail as she was working out her ideas. Particularly useful are some of the papers given to non-analytic audiences, because here she wrote without technical terms, and with everyday examples which most people can readily understand.

*Normality and Pathology* was not Anna Freud's final statement of theory. For another decade and a half she continued to advance her thinking about development. Both the book and the later papers were based on her earlier theory and work in the war nurseries, but they are honed by the controversial discussions, influenced by the work of colleagues from the early days in Vienna, many of whom had fled to the US, and facilitated by her interactions with staff and students in the many research groups of the Hampstead Clinic. She was an active participant in many of the research groups, but also kept in close touch with the work going on in all of them, as well as all the clinical work. Anna Freud had a huge capacity for reading and digesting vast amounts of material. She routinely read all the weekly treatment reports (as many as eighty or ninety a week when the caseload was at its maximum), diagnostic reports on new referrals, minutes of weekly research meetings (often a dozen or more), and minutes of clinical and educational meetings (at least three a week), in addition to papers and drafts on which her opinion was being requested not only by staff and students of the Clinic, but by colleagues all over the world. As students, we were sometimes unnerved to realise how closely she followed our work when, as she passed by, she would stop for a word about some development or problem in a case which had interested her, or to comment on some discussion in a group. This close reading and discussion meant that she, more than any of us in the Clinic, had access to a huge amount of clinical material as well as theoretical ideas which influenced and were integrated into her own developing thinking. It was her forte to be able to integrate and summarise the work of many colleagues so that it blended seamlessly into her own thinking. But this capacity does add to the density of her formulations, so that unpicking them in order to understand the details often means reading not only Anna Freud's earlier papers, but those of others to whom she refers.

*Normality and Pathology* gave expression to the developmental point of view which had by now become the hallmark of her work. It is a coherent theory which gives due weight to all stages and areas of development from infancy to adolescence. It is a natural extension from the work of Sigmund Freud and Abraham on libidinal phase development. Anna Freud's own work began with the development of ego and superego functions, went on to include the development of aggression, and finally to distinguish many lines of development in specific areas of functioning within which internal and external factors interacted. Her theory allows the analyst to distinguish material from different areas and levels of development and to view psychopathology against the background of normal development. This developmental point of view is what most distinguishes Anna Freud's students from the Kleinians. It also characterises the Contemporary Freudian Group in the British Psychoanalytic Society, because even those who are not close followers of Anna Freud are indirectly influenced by her thinking as an interpretation and extension of Sigmund Freud's theories.

By 1945 Anna Freud's writing about psychopathology in childhood was already demonstrating her belief that the emphasis should be shifted from clinical symptomatology to interference with normal development (Freud, A. 1945).

In 1954, but in a paper not published until 1974, she set out three basic principles for assessing childhood disturbance: (1) is the child progressing or retarded in normal drive and ego development? (2) is his behaviour towards his objects progressing normally? (3) are his conflicts at the level (external, internalised, internal) to be expected for his age and stage of development? (Freud, A. 1974b [1954], pp. 53–55).

In her Foreword to the 1979 edition of *Normality and Pathology* Anna Freud noted the difficulty of turning analysts' attention away from pathology towards the problems of ordinary personality growth and adaptation to reality, which she saw as 'the task for the future', and her book as a first step in that direction (Freud, A. 1965a, pp. 1–2). Later papers pursued the same themes.

## Uses of observation

The book begins with a history of changes in psychoanalytic ideas about development as viewed first from reconstruction in adult analyses, which prompted early analysts to observe their own children for corroboration of these ideas; then from reconstruction in child analyses, and finally from direct observation of growing children. She noted the trial and error nature of early attempts to apply psychoanalytic ideas, especially about childhood sexuality and superego development, to the upbringing of children, when successes were mixed with failures due to the incomplete state of knowledge. The advent of child analysis provided a better understanding of the working of a child's mind and the impact upon him of his experiences. Direct observation gave the opportunity to view development in progress rather than from reconstruction.

She discussed the pros and cons of observation, which analysts at first rejected as too superficial, and not relevant for understanding the unconscious. She pointed out that psychoanalytic theory equips the observer with a greater capacity for understanding what is seen, and over the years close correspondence between overt behaviour and unconscious meanings has been established for certain manifestations; though other surface manifestations may have many meanings (ibid., pp. 3–15). Anna Freud stressed, however, that observed behaviour cannot be used for interpretation without appropriate analytic material. The study of defences and of other ego functions, she suggested, has added much to our understanding in recent years; some aspects of ego and superego functioning can be observed from surface behaviour. For example, some reaction formations and sublimations are fairly obvious transformations of more primitive feelings, wishes and impulses (ibid., pp. 16–17). Parents and teachers are familiar with the pleasure small children can derive from play with mud, sand and hand painting as they become toilet trained. They develop disgust at soiling, but shift their enjoyment to substitute forms of messing which are more acceptable, and which in some cases are developed much further into talents for painting, modelling or sculpting of a truly sublimated nature.

Other manifestations are more complex and require depth analysis. For best understanding of development the combination of observation, analysis and longitudinal follow-up serve as checks on each other as well as amplifying information (ibid., pp. 16–24). Such a combination was, of course, available at the Hampstead Clinic, where some children seen in the Well Baby Clinic might also attend a toddler group and the nursery school, and a small number would be taken into analysis. Some war nursery children were also followed up and/or subsequently analysed. In some families two or three generations have attended various departments of the Clinic.

> Derek, for example, who will be mentioned again below, attended the Well Baby Clinic and Nursery School and then entered analysis. His parents approached the Clinic for advice and help having been pleased with the results of his elder brother's therapy. Derek's nephews and nieces subsequently made use of various Clinic services.

In an earlier paper Anna Freud had discussed how vividly observation reveals the child's gradual development through the libidinal phases, albeit with marked overlaps, persistence of earlier phases and regressions according to individual predispositions and circumstances. She noted that this progress can be seen particularly clearly in the child's relationship to his mother or her substitute. She made the very important point that this phase progression cannot be as easily seen in analysis. In adult analysis early forms of relationship in the transference are intermingled with and distorted by later reactions. Even in child analysis the dominant fixations and regressions obscure the other phases (Freud, A. 1951a). Some analysts today express doubt about the correctness of the theory of libidinal phase development, on the grounds that oral, anal and genital manifestations are often all present simultaneously. The distinction between the intermingled way analytic material appears, and the progression that can be seen in direct longitudinal observation, helps to clarify this issue.

### Differences between the mind of the child and the adult

Anna Freud stressed the enormous complexity of normal development, with many strands of drives, ego/superego and object relations combining to produce each small achievement. The developmental lines (see Chapter 6) describe these interactions in some of the main sequences of development. She also stressed the importance of understanding the differences between the mind of the child and the adult, especially when attempting to determine a child's readiness for and likely reaction to ordinary experiences like school or holiday separation from parents, or for less ordinary ones like medical treatment or hospitalisation (Freud, A. 1965a, pp. 54–58).

In a 1962 paper for teachers she described the differences between the thinking of a child and an adult (Freud, A. 1962b), and in 1965 she summarised these ideas. She noted four main areas in which a child's thinking (especially that of a young child) differs from that of normal adults:

1   Before the child achieves object constancy, and can understand that his objects have their own separate life, his relationships are governed by *egocentricity*: everything his mother does is experienced as directed at satisfying or frustrating the child's needs and wishes. So her illnesses or absences are felt as rejection or desertion; the birth of a sibling is experienced as unfaithfulness. The child may react with disappointment or hostility expressed in emotional withdrawal or demandingness. (Freud A. 1965a, pp. 58–59)

> Derek was referred at age three for a major sleep disturbance with nightmares, many daytime fears, desperate clinging to his mother and tantrums which she could not manage. This had followed the birth of a younger sister to whom he was aggressive. Treatment material soon showed that he felt abandoned and enraged with his mother, convinced that she had another child to replace him; and he assumed that he must have been somehow bad to deserve this.

2   The child's *sexual immaturity* leads him to misunderstand parental intercourse as violence or perverse behaviour. Even when told the 'facts of life', the child's own oral or anal fantasies may override this 'enlightenment' so that he does not give up his theories of oral impregnation, anal birth, intercourse as castrating, etc. This can contribute to later difficulties of sexual identification with parents seen as 'aggressor' or 'victim'. (Ibid., p. 59)

Derek's parents were careful to explain to him how babies were conceived, carried and born. But he continued to play games in which eating something resulted in a baby in the mummy's tummy. Or, as a variation, he blew on a building block and announced that it would have a baby. What could be understood in his therapy was that these theories seemed safer to him than what he had understood about sexual intercourse. For example, in one of his fantasy games a mother bird took the father bird's penis, kept it in the nest, and cut off a bit each time she wanted to make another baby.

3   The *relative weakness of secondary process thinking* compared with the power of impulses and fantasies, means that even when the child is capable of rational understanding he may still at times of stress be swamped by fantasies. Thus, for example, at his best he may understand the doctor's helpful intent, the need for an operation, medicine, or dietary restrictions; but he may be unable to maintain this understanding, and then feels attacked, mutilated, imprisoned or deprived; his own parents who failed to stop these things happening may be felt as hostile, and the child retaliates with his own hostility. Even a minor illness may be experienced as an attack in some cicumstances. (Ibid., pp. 59–60)

Derek sometimes stammered, and in therapy this had been linked with his holding back aggressive words and thoughts. One day he told me a story about a clown whose nose was cut off. Next day he arrived with a sore throat and anxiously whispered: 'I'm n – not g – going to tell you that story any more b – because it hurt my throat'.

4   The child's *sense of time* varies according to the extent to which it is governed by id or ego. When id impulses and needs are dominant he becomes unable to wait and a few minutes may seem like a lifetime. But when the ego is dominant he is able to wait, to anticipate future pleasures, and the periods of waiting seem shorter and more tolerable. (Ibid., p. 60)

This was evident in Derek who, when anxious, could not bear his mother to disappear for even a minute or two without becoming unable to concentrate on anything other than when she would return. But when in a good state, he thoroughly enjoyed activities all day in the Nursery School and could easily accept that she would surely fetch him at the end of the day.

It is these characteristics which often account for parents' failure to understand the importance of events for their child (Freud, A. 1965a, pp. 58–61). Other aspects of development also have to be taken into account. For example, in planning any separation of the child from mother, account must be taken of whether the child still needs his own mother for help with eating and toileting, or whether he can accept help from other adults. This is important for entry into nursery school, as is the progress of his capacity to relate to other children. These are the kinds of factors which Anna Freud pursued in the developmental lines.

### Normal regression

In a more general way, good behaviour whether at home, in nursery school or elsewhere (being able to wait, take turns, share, cope with anxiety, tolerate disappointments without tantrums, etc.) depends on general ego maturation and the extent to which the child is able to master his feelings and impulses. But in this respect Anna Freud pointed out that no young child can be expected to maintain best behaviour for lengthy periods, because of normal regression. Psychological development is not a straightforward progression. Under stress, for example, because of anxiety, illness or ordinary tiredness, a child regresses to earlier states of mind and ways of behaving. Fixation points at earlier stages of drive and object relations development may have been caused by excessive frustrations or gratifications, or other traumatic experiences, leaving the child vulnerable to regression to these points; for example, a well-functioning latency child may revert to anal stubbornness or oral demandingness; he may treat his mother as a mere satisfier of needs instead of loving her as a person in her own right. Ego functioning may also regress as the child loses the most recently acquired and therefore most precarious achievements when under stress. Rational speech may deteriorate to baby talk, bowel or bladder control may be lost, social adaptation may disappear. Frightening or unpleasant experiences may cause the child to bring into play defences such as denial, repression, reaction formation and projection, all of which interfere with ego functions such as reality orientation, memory and the synthetic function.

When such regressions are temporary they may serve to give the child respite from unbearable pressure, and the child recovers once the cause of strain is removed: someone deals with the anxiety-provoking situation, his health improves or he has a good sleep and wakes refreshed. This type of regression is normal, and helps to explain some of the occurrences of disharmony between developmental lines and temporary unevenness in development. It is only the more permanent regressions which become pathological (Freud, A. 1963b, 1965a, pp. 93–107). She noted that even in adults the line between mental health and illness is often a quantitative matter as much as a qualitative difference, and with developing children much more so. The descriptive categories used in adult psychiatry emphasise manifest symptomatology while neglecting underlying pathogenic factors.

### Symptoms may have many meanings

In children, symptoms may have a range of meanings dependent on the child's stage of development. The *temper tantrum* is one of the examples Anna Freud gave. In a young child it may simply be a way of discharging chaotic drive impulses and feelings, which will disappear with ego development and be replaced by speech or other more organised channels of expression. But if it is an outburst specifically of aggression or destructiveness, being deflected on to the child's own person or his surroundings, relief will come only from understanding the original frustration and who caused it. (Ibid., p. 111)

> Early in therapy Derek could not separate from his mother so she was in the treatment room with us. The first time in treatment he threw a tantrum, she looked helpless and was unable to calm him. I drew a picture of him having a tantrum. He immediately became interested, calmed down and instructed me: 'Draw mummy saying "No"'. I did, and he added his own drawing. We could thereafter use this technique when a tantrum threatened. His additions to the pictures made clear his wish for help in containing himself, his conflict about his

destructive anger with his mother and baby sister, and his fear of retaliation.

Temper tantrums also have to be distinguished from anxiety attacks which may look the same, but which are due to a phobic child being subjected to the situation which terrifies him, for example, going into the street, or facing an animal which frightens him. These anxiety tantrums are relieved only by letting the child reinstate his defensive avoidance or by the analytic understanding and dissolution of the original source of the displaced anxiety. (Ibid., p. 112)

> Derek subsequently developed a temporary refusal to walk past a certain cupboard in the Clinic. He would have an anxiety tantrum unless we used a different route to the treatment room. He gradually told me about the frightening ghosts who lived in the cupboard. In the course of various fantasies they gradually changed into policemen coming to get him. I could interpret them as his own 'inside policemen' coming to tell him off for the secret wishes he believed were dangerous. Upon realising that the policemen were inside, not outside, he literally danced for joy, pleased at the discovery that they belonged to him, and that they could give him the power to control his bad wishes, rather than to be afraid of punishment.

Another example Anna Freud gave was *separation anxiety*, a term she thought should be reserved for the legitimate distress of an infant separated from the mother who satisfies his major needs. The reaction to separation in older children has far more complex meanings. 'Homesickness' or 'school phobia' is usually due to excessive ambivalence towards the mother, so that the child can tolerate the hostile side of his fantasies and feelings only when in the reassuring presence of the mother. (Ibid., pp. 112–113)

She also discussed symptoms such as *lying and stealing* which do not have the same meaning in children as in adults. For example, as the wishful thinking of the young child means that he cannot reliably distinguish fantasy from reality it is not appropriate to call him a liar when he tells an objectively incorrect story. It is only as he develops such ego functions as secondary process thinking, reality-testing and the ability to differentiate between the inner and outer world that 'truth' can have any meaning for him. Children vary in the length of time it takes them to develop these ego functions. Some older children who have developed normally in this respect may regress to wishful thinking if they encounter frustrations and disappointments which they cannot bear, and they become fantasy liars. These have to be distinguished from children who become delinquent liars: those who are neither developmentally delayed nor regressed, but who avoid or distort truth for their own advantage, for example, to escape punishment or criticism, to aggrandise themselves or gain material advantage. Clinic cases often have a mixture of these forms which then have to be disentangled.

In general, symptoms by themselves cannot be used for making diagnoses in children. They may be signs of developmental strain which the child will 'grow out of' as he resolves the issues of that particular stage. Even where there is an underlying disturbance, the symptomatic expression of it may change from one phase to another, or symptoms may disappear under the threat of investigation by a clinic. Further, young children do not usually suffer from their symptoms, except for nightmares and anxiety attacks. It is the environment which suffers. What children suffer from are the ordinary deprivations, frustrations and frights of life so that, in childhood, suffering cannot be taken as a measure of severity of psychopathology. Indeed, to be too 'good' or uncomplaining is more likely to be a sign of disturbance in children than is the presence of suffering (Freud, A. 1965a, pp. 108–123).

Since the use of rigid, static or descriptive categories is not useful for analytic diagnosis of childhood psychopathology, Anna Freud went on to discuss the various points of view from which development should be examined in order to make an appropriate assessment (ibid., pp. 123–147). These are what appear in the metapsychological profile.

## The profile: clinical and research uses

The profile was developed by a research group under the chairmanship of, first, Liselotte Frankl, then medical director, and later Humberto Nagera, director of research. Renate Putzel, the first secretary of the initially small, informal group trying to improve diagnostic skills, has described the group's transformation into a major research group (personal communication). It is typical of the way many of the groups arose. Using the minutes of meetings in which Anna Freud had described her own way of thinking about assessment, Putzel made the first attempt at a 'profile' on one of her own cases. Anna Freud was 'quite kind' about it but thought that it needed rewording. This led to discussions about how best to formulate what needed to be covered in the various aspects of a child's development. Renate Putzel, at that time still a student, felt proud that her effort had prompted Miss Freud to proceed to a larger study group and articulate her own ideas into a formal framework for use by others (Freud, A. 1965a, pp. 140–147).

Properly used, the diagnostic profile is simply a mental framework for thinking about the assessment of a patient. Its aim is to prompt the diagnostician to think about all areas of the child's life and development, so as to arrive at a balanced view of his normal as well as pathological functioning. Anna Freud was very concerned about the misdiagnoses which could occur if people placed too much emphasis on symptoms only, were insufficiently aware of the multiplicity of developmental factors affecting psychopathology in children, or were biased by particular beliefs, interests or adherence to currently fashionable diagnoses. The profile is not a questionnaire to be filled in so as to provide an automatic diagnosis. It is a framework for directing attention to each important area of the child's life and development in turn, so that the importance of each and their interaction can be evaluated. It also serves to make the diagnostician aware of the gaps in his knowledge about the child.

From its initial clinical use the profile developed into a research tool which could be used to compare cases, to assess changes during treatment, to check the accuracy of the original assessment, or to explore specific problems (see below). Because it is a framework for thinking, diagnosticians and research workers are also made aware of gaps or unclarities in the profile itself so that it undergoes continuous modification while retaining its basic format. This can be seen in different published and unpublished versions of the basic developmental profile for children (e.g. Freud, A. 1962a, 1965a; Eissler *et al.* 1977), quite apart from the more major changes introduced in the versions produced for other age groups or specific research areas. Advances in theory also give rise to modifications of the profile to encompass new ideas. The version I use in the illustrations below is the one I currently favour: a slightly modified version of the profile given in *Normality and Pathology* (Freud, A. 1965a, pp. 140–147).

The usual diagnostic procedure at the Hampstead Clinic (and now the Anna Freud Centre) is for the parents to have several interviews with a social worker, in which they present the problem and tell their story in their own way. The social worker asks questions to clarify unclear points, fill in gaps in the child's developmental history and family background, and makes comments to get the parents thinking about what might be going on in their child's mind, and whether there are things they themselves could do to help. The child is then seen by a diagnostician (either alone or with a parent if he cannot separate), usually twice, in relatively unstructured interviews in which the child can talk or play. Some children are able to talk about themselves and their lives, and to describe their own problems, or indicate them in play; others need help from the diagnostician who may ask questions, join in the play, make comments, etc. The child is usually also seen by a psychologist for more formal intellectual and personality testing. Relevant information is also sought from the child's school, and from hospitals or other agencies who have been involved with the child. All the Clinic interviews are first written up as process recordings, because the flow of the interviews, and the ease or difficulty with which members of the family can think and talk about themselves, and their interactions with the interviewers, are important indicators of the dynamics of their difficulties, and of the degree of insight they have or might be capable of developing.

Only after that does the team move on to breaking down the material into profile format. This is important to understand, because many people on first acquaintance with the profile think of it as an alternative to process recording, or as a questionnaire to be filled in while interviewing the members of the family, which would, of course, stifle the spontaneity of interactions between patients and professionals.

Many people also find the profile too time-consuming on their first acquaintance with it. When used as a research tool for purposes of comparing cases, or examining the same case at different stages of treatment, the profile is, indeed, time-consuming, since all sections must be written out in detail. It is, however, no more laborious than completing and scoring a battery of research questionnaires and analysing the results. For everyday diagnostic purposes clinicians soon find that their speed improves with practice, as the user becomes familiar with headings of the profile and the way of thinking about mental life embodied in them. Nor does the profile need to be in written form. Often in diagnostic meetings where all participants have read the process records of interviews, the diagnostician simply leads the discussion by considering the material relevant to the various sections of the profile. Nor is it necessary for the Centre's particular interviewing format to be used. The profile is helpful for analysing and integrating material gained in any form of interviewing or reporting, and for identifying gaps in the information which would be needed to make a thorough assessment.

### Reasons for referral

The profile begins with a section on the referral, going beyond the presenting complaint to consider who referred and why, what prompted the referral at this particular time, and whether there might be other, underlying motives for seeking help, as well as other problems that emerge only in the course of the assessment.

### Description of the child

Next comes a general description of the child's appearance, moods and manner, and what this might signify about him. Where different people give different descriptions this may signify differences in the child's experiences or expectations and approach to different categories of people. For example, in the relatively unstructured diagnostic interviews a child may welcome the opportunity to engage the diagnostician in lively and enthusiastic fantasy games. But in the more structured psychological assessment he may become anxious and timid, fearful of 'failure' in answering questions or performing tasks. Whereas a different child may seem comfortable and confident in the structured psychological testing, but become scared and withdrawn in the unstructured diagnostic interview, uncertain what he is supposed to do and fearful of getting it wrong.

### Family background and personal history

Next, an examination of a detailed developmental history and family background is used to suggest possibly significant environmental factors, both positive and negative, as well as organic factors, which might be influencing the child's development and disturbance. Some parents are able to give this information in an orderly, thoughtful way. But others may be unable to clearly remember milestones, important events, illnesses, etc., or may never have thought about connections between events and their child's reactions, or about the implications of their child's behaviour. This gives the diagnostician clues about the nature of the parent–child relationship, but also makes it difficult to achieve a clear picture of the child's development. Some parents are able to use the history-giving process as a first step to making sense of their child and their own relationship to him, while others are unable to see the point of all these questions. This, too, gives clues about the likely interaction between parent and child.

### Possibly significant environmental influences

This section extracts the most important points from the history and family background to determine possible sources of pressure and influences on the child. They include things the parents have stressed, as well as those the assessment team thought could have been important, such as disruptions of family life through illness, death or separation, parental unemployment, features in the parents' personalities which impinge on the child, parental anxiety about the child 'taking after' a disturbed, delinquent or ill member of the family, traumatic accidents, moves of home, especially those involving loss of family and close friends, and any other factors which seem to have influenced the child's development. Together with physical disabilities, they represent factors outside the child's own psyche to which he has to adapt.

Against these are set the positive influences within or outside the family (e.g. school) which have had a supportive and stabilising effect on the child's development.

The sections of the profile thus far have set out the context for the child's difficulties as seen from the outside, as well as giving pointers to possible areas of vulnerability in the child, and possible areas of strength in the environment.

### Assessments of development

After this the profile has several sections which examine the child's internal world, trying to assess his emotional development and personality structure, taking into account not only his fears and fantasies, but what he has made of his own history and family background. The sections are based on Sigmund Freud's drive/structural theory in which the drives are seen as developmental forces motivating both the formation of relationships and the building of the personality structures needed to mediate and control the drives: the ego and superego. The conflicts between drives, ego and superego influence character formation and symptom formation. Anna Freud's particular contribution to this framework was to show the importance of the child's adaptation to his environment: the interactions between the child's need for relationships and his struggle to find ways of expressing his drives which do not alienate the objects of his love and hate; also how elements of his relationships are built into the ego and superego together with elements coming more directly from the drives. All these sections may make use of information given by other people, but the most important indicators come from the child's own material in his interviews.

## Drive development

First comes a section on drive development which assesses the child's progression through the phases of libidinal development and whether he has reached the age-appropriate one; or whether his development has become arrested at early levels or has regressed from higher levels; also whether expressions of aggression are age appropriate, overt or covert.

The most contentious section is that labelled 'drive distribution', because it is here that Anna Freud located the main assessment of the child's relationships. Other aspects of relationships are picked up in the ego and superego sections, but the basic assessment is in terms of libidinal cathexis of self and objects. Many people think that object relations should have a section in its own right – even those who do not believe that the child's entire development and psychopathology can be described in terms of his object relations. In the developmental lines (see Chapter 6) Anna Freud did spell out in greater detail the sequence of levels of relationships, and related achievements in other areas. But here, in the profile, her formulation emphasised the importance of the economic point of view in metapsychology: whether there is enough libido invested in self and object to create a state of healthy narcissism on the one hand, and stable attachments to objects on the other.

Whether or not the libidinal attachment to the object is strong enough to promote ego and superego development, or to provide a motive for curbing aggression (which she formulates in terms of fusion of aggression and libido) is described here and followed up in the ego and superego sections.

Likewise it is considered whether the child's libidinal investment in himself is good, or so poor that he either suffers from low self-esteem with all the consequent doubts about his capacities to achieve, and to be lovable and admirable, or defends against recognising his poor image of himself by means of grandiose ideas and omnipotent fantasies. In the 1972/1973 Index discussions, Anna Freud gave a simple definition of 'narcissistic homeostasis': it means that 'the person is pleased with himself' (Sandler and Freud 1985, p. 530).

Whether or not one agrees with the detail of Anna Freud's way of formulating this section matters less than the fact that it directs attention to the crucially important issues about the child's inner world of self and object relationships.

Pat Radford made particular use of these sections in a comparison of two deaf boys, both with potentially high IQs, both referred for learning difficulties, and aggressive and disruptive behaviour in school of a severity which could not be contained even by experienced teachers well used to handling the specific personality disorders of the deaf (Radford 1980). Radford makes the point that it is not the disability *per se* which is responsible for the psychopathology, but its impact on the child's objects and on his own feelings about himself.

> Both boys were much wanted. David, referred at age 9, had been a healthy baby when adopted, but became critically ill with a brain tumour at 3-and-a-half months, which left him profoundly deaf. Peter, referred at age 8, was a rubella child, and his mother had been reassured that he was not damaged. But eventually he proved to be profoundly deaf and partially sighted.
>
> Both sets of parents were devastated. David's parents were convinced he would die, and adopted another child while he was in hospital. On his return home he was cared for by a succession of nurses. He became hyperactive and demanding, unable to benefit from deaf aids or speech therapy. Peter's parents fought to obtain a correct diagnosis and get the

maximum help for him, but emotionally could not accept his disability and tried to treat him as a normal child. They found it hard to cope with the hyperactivity caused by the rubella. Peter managed to integrate into a normal nursery school, and apparently coped well with hospitalisations for eye operations.

David's family was further disrupted by his adoptive mother's death and father's lengthy incapacity with a severe illness when David was 3 years old. He was fostered until age 4 when his father remarried; his new step-mother took charge and cared for him well, and ensured that he got intensive educational help. He finally learned to speak at age 5, but was retarded in comparison with deaf peers, and his behaviour continued to deteriorate. He was angry, unhappy, bored and restless. He was unwilling to learn in spite of a high IQ, and could not be influenced by others because of his lack of concern for them. He was excessively jealous of his younger sibling.

Peter's parents found their marriage endangered by their reactions to his disabilities, but he forced them to stay together by panicking when either was absent. Confronted with other deaf, non-speaking children on entry to school at age 5, Peter withdrew from his peers, and refused to wear his hearing aid or glasses. He refused to do schoolwork, would not lip-read, and his behaviour deteriorated at home and school to the point where both school and parents wished to send him away to boarding school. To help herself cope his mother sought psychotherapy for herself and then for him.

Thus both boys had to cope with the distressed, uncomprehending and rejecting reactions of their parents, as well as with traumatic events, David more so than Peter. The fact of David's adoption, a significant factor in the development of most adoptive children, in David's life became only one of a series of losses and separations which contributed to the disruption of his development. On the surface they presented very similar pictures of aggressive, disruptive behaviour and refusal to learn. Both seemed more handicapped than their peers with a similar degree of physical disability. But marked differences between them emerged in the profile sections on self-cathexis and object relations.

David was physically well co-ordinated and showed some pleasure in bodily activity. But in all other ways he was dissatisfied with himself. He wanted to be 'lovely' and could not bear to be thought 'horrible'. He could not bear frustration or failure of any kind, and used constant physical movement to evade recognition of either. He could not be encouraged by his objects to persevere. He was dominated by omnipotent fantasies, for example, of being an ice-skating champion, though he rarely practised. He seemed to deny his disabilities, while simultaneously using his deafness as a weapon for getting his own way. He seemed unaware of the consequences of his actions, and may have lacked a sense of wrongdoing. But he seemed overwhelmed by a sense of shame, unable to improve his self-esteem because he could not come to terms with his lack of perfection.

Peter, by contrast, did seem to like himself and expect to be liked, for example, wanting to wear attractive clothes, being friendly and wishing to communicate. He was sufficiently self-confident to organise his activities in diagnostic interviews, in contrast with his unco-operative attitude in school. It seemed that he felt better in settings where his defects were not stressed. He also got on better with hearing than with deaf children. Clearly his physical defects were a narcissistic hurt to him, but in other areas his self-esteem was better, perhaps reflecting his parents' view of him.

David had a major disturbance in object relations, unsurprising in view of his many losses and separations. He functioned largely on a need-satisfying level, making no attempt at getting on with others. His relationships consisted mainly of attempts to control and manipulate others, with the exception of his step-mother to whom he showed a degree of attachment. He was sadistic to other children.

Peter, however, had progressed through the appropriate levels of object relationships although with some delay in becoming established in latency. His fantasies still contained open Oedipal rivalry with his father for mother, and protectiveness and concern for his mother. In his reality behaviour, however, he was aggressive and demanding towards his mother, and this seemed linked with blaming her for his deafness, though not for his visual impairment, yet he also trusted her and expected her help. His reality relationship to his father was on a more pre-Oedipal level, seeing him as a caring person. Peter also had good relationships with his grandparents and with hearing peers. But with deaf peers he was either aggressive or withdrawn.

It was clear that Peter's difficult behaviour arose primarily from conflicts around his deafness which affected limited aspects of his self-esteem and relationships to others. He needed to resolve these conflicts to make the most of his potential.

David, however, had a primary disturbance of object relationships, with his deafness serving to increase his lack of trust. All areas of development had been affected, and lengthy therapeutic, developmental and educational help would be required, all dependent on the appropriate workers being able to establish some form of relationship with him.

## Ego and superego development

There follows a section on ego and superego development, which considers whether the basic 'ego apparatus' is intact; i.e. whether or not there are organic defects which will interfere with the development of ego functions (memory, reality testing, synthesis of wishes, urges and experiences, control of motility, speech and thinking). For example, we would expect both Peter and David, because of their lack of hearing, to experience some interference and delay in the development of speech, possibly of thinking, and perhaps with some repercussions on other ego functions, all of which could have been largely overcome by appropriate special needs provision.

This section considers whether ego functions have developed to the age-appropriate level or whether there are primary deficiencies (which are largely those deriving from failures of the early mother–child relationship, traumatic events or physical illnesses, ranging from inadequate stimulation and nurturing of the baby's maturational moves to active interference with developing functions). David's primary disturbance in object relations meant that his ego functioning suffered more widespread delay and disturbance than Peter's.

In this section particular attention is also paid to the defence organisation, in terms of the range of defences the child has developed, whether they are age appropriate, whether they are effective and well balanced, whether they are flexible or rigid, whether specific drives or affects are more defended against than others; also whether defences are interfering with ego achievements. Both David and Peter were using defences which prevented them from making the most of their capacities and abilities.

The child's identifications are also examined to see whether he is making the normal identifications with his objects; much of a child's way of thinking, understanding and behaving is modelled on his parents or other important carers, so these identifications influence both ego and superego functions, as well as shaping his self-development. The failure to develop close relationships will interfere with this process. Identification with people who are themselves disturbed, defective or ill can produce a surface appearance of mental illness or defect which is not an accurate assessment of the child's actual functioning capacity.

The child's affective development is also considered, both from the point of view of the range of feelings available to him, and whether and in what way these feelings are overtly expressed.

Concerning the superego the profile considers whether it is age adequate, which involves the extent to which it is still dependent on reinforcement from external objects, and to what extent it has become independent (i.e. internalised); whether it is harsh and primitive, or whether it has benign, rewarding aspects as well as punitive ones.

It is to be noted that the profile makes a clear distinction between 'ego' and 'self', a distinction which was not always clear in Sigmund Freud's own writings, but which was clarified by Hartmann, Jacobson and others including Anna Freud; in the Hampstead Clinic Joseph Sandler's work was particularly important in this respect. It is a distinction which permits the cognitive aspects of a child's development to be distinguished from the development of aspects of internal self and object representations. Thus a child's development may be described in terms of his internal fantasy life in which he and his objects have roles, or in terms of his reality interactions with objects, or in terms of the development of specific ego and superego functions which depend partly on maturation, partly on interaction with objects. This distinction allows for finer assessments of which elements in a child's development are going wrong, and what forms of therapy or other help are required for them.

This section can be illustrated by excerpts from a terminal profile on a boy in analysis from age 6 to 9 (Edgcumbe 1980). George was referred for soiling. Other problems not originally mentioned by his parents included major rages and temper tantrums. Under 'description', dramatic variations in appearance, moods and behaviour were recorded. He could be a neat, tidy schoolboy, well behaved and self-possessed, or a scruffy, wild, unmanageable ruffian, or a drooling, snivelling, smelly, neglected-looking half-wit. Among the 'environmental factors' a family secret concerned his older brother, severely disabled and sent away at birth. George was not supposed to know of this child, but his anxious parents constantly watched over him for signs of handicap, and much of George's behaviour seemed to mimic a defective person.

Under ego functioning the diagnostic profile noted a speech impediment whose severity varied; poor muscular co-ordination and manual control resulting in clumsiness and awkwardness, also variable; occasional failures of reality-testing, poor concentration and other interferences with his learning ability. His school performance was thought to be commensurate with an IQ in the average range. All these difficulties were thought to be due to interference from conflict. All improved during treatment, reappearing only at moments of high anxiety.

Denial was a prominent defence at the diagnostic stage, particularly in connection with object loss and curiosity. He also denied any concern about his soiling. Denial of affect was pronounced and gave way only slowly with analysis of fears of rejection. Regression in drives, ego and superego was for a long time the most intractable defence, used to avoid conflicts about loss of love, and about phallic-Oedipal wishes. It transpired that his mother could tolerate his soiling better than his phallic masculinity, and was unrealistically terrified of his rages and tantrums. He also used projection a great deal. This primitive constellation of defences was seriously interfering with his ego functioning. The reorganisation of defences during treatment permitted the improvements in all his ego functioning. Further, his school performance rose to a level suggesting an above-average IQ, he developed interests in hobbies, and mastered new skills such as games and playing musical instruments.

The improvements in ego-functioning paralleled an improvement in self-esteem noted in the section on libido distribution. This arose from the modification of his alternating self-images which had, at the diagnostic stage included a denigrated, faecal self, arising from defensive regression, and a dangerously aggressive, destructive, phallic self. Both these self-representations had been reinforced by his mother's attitudes and fears, and work with her had helped to modify her relationship with George.

Concomitant with these self-images and fears of loss of love, George's superego was harsh, critical and punitive at the diagnostic stage. Analysis of his conflicts, perhaps boosted by identification with more benign internal objects, helped to produce a more balanced superego including some benign rewarding and aim-giving aspects.

Having examined these separate areas of development, the profile moves on to several sections which assist the diagnostican to integrate the data so as to arrive at overall conclusions about crucial areas of psychopathology.

### Genetic assessments: regression and fixation points

The term 'genetic', as used by psychoanalysts, does not refer specifically to genes, or to characteristics or susceptibility to diseases determined by a person's physical genetic makeup. When Sigmund Freud was developing his metapsychological theory, the science of genetics was only dreamed of; Freud often expressed the hope that one day biology would answer his questions about the physical basis of mental functioning. For him, the genetic point of view referred in a more general way to the origins or mode of formation of personality traits or psychological characteristics. It might include a constitutional factor which could not be measured at the time Freud was working, but it mainly referred to the psychological factors which he could discern, especially the fixations and regressions.

In Anna Freud's profile a section on fixation and regression puts together various aspects of the material which can indicate vulnerable points in development at which the child has had special difficulty and to which he may regress under stress. Aspects of the child's behaviour as described by parents and others as well as witnessed by the diagnostician, certain symptoms which have known connections with particular phases of development, as well as the child's fantasies, can all be used to pinpoint libidinal phases and levels of object relationships to which the child tends to regress, or from which he has not been able to move forward; this material can also indicate at what levels the child encountered problems he could not resolve, so that he avoids the issues by regressing.

Anna Freud stressed that pathology results not from normal, temporary regressions, but from regressions that become permanent and therefore have repercussions in harmful readjustments of the personality. Regressions which begin in the ego/superego may be caused by traumatic shocks, highly anxiety-arousing events, separations, severe disappointments in love objects or severe disillusion in people with whom the child has identified in his functioning (Jacobson 1946). A regressed ego loses its power to control feelings and impulses; defences break down and the child may have outbursts of uncontrollable aggression or emotions and other irrational behaviour.

When regression starts in the drives, the outcome depends on the way the ego reacts. If it also regresses, there is a general lowering of the standards and demands the child makes on himself. The regression is 'ego-syntonic'. This was the case with 'George', described above. The total personality may become less mature, resulting in forms of infantile, delinquent or other atypical behaviour, depending on which ego and superego functions are most affected, and how far the regression goes. But if the ego and superego have reached 'secondary autonomy' (Hartmann 1950b), i.e. they have become sufficiently independent of id pressures (as well as of dependence on the child's objects), the regression will be 'ego-dystonic'. Then the child will be horrified, anxious and guilty about his regressed wishes and feelings, and will attempt to defend himself against them; if that fails he will develop symptoms or other compromise forms of behaviour, i.e. he will be in conflict, and will develop one or another form of infantile neurosis. 'The anxiety hysterics, phobias, pavor nocturnus, the obsessions, rituals, bedtime ceremonials, inhibitions, character neuroses belong in this category' (Freud A. 1965a, pp. 127–131).

### Dynamic and structural assessments: conflicts

This section pulls together the material to determine the dominant conflicts in the child's life at this time, and whether they are age appropriate and within his capacity to resolve.

Anna Freud described how the progress of structuralisation of the personality, i. e. the development of ego and superego through maturation and via identification with the parents, can be assessed from the nature of the conflicts and anxieties discernible in the child. The earliest form of conflict is 'external', in which the child's immature ego is still siding with his wishes and impulses. Control depends on the child's objects, and he gets into battles with them over satisfaction of his needs and wishes. This type of external conflict is considered infantile if it remains the dominant form, or the child regresses to it at later ages. While external conflicts are dominant the child's anxieties are aroused by the external world: he fears, in sequence, loss of the caretaking object (separation anxiety), loss of the object's love (after the establishment of object constancy), criticism and punishment by the object (this becomes reinforced by projection of his own aggression), and finally castration.

But as the conflicts become internalised, they are played out between his own ego/superego and id. What he then fears is his own superego, i.e. he experiences guilt.

The third type of conflict is independent of external pressures. The conflict lies between opposing drive trends: love and hate, activity and passivity, masculinity and femininity. These are not conflictual early in life. (I have already mentioned, in Chapter 4, Anna Freud's disagreement with Melanie Klein on this point, since she believed that opposing trends only become conflictual as the ego matures enough for the development of the synthetic function. Then the opposition between the trends, now perceived as incompatible, can no longer be tolerated by the child.) These internal conflicts arouse great anxiety in the child.

The external conflicts can sometimes be improved via changes in management of the child, not through analysis. But the internalised and internal conflicts can only be influenced by analysis of the internal situation, with the internalised conflicts being less difficult to deal with than the completely internal ones (Freud, A. 1965a, pp. 131–134).

The assessments in the last two sections begin to indicate the general level of the child's maturity and the severity of his disturbance. The following section assesses some factors which influence the child's chances of spontaneous recovery and likely reaction to therapy.

## Assement of some general characteristics

Predictions of future mental health or illness depend not only on assessment of the type of disturbance, but also on certain general characteristics which are innate or acquired through experience very early in life. Children who cannot tolerate frustration rapidly become unhappy and angry; they are in greater danger than those who can accept waiting, or find substitute satisfactions. Children who can sublimate their drive energy have an additional safeguard for mental health.

The way children deal with anxiety is of greater importance than the level or strength of it. Children who can tolerate and find ways of mastering anxiety have a better chance of remaining healthy than those who have to avoid anxiety at all costs; the latter will set up defensive patterns (of denial, projection or other primitive mechanisms) which promote pathology (Freud, A. 1965a, pp. 135–136).

- *Frustration tolerance* for tension and frustration of wishes or needs determines how much anxiety or unpleasure a child can cope with before he gets upset and resorts to potentially pathological adaptations.
- *Sublimation potential* determines how readily a child can avoid pathological solutions to conflict by displacing drive energies into other activities which bring different kinds of rewards.
- *The overall attitude to anxiety* indicates whether the child uses mainly avoidance measures to escape anxiety, either about his own inner urges, wishes and fantasies or about the external world; or whether he uses more active forms of mastery which are likely to be less pathological.
- The balance between *progressive developmental forces and regressive tendencies* indicates the chances of spontaneous recovery or active use of therapeutic help. Children who find pleasure in new experiences and in being 'big' find it easier to cope with the frustrations and disappointments of growing up, and therefore to remain healthy. But those who are fearful of new experiences, and prefer to remain small, are more likely to experience growth in terms of losses and deprivations, to become arrested or to develop fixations which leave them vulnerable to serious regression (Freud, A. 1965a, pp. 137–138).

### Diagnosis

In the final section all the conclusions of the previous sections are integrated to suggest a diagnosis and recommendation for treatment. This may be either in the form of a diagnostic statement assembling the main points which have emerged about external and internal factors to summarise the way these have successively influenced the child's development and what sort of outcome they have produced. Or the diagnostician may choose to place the child in one of the categories devised by Anna Freud, giving reasons for this choice from the assembled pointers in the profile. The categories are:

1    that, in spite of current manifest behaviour disturbances, the personality growth of the child is essentially healthy and falls within the wide range of 'variations of normality';
2    that existent pathological formations (symptoms) are of a transitory nature and can be classed as by-products of developmental strain;
3    that there is permanent drive regression to previously established fixation points which leads to conflicts of a neurotic type and gives rise to infantile neuroses and character disorders;
4    that there is drive regression as above, plus simultaneous ego and superego regressions which lead to infantilisms, borderline, delinquent or psychotic disturbances;
5    that there are primary deficiences of an organic nature or early deprivations which distort development and structuralisation and produce retarded, defective and non-typical personalities;
6    that there are destructive processes at work (of organic, toxic, psychic, known or unknown origin) which have effected, or are on the point of effecting, a disruption of mental growth.

(Freud, A. 1965a, p. 147)

The contribution of the final sections of the profile in arriving at a diagnosis and recommendation for treatment can be illustrated by comparing two children.

Timothy, aged 7, was referred for anxious, hyperactive and aggressive behaviour. He had fractured his skull in an accident, but on neurological examination no abnormalities were found. Not long after he had needed to be circumcised. He had also had to adapt to various upheavals in his life including the death of a sibling, his parents' divorce and various moves of home and country.

The diagnostic assessment showed that progressive forces predominated over regressive ones, that conflicts were not marked, though problems might yet arise from conflicts between passivity and activity. The general characteristics section suggested evidence for both high and low frustration tolerance in different situations. His sublimation potential was good. His overall attitude to anxiety was to attempt to master it, though not always successfully.

The diagnostic conclusion was that he had been exposed to developmental strain throughout his life. His symptoms could not be considered transitory, but he had not yet developed a neurosis. He would need help to avoid a more permanent disorder, and was considered capable of using analysis.

(Earle 1979)

Susan, aged 8, was referred for deteriorating schoolwork and frequent minor illnesses and absences from school. She, too, had had to cope with many stresses in her life, including her parents' divorce, changing partners and moves of home.

The diagnostic assessment showed her still in conflict with the external world, desiring to reunite her parents. Her attempts at resolving internalised, Oedipal conflicts were being distorted by her life situation.

Her frustration tolerance was good in a one-to-one situation, but without individual attention she became anxious and unable to concentrate. Her sublimation potential seemed low, perhaps due to her poor self-esteem and reliance on the object to facilitate concentration. Her overall attitude to anxiety was not good, she did not cope with it except by avoidance. Her struggles to deal with internal and external problems was impeding progressive movement.

Diagnostically it was difficult to discern the balance between developmental disharmony and neurotic conflict. It was thought that she might be able to use analytic help, but only if her mother could support it.

(Lament 1983)

Both of these children had been exposed to stressful life events, Timothy perhaps more so than Susan. But Timothy was coping in a more active way, independently attempting to overcome difficulties and likely to make active use of analytic help. Whereas Susan was becoming more overwhelmed, passive and dependent on others, unlikely to cope with the challenges of therapy without a great deal of support.

## Modifications of the profile

Since the profile is a way of thinking rather than a specific formula, it is capable of modification in many ways to accommodate the diagnostician's or the research worker's special requirements. Anna Freud initially devised it for the clinical assessment of disturbed children, but it was subsequently extended to babies at one end of the age range, and to adolescents and adults at the other. The basic metapsychological framework remains the same, but in the sections on development different phases of life require emphasis and elaboration. Thus the Baby Profile was developed by Ernst Freud from his work with mothers and infants, and it places special emphasis on the early forerunners of later personality features, on the earliest developments in object relationships, expressions of drive and affect, and ego development. Ways of observing these features are described in terms relevant for young babies (Freud, W.E. 1967, 1971). Similarly, Erna Furman has developed the toddler profile, which not only goes into detail about the many areas of development the toddler has to pass through, but also gives a parallel series of headings for the mother's capacities for supporting and aiding her child's development (Furman 1992). The adolescent profile was developed by Moses Laufer, and extended the sections on development to include examination of the way the adolescent deals with the particular tasks of adolescence: to integrate physical sexual maturity, the changing relationship to parents, the development of mature peer relationships, the finding of a sexual object, and the acceptance of responsibility for one's own behaviour (Laufer 1965). The adult profile extends this even further to examine whether the ultimate developmental stages have been reached and whether the quality of functioning is adequate in work, sexual life and sublimations (Freud A. *et al.* 1965).

The profile has also been modified to elaborate in greater detail on sections which are especially relevant to children with a specific handicap. Dorothy Burlingham, for example, developed a profile for blind babies which stressed the different way blind babies experience their environment, their different needs, the special problems parents will have in raising their babies, the repercussions of the parents' own feelings about their child's blindness (both their reactions to discovering it, and their potential guilt about it) (Burlingham 1975). Humberto Nagera and Alice Colonna used the profile to study the role of sight in children's development (Nagera and Colonna 1965). Paul Brinich has developed a profile for deaf children which similarly stresses the additional factors that must be taken into account when assessing a deaf child (Brinich 1981).

As in the Hampstead Index, theoretical problems were thrown up by the application of the profile to a wide range of clinical problems. For example, Ruth Thomas, in a paper based on the work of four therapists treating a group of psychotic children (Hansi Kennedy, Maria Berger, Lilian Weitzner and myself, with Ruth Thomas as consultant and co-ordinator), notes that on the one hand the profile was useful for highlighting aspects of the children's chaotic development and reactions to treatment; on the other hand, some apparently significant chararacteristics also appeared in other forms of disturbance deriving from the earliest period of development. Focusing on selected aspects of the profile, she attempted to modify it 'where it has not proved a fine enough sieve to differentiate between the degree of disturbance we are studying and lesser disturbances which are better understood' (Thomas *et al.* 1966, p. 544). In particular, it proved necessary to elaborate on stages in the development of self and object relationships, especially the very early ones, together with aspects of the family background, and the distortions of development found in our children. Both Anna Freud and Joseph Sandler took part in the discussions of these issues (ibid., pp. 544–579).

This was one of many research studies at the Hampstead Clinic which focused on childhood disturbances or on comparison of adult and childhood psychopathology (Freud, A. 1969b). Many of these studies contributed to different forms of the profile, as well as to Anna Freud's own thinking (Freud, A. 1965a, pp. 108–147).

The profile was modified for use in comparative studies of adult psychotics (Freeman 1973, 1975), and mainline heroin addicts (Radford *et al.* 1972; Wiseberg *et al.* 1975), as well as for comparison of child and adult psychopathology (Freeman 1976). It has also been used in a comparative study of the results of intensive and non-intensive therapy (Heinicke 1965).

## Developmental lines

Shortly after publishing the diagnostic profile, Anna Freud published the developmental lines (Freud, A. 1963a, 1965a, pp. 62–92), another useful framework. It was one which opened the way for further developments in theory and modifications in technique, and therefore deserves a chapter to itself. I go on to consider the lines and their importance in Chapter 6.

# The developmental lines, further elaboration of developmental theory and later applications

In the last two decades of her life, the developmental point of view permeated all areas of Anna Freud's work. The developmental lines are one manifestation of it. They have both practical and theoretical roles. They can be used by non-analysts as well as analysts to examine a child's readiness for various life experiences, or to see in detail which necessary capacities are well developed in him, and where there are deficits. They can also be used to pinpoint areas of deficit in adults, and to promote the expansion and modification of theory.

The lines examine in detail particular sequences of drive and structural development in specific areas. 'Whatever level has been reached by any given child in any of these respects represents the results of interaction between drive and ego–superego development and their reaction to environmental influences, i.e. between maturation, adaptation and structuralisation' (Freud, A. 1965a, p. 64). We can see how the child has progressed through the various developmental tasks involved in each line, and whether development is even or uneven among the various lines. Although the lines place more emphasis on observable behaviour, they also spell out the internal, psychological development required to achieve each step on each line. The lines are sometimes used in conjunction with the profile, or even instead of it, to assess disturbance in development. They are especially useful for highlighting developmental delays and distortions.

The developmental lines are not a substitute for the meta-psychological approach to assessment. Nor, as Neubauer points out, are they simply an additional metapsychological point of view, to be added to the dynamic, genetic, economic, structural and topographic. Rather, the developmental approach is supraordinate to the metapsychological dimensions. It is an endeavour to address the enormous complexity of human development by scrutinising smaller areas and sequences of progress (Neubauer 1984).

It is noteworthy that the lines have a marked focus on the role of the child's object relations. To anyone who has read Anna Freud's publications from the war nursery years the lines immediately seem familiar, for they are a development of her thinking about the observations made during those years (see Chapter 3). They are, however, extremely condensed statements which cannot be understood without elaboration and illustration; and their deceptive simplicity contains a view of the complexity of human development.

## THE DEVELOPMENTAL LINES: THE INITIAL PRESENTATION

Over the years Anna Freud described many developmental lines in greater or lesser detail. But her original discussion listed six lines which she regarded as prototypes and gave in some detail:

1   From dependency to emotional self-reliance and adult object relationships.
2   From suckling to rational eating.
3   From wetting and soiling to bladder and bowel control.
4   From irresponsibility to responsibility in body management. (lines 2 to 4 are aspects of development towards body independence).
5   From egocentricity to companionship.
6   From the body to the toy and from play to work.

(Freud, A. 1965a, pp. 64–87)

### Line 1. From dependency to emotional self-reliance and adult object relationships

(Freud, A. 1965a, pp. 64–68). Anna Freud viewed this line as the 'basic developmental line which has received attention from analysts from the beginning . . . the sequence which leads from the newborn's utter dependence on maternal care to the young adult's emotional and material self-reliance' (ibid., p. 64). The line describes the observable, external relationship between child and mother (or mother-substitute), as well as the developing internal world of object representations which become templates for subsequent relationships. It takes further the ideas about the early stages of development which she had expressed in an introduction to the discussion at a symposium on the mutual influences in the development of ego and id. The main presenters were Hartmann (1952) and Hoffer (1952); Melanie Klein was among the participants (Freud, A. 1952c).

### Stage 1

> The biological unity between the mother–infant couple, with the mother's narcissism extending to the child, and the child including the mother in his internal 'narcissistic milieu' (Hoffer 1952).
>
> (Freud, A. 1965a, p. 65)

Anna Freud meant by this that in the earliest months of life the baby has a built-in physical relationship to his mother, but psychologically is not yet aware of her as a separate person. From the baby's point of view this phase may be called narcissistic in that he has not yet discovered that mother is not part of himself, not under his control. From the mother's point of view it may be called narcissistic because the baby that was part of her body continues to be experienced psychologically as part of herself, an experience that changes gradually as she begins to perceive his individuality and difference from herself. This phase is the foundation on which are built subsequent developments of emotional attachment to objects. Loss of the mother during this phase gives rise to 'separation anxiety proper' (ibid., p. 66): the generalised psychosomatic distress and disturbance suffered by the baby in the hands of strangers, and the loss precipitates the baby into premature experiences of separateness from the object. The provision of a stable mother-substitute helps a small baby recover, as does reunion with the mother. But if neither of these events happen quickly enough there may be serious repercussions on later development. Hansi Kennedy has suggested that Anna Freud initially placed the development of attachment rather late, around six months, because she began by observing institutionalised children in whom it was delayed. But her later observations of family babies in the Hampstead Well Baby Clinic led her to place the development of attachment much nearer to birth (personal communication). In addition, the received neurological wisdom of the time suggested that neurological pathways were not sufficiently mature to support psychological functioning. All this pre-dated the recent research on the newborn's sensory abilities to differentiate mother from others. In the 1972/1973 index discussions Sandler and Anna Freud agreed that in 1936 'earliest infancy' would have meant childhood rather than babyhood, whereas now it means the first few weeks of life (Sandler and Freud 1985, p. 435).

Perhaps the most eloquent of Anna Freud's discussions of this early stage in the mother–child relationship, and the repercussions from disruption of it, is to be found in her paper 'About losing and being lost', written in 1953 but not published until 1967. In this paper the concepts of 'object cathexis' and 'narcissistic cathexis' were clarified as referring to the infant's developing attachment to his object, his mother or her substitute, and his initial inability to make a clear psychological distinction between her and himself. Transitional objects, toys and other possessions come to symbolise self or object. The mother is the child's most important 'possession' to which he clings, and he needs to feel 'possessed' by the mother in order to feel safely cared for and held. The child who frequently 'gets lost' or loses his possessions is demonstrating his sense of feeling insecurely held and valued, and his consequent inability to value himself and the possessions which symbolise his self (Freud, A. 1967a).

Anna Freud did not believe that a baby of a few weeks or months was yet capable of having fantasies about objects of the sort described by Melanie Klein. She places these into her own second stage. But several of her papers indicate that she placed the early introjective and projective processes in the first stage (see p. 73); her own thinking would have included Sigmund Freud's description of the early differentiation of ego and external world in terms of what is pleasurable and unpleasurable (Freud, S. 1915, pp. 135–136).

In her summary of the stages, Anna Freud also places all of Margeret Mahler's autistic, symbiotic and separation–individuation phases (Mahler *et al.* 1975) within her own first stage, to my mind wrongly. Present-day thinking refutes the existence of normal phases which can be called autistic or symbiotic. Before this doubt arose, however, the autistic and symbiotic phases might have been thought to belong in these early months. But Mahler's descriptions of the separation–individuation process, which is still accepted as valid, place it as continuing into the second year of life, i.e. into Anna Freud's second stage; and, indeed, Anna Freud links break-downs in individuation with failures in her own stage 2 (Freud, A. 1965a, p. 67).

### Stage 2

> The part object (Melanie Klein), or need-fulfilling, anaclitic relationship, which is based on the urgency of the child's body needs and drive derivatives and is intermittent and fluctuating, since object cathexis is sent out under the impact of imperative desires, and withdrawn again when satisfaction has been reached.
>
> (Freud, A. 1965a, p. 65)

This extremely condensed statement is meant to cover the still egocentric child's growing awareness of the mother's separateness and her role in satisfying his many and varied bodily and emotional needs. The urgency of the infant's need for his mother at any given moment depends on the number and urgency of his physical and psychological needs at that moment. At moments when his needs are quiescent, or are ones that he can satisfy for himself, for example, gaining pleasure through autoerotic activity or visual and tactile exploration of the world around him, he has no need of an external object. It is, however, during this phase that the infant is beginning to build up internal images of 'good' and 'bad' mother who satisfies or frustrates his needs and desires (Edgcumbe and Burgner 1973). These images have not yet coalesced into a stable object representation in the child's mind of an object who exists in her own right, not merely as the baby's servant. The internal image may be good enough to help the baby recognise the sounds of a feed being prepared, and to wait for a short time; but not for long, because the real external mother with a real feed is required to stem hunger. That babies soon come to prefer their mother (or their main caretaker) to other people is demonstrated by the obvious caution or even anxiety shown towards strangers. The infant has a good enough internal image to recognise his mother, long before the image is stable enough to recall it in her absence and use it as a source of comfort or reassurance. The needs remain more import-ant than the person, which is why Anna Freud said that the very young child who is separated from his own mother has no choice but to accept a substitute mother (see Chapter 3).

Anna Freud did not date the stages on developmental lines in terms of age, because of the wide variations in normal development, and because the moves are very gradual. In this line, from dependency to emotional self-reliance, the timing of the beginning moves from stage one to two depends on the personality and circumstances of each mother–child couple, but is usually underway before the second half of the first year. Although the needs remain more important than the person for some time, the crucial internal developments in Stage 2 are the establishment of the mother representations in the child's mind linked with gratifications and frustrations which help him to become aware of her separateness from him and to develop an attachment to her. Anna Freud stated that failures in the mother–child relationship at this stage could cause breakdowns in individuation, anaclitic depression (Spitz 1946), various manifestations of deprivation, precocious ego development (James 1960) or a 'false self' (Winnicott 1960b). Winnicott, however, would probably see the false self as liable to begin developing as early as Stage 1 if the child is forced to accommodate to the mother's needs and his own needs are insufficiently met (Freud, A. 1965a, p. 67).

## Stage 3

> The stage of object constancy which enables a positive inner image of the object to be maintained, irrespective of either satisfactions or disatisfactions.
>
> (Freud, A. 1965a, p. 65)

This stage is pivotal for the whole future development of relationships (Burgner and Edgcumbe 1973) since without the capacity for object constancy the individual will never achieve the ability to make and maintain reciprocal relationships which can survive disappointments, disillusionments or frustrations, and within which he can willingly care for the object as well as demanding to be cared for.

For the small child this capacity allows temporary separations to be lengthened as the child becomes able to use the inner image of mother to substitute for her actual presence for gradually longer times. Very young babies may imitate things their mothers do for

them. But it is only with the stabilisation of the internal representation of mother that the child's imitations can consolidate into a
useful identification which gives the child the capacity to mother
himself and others. For children who have been brought up at
home exclusively or mainly by the mother, the capacity for object
constancy is the minimum requirement for entry into nursery
school, since it allows the child to have confidence that mother
continues to exist and will return; without it the child cannot feel
safe enough to enjoy the new experiences offered by the nursery
school. For the child whose care has been shared, whether through
day nursery care or by a another person in the home taking an
equal or greater role than the mother in the child's upbringing, the
situation is more complicated. Children are capable of developing
constant relationships with more than one person provided they
are reasonably stable and predictable. Thus a child may develop
attachments to father, grandparents or an au pair. Practice in
managing more than one dependent relationship may even help in
making the transition to new situations without feeling lost. But
too many changes or losses delay the development of object constancy, and in extreme cases prevent it altogether. The child then
cannot develop an internal model for reliable relationships, and
may end up unable to trust anyone, or to expect any relationship to
endure. He may feel unable to look after himself or anyone else, or
to let anyone look after him. Such a child may, depending on other
factors, be suspicious of nursery school and reluctant to engage
with people or in activities; or alternatively he may prove promiscuous in forming transient attachments to many people and
drifting from one activity to another. The child with good enough
object constancy usually chooses a particular teacher to whom he
forms a special attachment, and this choice of a substitute helps
him manage the separation from mother.

### Stage 4

> The ambivalent relationship of the preoedipal, anal-sadistic
> stage, characterised by the ego attitudes of clinging, torturing,
> dominating and controlling the love objects.
>
> (Freud, A. 1965a, p. 65)

Often known as the 'terrible twos' (though it may begin earlier
than that), this is the stage in which all a toddler's love and hate,

needs and wishes can be focused on the same person, and many conflicts are visible. Demanding to be looked after alternates with 'me do it'. Clinging alternates with struggling to get down from mother's lap and running off. Battles to take charge of his own body may focus on toilet training, eating, bathing or dressing, and may alternate with passively wanting to be fed, cleaned, etc. Anna Freud pointed out that this behaviour is not due to mother spoiling the child, but to normal ambivalence. It is also due to the child's rapid ego development which makes him want to practise all his maturing motor skills, as well as the skills he is learning in identification with his parents. This development also leads him to be full of curiosity and wishes to explore and to try out whatever looks interesting, but at the same time to be more aware of external danger.

The internal danger in this phase is the failure to resolve ambivalence sufficiently to control aggression and hatred within relationships. Anna Freud continued a line of thought discussed in an earlier paper (Freud, A. 1949a), stating that 'unsatisfactory libidinal relations to unstable or otherwise unsuitable love objects during anal sadism . . . will disturb the balanced fusion between libido and aggression and give rise to uncontrollable aggressivity, destructivness, etc.' (Freud, A. 1965a, p. 67). This is another statement that needs to be unpacked if it is to be fully understood. The work in the war nurseries (see Chapter 3) had already led Anna Freud to formulate her view that the child can learn self-control and consideration for others only within a close and stable relationship; that children accept frustration and become willing to make sacrifices only for someone they love and feel loved by; that an inner moral sense and acceptance of the rules of society develop best in a safe and stable attachment to the family as the representative of society. Her later works clarify her view of aggression as an essential drive which, used positively, serves mastery and achievements of various kinds. Among other things, as I once heard her put it, aggression 'gives the power to grasp the object'. In other words, it has an important role in the child's active search for object relationships. But if it is not 'balanced' with libido, i.e. bound by feelings of love and concern for the object, it becomes sadistic and destructive. Children who are violent to others, whose only pleasure seems to lie in destroying or defacing property, who torment animals, other children or vulnerable adults, are those whose attempts at relationships have failed to result in a balance in which love can control hate. They are children who have been deprived of a loving, stable relationship at crucial periods of their development.

Collectively, these first four stages are often referred to as 'pre-Oedipal', as coinciding with the oral and anal phases of drive development; forms of disturbance which have their roots here are loosely thought of as 'non-neurotic'. In the early days of psycho-analysis they were considered unsuitable for psychoanalytic treatment, though this view changed with awareness of the possibilities of treating developmental delays and deviations (see Chapter 7).

### Stage 5

> The completely object-centred phallic-oedipal phase, characterised by possessiveness of the parent of the opposite sex (or vice versa), jealousy of and rivalry with the parents of the same sex, protectiveness, curiosity, bids for admiration, and exhibitionistic attitudes; in girls a phallic-oedipal (masculine) relationship to the mother preceding the oedipal relationship to the father.
>
> (Freud, A. 1965a, pp. 65–66)

Here, Anna Freud finally arrives at the stage of object relationships which Sigmund Freud and the early analysts considered of crucial importance in the development of neuroses. Anna Freud herself maintained that view. But her awareness of the things that can go wrong in the preceding stages made her (and many modern analysts) regard infantile neurosis as not merely a form of emotional disturbance but as an achievement, only possible in an individual who has successfully negotiated the earlier stages and developed the personality structures capable of producing internalised neurotic conflict.

The simple formula of unconsciously wishing to murder one parent in order to marry the other does not suffice to make clear what has to have been achieved by this stage. To be in conflict about these wishes requires that the child has moved on from regarding each love object primarily as a source of need satisfaction, to be discarded when not needed and retrieved again on demand, to an acceptance of the object's separate existence and concern for the needs and rights of the object. The child also has to be aware of the existence of aspects of relationships between his two parents from which he is excluded, i.e. he has to have moved beyond a capacity only for one-to-one relationships with one person at a time, to the capacity for being in a triangular relationship with two other people at a time. He has to have developed a complex internal world which can encompass all these different types of relationships with their accompanying wishes and affects. He has to have developed a good enough ego and superego to be aware of the forbidden nature of his incestuous wishes, to feel anxiety and guilt about them, and concern about the effects on his objects of acting on his wishes. In addition, there are all the internal and external influences that determine the child's moves between positive and negative Oedipal positions, i.e. heterosexual or homosexual object choices.

If the child does not develop the conflicts appropriate to this phase it means that he has developmental deficits which lead to non-neurotic forms of personality disorder. The child who develops the conflicts but fails to resolve them adequately has the basis for developing a neurotic character or a symptom neurosis. The child who both develops and resolves the conflicts has the basis for subsequent healthy development.

### Stage 6

> The latency period, i.e. the post-oedipal lessening of drive urgency and the transfer of libido from the parental figures to contemporaries, community groups, teachers, leaders, impersonal ideals, and aim-inhibited, sublimated interests, with fantasy manifestations giving evidence of disillusionment with and denigration of the parents ('family romance', twin fantasies, etc.).
>
> (Freud, A. 1965a, p. 66)

This is a description of a healthy schoolchild whose interests are widening to embrace love of learning in many areas as well as the development of talents and skills. Awareness of social, political and legal issues in less personal terms can be seen in the passion for 'causes' and campaigns of one kind or another. The child develops strong involvements with peers and admiration for adults outside the family circle. Anna Freud states that 'no child can be fully integrated in group life before libido has been transferred from the parents to the community' (ibid., p. 68). A child who is not well established in Stage 6 is liable to be uninterested in schoolwork, not integrated into the peer group and often reluctant to go to school, or seriously homesick if at boarding-school.

## Stage 7

> The pre-adolescent prelude to the 'adolescent revolt', i.e., a return to early attitudes and behaviour, especially of the part-object, need-fulfilling, and ambivalent type.
>
> (Freud, A. 1965a, p. 66)

This is the stage at which previously reasonable latency children alarm their parents by reverting to demanding, contrary, inconsiderate behaviour. It represents a regression to earlier forms of relationship to the parents, which the child had outgrown, but which still exist in his mind as ways of relating to which he is tempted to return at times of stress. As Anna Freud described in an earlier paper on pre-adolescence, the stress the child now faces is the beginning of the adolescent upsurge of drives. Initially, before the child can mature into the genital phase of drive activity, this upsurge strengthens the oral, anal and phallic drive components reviving the primitive fantasies directed towards the parents that belong to these phases. The child's ego and superego are plunged into the struggle to give up these infantile ways of relating. But it takes some time before the ego and superego can find more mature ways of integrating drives, finding sexual objects among peers, and moving on to a more adult relationship with the parents. At first, in repudiating the infantile and incestuous fantasies, all the child can manage is to distance himself from the parents' influence altogether, often including their companionship and authority over him. Sublimations may be temporarily lost and interest in school-work may diminish (Freud, A. 1949b).

## Stage 8

> The adolescent struggle around denying, reversing, loosening and shedding the tie to the infantile objects, defending against pregenitality, and finally establishing genital supremacy with libidinal cathexis transferred to objects of the opposite sex, outside the family.
>
> (Freud, A. 1965a, p. 66)

This is yet another densely packed statement of what is involved in the complex transitional state between childhood and adulthood. In 1936 she had described the ego's struggle to master the upsurge of sexuality and aggression in adolescence; and she had discussed two forms of defence which emerge in adolescence: intellectualisation and asceticism, both of which aim to distance the individual from the instinctual demands of the body (Freud, A. 1936, pp. 152–165).

She also stressed the importance of internal changes in object relations during adolescence: the need to withdraw from the now 'incestuous' love for the parents may also lead to a repudiation of the superego insofar as it is based on parental example and demands (ibid., pp. 165–172). She takes this aspect further in a later paper. Discussing the difficulties of treating adolescents, she partly attributed them to the adolescent's inability to become fully involved in the transference to the analyst because he is preoccupied with the internal struggle to detach himself from his parents and transfer libido to new objects (Freud, A. 1958b, pp. 145–148). She likened this to the processes of mourning and being in love: in these states the individual is preoccupied with either giving up a lost relationship or establishing a new one. In both cases the person's interest is fully centred on a real object with little interest to spare for the analytic exploration of transference to the analyst. The mourning for the lost parents of childhood has to take place to allow the finding of peer relationships and a changed relationship to the parents.

Anna Freud described various forms of defence which the adolescent may use in the attempt to break away from the infantile tie to the object, and the effects these may have on behaviour. Instead of gradually withdrawing libido from the parents the adolescent may do it suddenly, either actually taking flight and leaving home, or emotionally switching his allegiance to another adult who seems diametrically opposed to the parents, or attaching himself to peers and adopting their values. He may act out his opposition to parental ideals in ways which may be harmless or delinquent, depending on who is the new object of attachment and identification. He may reverse affects, feeling hate towards his parents in an attempt to escape from his loving attachment. This leads him to be unco-operative and hostile. He may also project his feelings on to his parents, experiencing them as hostile and persecuting. Or he may turn the feelings on himself in suicidal or other self-injurious tendencies. If he withdraws libido from parents to his own self, he may become narcissistically grandiose and omnipotent; or if he cathects his body rather than his psychic self he may become hypochondriacal. If, to escape the oedipal level conflicts, he regresses to 'primary identification' which involves disintegration of ego functioning as well as drive regression, he may lose the boundaries between self and object, the distinction between the internal and external world, between reality and fantasy, and may eventually suffer from fears of loss of self (ibid., pp. 155–164).

In a later paper she describes adolescence as a developmental disturbance, in the sense that sweeping physical and psychological changes in this phase may upset a previously healthy balance. Even when this is transitory it can be damaging to the individual since this upheaval coincides with educational and social demands for academic achievement, choice of career, and increased financial and social responsibility for oneself (Freud, A. 1969g).

This developmental line, from dependency to emotional self-reliance and adult object relationships, is the most important one, not only because all the others cluster round it, but because it is the only place where Anna Freud pulls together into a sequence her various formulations about object relations made in many other places in her work.

## Lines 2 to 4; Towards body independence

Anna Freud described three lines 'towards body independence': 'from suckling to rational eating', 'from wetting and soiling to bladder and bowel control', and 'from irresponsibility to responsibility in body management' (Freud, A. 1965a, pp. 68–77). In each of these three lines the child goes through several stages in the process of taking over from his mother the management of his own functioning as his own ego development proceeds. The first two lines are based on ideas about attitudes to eating and toilet training derived from the war nursery work (see Chapter 3). Transient difficulties may occur in all of them as a normal reaction to the developmental stresses, but more serious delays and regressions may reflect failures or difficulties in the mother–child relationship.

For example, in the line from suckling to rational eating (ibid., pp. 68–69), as long as food and mother are equated in the child's mind, any conflict with mother may be fought out on the battleground of meals. Thus in stages 3 and 4 battles about quantity of food, table manners, food fads, craving for sweets, etc. may represent battles about independence, spillover of conflicts from toilet training, demands for substitute comforts, etc. Because these battles are about the mother–child relationship rather than about food, children in these stages will often eat better when with other people, for example, in nursery school. But traumatic separations during these early stages may result in refusal to eat because the child eats only for mother, or in excessive greed as the child treats food as a substitute for mother.

The equation food = mother fades out in Stage 5. But this coincides with the Oedipal phase, and irrational attitudes may be determined by infantile sexual theories: food refusal may reflect fantasies of impregnation through the mouth, fear of getting fat may represent fear of pregnancy, or there may be reaction formations against cannibalism and sadism in refusals to eat meat. At this stage, eating with other people than mother will not solve the problems, because these problems are now internalised and based on conflicts in the child's own mind, no longer between him and mother.

Only in Stage 6 does the individual's eating become relatively rational. But all adult preferences and food habits are partly shaped by earlier experiences, and severe difficulties may leave permanent, serious vulnerabilities connected with eating.

In a similar way Anna Freud traced the other two lines towards body independence, noting the normal transitory difficulties as well as the more severe pathology which may be linked with each. She went on to describe two further lines.

## Line 5: 'From egocentricity to companionship'

(Freud, A. 1965a, pp. 78–79). This traces four stages from the selfish narcissistic outlook on the object world in which other children are ignored, or seen only as rivals for the mother, through using other children like toys without expecting a response, and through using children as helpmates with a particular task, to taking other children as partners and objects in their own right. Only at this fourth stage does the child admire, fear and compete with the other child whom he can love and hate, and with whom he can identify, share possessions and respect the other's wishes. The third stage, the ability to use other children as helpmates, is required for integration into a nursery group, but only the fourth stage equips the child to make lasting friendships.

## Line 6: 'From the body to the toy and from play to work'

(Freud, A. 1965a, pp. 79–84). This is another densely packed summary, which there is not space to discuss in detail here. It traces the stages from the infant's play with his own and mother's body, to the transitional object (Winnicott 1951), then the use of soft toys which serve as symbolic objects and allow the child to express a full range of ambivalent feelings and wishes because they do not retaliate. Cuddly toys gradually fade out except at bedtime, but in daytime their place is increasingly taken by play materials serving ego activities and fantasy life. Anna Freud described the many kinds of ego and drive needs which can be displaced from objects and satisfied by different kinds of toys and material. Eventually direct drive gratification is replaced by pleasure in achievement which becomes relatively independent of the praise and admiration of the object. Finally the ability to play develops into the ability to work when the child is able to control, inhibit and modify instinctual impulses, so as to use them constructively in shared communal life, to tolerate frustration so as to carry out longer term plans and find pleasure in the final outcome, and to achieve pleasure in sublimation in accordance with the demands of reality. *En route* to this final outcome Anna Freud also described how various activities in between play and work branch off: daydreaming may take the place of fantasy play with toys, organised games serve to provide alternative, socially acceptable outlets for aggression and competitiveness, and hobbies develop as activities halfway between play and work. She did not, I believe, mean to imply that once the ability to work was achieved the individual would give up playing, though that play might be with ideas and fantasies rather than toys and games.

In the 1980s Hansi Kennedy ran a study group on the role of play, and, at an International Colloquium held at the Anna Freud Centre in 1987, the topic was the role of play in child and adult analysis. There was also a good deal of more general discussion about the nature of play and work. In his summing up, Robert Wallerstein noted that in many of the discussions play and work were not taken as opposites which exclude each other, but as often being intermingled. Creativity depends partly on the capacity to play with ideas even in the most serious scientific work. A work inhibition may derive from an inhibition of the playful aspect of work: the ability to take the first creative step of playing with ideas (Wallerstein 1988).

## The use of developmental lines

Anna Freud used entry into nursery school as an example of how the child's status on relevant developmental lines can be used to predict readiness for a new experience (Freud, A. 1960b, 1965a pp. 88–92). The age of the child is less significant than whether he has reached Stage 3 on the line from dependency to emotional self-reliance: object constancy, which allows him to keep his mother in mind during separation. To be comfortable about eating in the nursery he needs to have reached Stage 4 on the line from suckling to rational eating, i.e. to be capable of self-feeding, and no longer equating food with mother. To use the nursery toilet he needs to have reached Stage 3 on the line towards bladder and bowel control, i.e. to have got beyond the anal stage of battling with mother and to have identified with the environment's attitude to cleanliness. To enjoy the company of other children he needs to have reached at least Stage 3 on the line from egocentricity to companionship, in which he can relate to other children as helpmates in play; and once he has reached Stage 4, in which he can accept other children as partners in their own right and form real friendships, he will be a constructive, leading member of the group. To enjoy nursery school activities he needs to have reached at least Stage 4 on the line from play to work, in which play material serves to develop ego activities and express fantasies.

Anna Freud used details from developmental lines to explain the child's capacity or incapacity to cope with various life events in many of the papers given to professionals in other disciplines (see below: Applications of the psychoanalytic developmental point of view, pp. 144–159). As well as being useful as indicators of a child's readiness for various life experiences, the lines are also an additional diagnostic tool, since the correspondence or lack of it between the lines gives information about whether the child's development is proceeding evenly, or whether there are discrepancies which can point to areas of particular difficulty for the child. The lines thus have a dual function. They help people to understand the minutiae of normal development, and how this affects the child's reactions to experiences; and they help to pinpoint both the areas of delay or distortion leading to pathology, and the time in the child's life at which they occurred, in the fine detail required for accurate and effective therapeutic approaches.

A certain amount of unevenness falls within the bounds of normality, simply indicating the tendencies and inclinations which are most favoured in each individual's personality; and this depends partly on endowment, partly on environmental influences in the family and cultural setting. For example, a mother can promote the development of language as against bodily activity, or vice versa, but only up to a point, depending on the strength of the child's own, innate tendencies.

Anna Freud described how more extreme discrepancies result in various distortions of behaviour. For example, children with high intelligence, but who are delayed on the lines towards emotional self-reliance and adult object relationships, companionship and body independence, may show acting out of sexual and aggressive tendencies (including those which in adults would be deemed 'perverse'), a profusion of organised fantasy, and clever rationalisation of delinquent tendencies. They tend to be labelled 'borderline' or 'pre-psychotic'. Children described as 'lacking concentration' or having a 'short attention span', are often found to be very delayed on the line from play to work whilst normal on other lines. Closer inspection of ego functioning may reveal one or many failures, for example, to achieve control of pre-genital drive components (so that drifting off into fantasy interferes with work), or to move to functioning according to the reality principle rather than the pleasure principle, or to take pleasure in the ultimate results of activity rather than in the immediate satisfaction (Freud, A. 1965a, pp. 126–127). This diagnostic use of the developmental lines was to be developed into a way of pinpointing the specific areas of delay or deficit which needed to be addressed in therapy, and hence had an important influence on technique (see Chapter 7).

## LATER WORK ON DEVELOPMENTAL LINES AND IMPLICATIONS FOR THEORY

The lines which Anna Freud included in *Normality and Pathology* are examples of the sequences of development which analysts had always regarded as important. But they are not an exhaustive list. Other colleagues took up her thinking about developmental lines. For example, a study group on adult psychopathology formulated a developmental line 'From diffuse somatic excitation to signal anxiety' (Yorke et al. 1989, pp. 5–10). Another group produced a line for the development of insight (Kennedy 1979). Another worked out the beginning of a developmental line for language (Edgcumbe 1981). Anna Freud herself went on to add further lines and indicated that there could be many more.

She always intended diagnosticians to have in mind what would be about normal for a child at the age of the one being assessed, so as to discern deviations from normal development. The profile gives an overview of the whole of the child's current developmental status and pathology, with the compromises in operation at a given moment deriving from the macrostructures or macrosystems: drives, ego/superego and external world. In the profile, it is the family background and personal history sections which provide the developmental background, and the section on significant environmental influences which attempts to assess the interaction between the external world and the child's developing internal structures. But the lines take a longitudinal view of the history of the series of interactions between microsystems, smaller elements from the drives, ego/superego and external world, showing how he arrived at his achievements on each line; for example, how he gained control of various areas of body management, or how near he is to reaching the ability to work.

In Anna Freud's later work further differences between the developmental lines and the profile may be seen. In spite of many discussions in the Clinic on the desirability of giving object relations and narcissism sections of their own in the profile, Anna Freud chose to retain their conceptualisation in terms of distribution of libido between objects and self.

In the lines, on the other hand, the 'object-related attitudes of the ego' are given more weight. Indeed, Anna Freud took it for granted that analysts were already familiar with the interaction between the libidinal phases and aggressive expressions of the id, and the object-related attitudes of the ego in which can be traced the development from the infant's emotional dependence to the adult's self-reliance and mature sex and object relationships (Freud, A. 1963a, pp. 245–246; 1965a, pp. 62–63). This is what she elaborated as the prototype developmental line 'From dependency to emotional self-reliance and adult object relationships' (Freud, A. 1963a, pp. 245–248; 1965a, pp. 62–66).

Object relations come to have an increasingly important role in Anna Freud's theoretical thinking in later years. She had always, of course, laid stress on the role of the object in the structuralisation of the child's internal world, where the object serves as a model for identification and internalisation in many aspects of ego and superego functioning, and is thus important in the control and transformation of drive impulses, wishes and affects. But after 1965, as she increasingly focused on the use of developmental lines to elucidate deficit psychopathology, there seems to have been a subtle shift in the importance she placed on interpersonal relations. Not that she ever went so far as to conceptualise the need for object attachment as primary, or as a more important motivator than drives. But some of her later papers do seem to indicate a move towards giving drives and object relations something closer to equal status in a theory of motivation.

Most of the lines she added in her later work are not written out in the same detail as the original ones she gave as prototypes. This is probably because she did not intend any of the lines to be used as scales in any rigid way. She was intent on exploring how the myriad small areas of interaction combine over time in a complex and initially fluid way to produce an individual's character. As maturation and development proceed, those areas gradually become more fixed, sometimes rigid, in recognisable aspects of normal and pathological personality development.

In her earlier papers Anna Freud, in common with other child analysts, thought about child analysis in relation to adult analysis, as a 'sub-speciality', seeing it as a way of confirming or correcting theories of development derived from reconstruction in adult analysis; and discussing technique in terms of its differences from technique with adults. But she later moved to the view that child analysts should 'go it alone' (Freud, A. 1971c [1970c]), and in her later papers views child analysis as a related but separate discipline with tasks of its own in both theory construction and the development of technique. There are three papers in particular in which she significantly advanced her ideas within the context of developmental lines: 'A psychoanalytic view of developmental psychopathology' (Freud, A. 1974c), 'The principle task of child analysis' (Freud, A. 1978a) and 'Child analysis as the study of mental growth, normal and abnormal' (Freud, A. 1981e [1979b]).

All these papers stress her own view that our knowledge of development is still too global. She cited Spitz (1965) and Mahler (1968) who had studied the details of stages in early development, and suggested that such an approach could be used to shed light on the whole of development up to maturity. She offered her own developmental lines as 'ladders leading up to every one of the expected achievements of the child's personality' (Freud, A. 1974c, p. 63). She suggested that a field of exploration which belongs exclusively to child analysts is the vicissitudes of forward development and exploration of the synthetic function of the ego (Freud, A. 1978a, p. 99). If the development of metapsychology is the 'crowning achievement' of classical psychoanalysis, child psychoanalysis can add a 'new, developmentally oriented psychoanalytic theory of child psychology' (ibid., p. 100). Developmental lines are 'the child analyst's domain' (ibid., p. 101).

She added many more lines in these later papers; for example, from physical to mental pathways of discharge, from animate to inanimate objects, and from irresponsibility to guilt (Freud, A. 1974c).

The line 'From physical to mental pathways of discharge' starts with the newborn in whom any excitation whether physical or mental is discharged via the body: sleep, feeding or elimination may be affected; babies respond to people by kicking or arm waving. During the first year, body–mind access remains easy, even while psychological life develops. Bodily upheavals cause mental distress, shown in crying; mental shocks, anxiety or distress cause physical upheaval. In the second year, as more mental pathways open up, the mind begins to take over from the body for discharging tensions of all kinds. But only during the third year, with the establishment of speech and secondary process thinking, is a clearer division between bodily and mental functioning established, though the division is never complete. Normal adults continue to have psychosomatic reactions such as tension headaches and intestinal upsets. Where the body–mind access remains easy it contributes to later psychosomatic, hysterical and hypochondriacal illnesses (ibid., pp. 64–65).

The line 'From animate to inanimate objects' is partly influenced by Winnicott's concept of the transitional object. Anna Freud believed that the use of inanimate toys can be seen as a normal sideline branching off from the development of the child's love–hate relationships to human beings. Such substitutes are useful to the child because as love objects they are under his control, and they do not retaliate to his aggression. She noted that these qualities are shared by placid dogs who are 'good with children'. But she speculated that children who lack satisfactory relationships might overemphasise the attachment to material possessions or to animals rather than to people; she also considered whether the destructiveness of toys and maltreatment of animals, and later the more serious destruction of property and cruelty to animals are the result of unmodified aggression being diverted away from human objects (ibid., pp. 65–67).

The line 'From irresponsibility to guilt' is the familiar series of interactions which eventually produce the mature internalised superego. But Anna Freud noted that we tend to miss an 'intermediate stage' at which the child becomes aware of internal conflict between wishes and superego but is unwilling to accept the painful struggle within himself; so he externalises the wishes on to other children and becomes censorious of his peers, until he can make the final move to accepting his own guilt (ibid., pp. 67–68).

In several places she indicated her ideas for a developmental line for defences against external and internal dangers, anxiety and unpleasure of various kinds. The most primitive defences are avoidance and denial used against external dangers, and later against internal dangers as well. Projection and introjection are processes used in the early differentiation of self and object, ego and id, which can be used as defences once a rudimentary distinction between self and object is established. Somatisation is another normal early process which can be used defensively by those with arrests or regressions on the line from somatic to mental discharge. All these primitive defences are used in relatively unstructured personalities. The more sophisticated defences such as repression, reaction formation and sublimation cannot come into action before structuralisation is well established. Obsessional defences, for example, can function only after the lines from somatic to mental discharge, and from irresponsibility to guilt have reached their highest stage (Freud, A. 1969f [1956], p. 313, 1974c, pp. 73–74, 1981a, pp. 141–144, 1981e [1979b], p. 124). The adolescent defences of asceticism, intellectualisation and removal from objects have already been mentioned above (p. 125).

The developmental line for insight proposed by Hansi Kennedy (1979) and discussed by Anna Freud (1979a, 1981a) is interestingly different from the other lines. It represents the unfolding of a capacity which is, however, relatively little used by the majority of people since defences work in the direction of reducing conscious awareness of troublesome wishes and feelings. Insight depends on ego function of self-awareness which, in the infant and young child, can take the form only of experiential awareness. The child is emotionally and cognitively egocentric, and uses this awareness in the service of maintaining a comfortable inner state, bringing his own defences into play against unpleasant or threatening feelings and wishes, and appealing to his objects to remove the situation which is disturbing or distressing him; for example he may want the new baby sent away.

The latency child, with well-developed ego and superego functions, is better equipped for reflective self-awareness, i.e. for understanding cause and effect in his own experiences and feelings, as well as the reasons for other people's reactions and for external happenings. But for defensive reasons most children do not use this capacity for insight into themselves, even though they may use it to improve their understanding of the world around them.

Adolescents are often more introspective and may use their intellect to understand themselves and others. But their absorption in their current adolescent difficulties often makes them uninterested in their past, and therefore in seeing patterns and making links between past and present.

Many normal adults manage their lives with only limited self-awareness. Creative artists tend to be especially aware of unconscious processes and motivations. But for ordinary people it is only when internal solutions to conflicts and deprivations have pathological results that insight needs to be widened in order to find new and different solutions. Thus analysis can be used to enhance unused potential for insight (Freud, A. 1979a, 1981a; Kennedy 1979).

Many of the lines concern ego and superego functions with which analysts are already familiar, deficits which are known to contribute to borderline, psychotic and other non-neurotic forms of adult psychopathology. Her contribution is to show what the findings of child analysis can add to the understanding of adult disorders. Thus in these papers her emphasis shifts beyond childhood psychopathology to include adult pathology as well. Yorke stressed the relevance of the developmental lines for understanding deficits in adult personality and functioning (Yorke 1983).

In several papers Anna Freud compared childhood and adult psychopathology, discussing both the point at which it becomes developmentally legitimate to apply the adult diagnosis to the child, but also showing how complex and difficult is the path to maturity. For example, in *Normality and Pathology* she discussed dissociality, delinquency and criminality, diagnoses which cannot be applied to young children, although their potential precursors may be discernible. In Britain the law considers children incapable of criminal intent before the age of 8, and even after that they should be given 'benefit of age'. From a psychoanalytic point of view the child must be able to understand the social setting to which he belongs and to identify with the rules that govern it. Social adaptation is a gradual process. But Anna Freud described some of the stages in this process, and the possible danger signs for failures in it (Freud, A. 1965a, pp. 164–184). Rather than 'causes' of dissociality she prefers to think in terms of *transformations* of the self-indulgent and asocial attitudes which are part of the child's original nature. 'This helps to construct developmental lines which lead to pathological results, although these are more complex, less well defined, and contain a wider range of possibilities than the lines of normal development' (ibid., p. 167).

The newborn is a law unto himself, governed by his built-in pleasure principle, striving to reduce unpleasant tension. Apart from autoerotic gratifications, however, he cannot achieve the satisfactions he seeks without his mother's help. So as well as becoming his first, need-fulfilling object, she also becomes his first legislator, confronting him with external laws about the timing and rationing of satisfaction. The infant experiences the regime as friendly or hostile according to his mother's sensitivity to him; and she experiences him as compliant and easy or difficult and self-willed according to how gracefully he accepts her rules.

Soon, to basic bodily needs, sexual and aggressive drives towards the mother and others become an additional source of tension between the internal pleasure principle and the demands of external reality. As the child learns about avoidance of dangers, and of harming himself or objects, damaging property, or transgressing social decencies, inevitable clashes occur between internal and external demands, manifest in disobedience, naughtiness and tantrums.

Up to this point the toddler is still dependent on the external world for his moral code. 'Almost the whole of personality and character formation, as it is known to us, can be viewed also in terms of remedying this humiliating situation and of acquiring for the mature person the right to judge his own actions' (ibid., p. 170).

Throughout life the pleasure principle continues to rule unconscious processes such as fantasy and dreaming, and is also involved in neurotic and psychotic symptom formation. But it becomes modified into the reality principle in governing normal ego functioning. If this does not happen, the individual remains impulse ridden and oblivious of social norms, unable to tolerate frustration. So this is an important step in socialisation, though not sufficient by itself. Individuals who are highly adapted to reality can make use of their capacity in antisocial ways.

The basic ego functions needed for adaptation to reality are: memory, reality-testing, understanding of reason and logic, and of cause and effect (the last two largely dependent on the acquisition of language), which permit anticipation and trial action in thought. Also important is the synthetic function of the ego which helps the infant pull together disparate and multitudinous experiences into some coherent and sensible pattern, and the development of defences which are flexible and balanced enough to control impulses and feelings without creating undue inhibitions. This level of functioning cannot be expected from very young children or those with intellectual defects or damage to ego functions.

But the final important steps to internalising the rules of society depend on the child's libidinal ties to the environment, i.e. his attachment to his parents. This leads him first to imitate, then to identify with them, which includes building their social ideals into his own ideal self, part of his conscience. It takes some years before these ideals are fully internalised, i.e. until the child will stick to his own moral principles regardless of whether or not the people around him support his stance. The lack of stable relationships may mean that this step is never taken to self-control and acceptance of society's laws. Alternatively, identification with love objects who are themselves criminal or otherwise antagonistic to the law may also result in some form of antisocial behaviour (ibid., pp. 164–180).

In an earlier paper Anna Freud had delineated at greater length a range of types of social maladjustment, differentiating between those based on early stunting of object love with consequent weakening of ego and superego functions, and those based on conflict. In the latter, antisocial behaviour may represent the displacement outside the family of unresolved Oedipal and pre-Oedipal conflicts occurring within the child's close emotional relationships, either in the form of irruptions of instinctual behaviour whenever defences fail, or in enactment of fantasies and fears (Freud, A. 1949d).

Trauma or excessive stress may cause regression in social attitudes. At a symposium on trauma in 1964 (published partly in 1967 with additions in 1969), she clarified her views on trauma, partly in a paper and partly in responses to other participants. She stressed the view that trauma cannot be defined objectively but only in terms of the individual's internal situation: being overwhelmed and helpless with one's ego functioning put out of action by a sudden excess of excitation for which the individual was unprepared. She discussed the importance of different levels of tolerance for excitation which may be partly personal, partly determined by environmental factors. Thus, during bombing, people may succeed in raising their 'stimulus barrier' so as to withstand much greater than normal amounts of stress. Ways of coping and recovering from trauma are also important in determining the role traumatic events play in people's lives. She gave examples from children in the war nurseries and in treatment at the Hampstead Clinic as well as discussing other participants' material. Some traumatic events have pathogenic results simply because they are so extreme; others trigger ordinary pre-existing conflicts into a more severe neurosis (Freud, A. 1969e [1964]).

Anna Freud cautioned against regarding aggression as a more important threat than the sexual drive to socialisation. It was her view that aggression is a positive force when fused with libidinal drives, because it gives tenacity to the child's reaching out and holding on to objects. It also underlies ambition, and it contributes to the strength and appropriate severity of the superego. All these are normal modifications of aggression. It is only a menace to social adaptation when it is not fused with libido, usually because of failures, real or imaginary in the child's important relationships: loss, disappointments, rejections or other upsets. This seems especially true if they occur in the anal phase, since they set free the child's sadism and destructiveness. These can become a major cause for delinquency if the object relation is not re-established (Freud, A. 1965a, pp. 180–181). She had discussed these issues in an earlier paper (1949c) where she had stressed the role of instincts as 'mind builders'. They exert a constant pressure on the individual to find ways of managing them: to achieve gratification or bear frustration, to control and redirect or suppress them in accordance with the demands of the family and social environment. The individual is constantly challenged to develop emotionally and intellectually by his experience of conflicts provoked by instinctual tensions. The transformations of aggression can make a positive contribution to personality development. But the lack of appropriate loving help in these transformations can lead to various forms of psychopathology, ranging from the suicidal impulses resulting from turning aggression against the self, to projection of aggression on to other individuals or groups, which contributes to intolerance in relationships, to racial and national discrimination, genocide and violence (ibid.).

Summarising an international psychoanalytic conference on aggression, Anna Freud clarified that aggression does not go through phases in the same way as libido, though aggressive manifestations may be coloured by libidinal phases (i.e. producing oral, anal or phallic aggression). A further difference is that libidinal aims are specific to the drive, whereas aggression can be used in the service of many aims, destructive or constructive. The transformations undergone by aggression derive from the use of defences which change with maturity, from concern for the object and the wish to preserve it, and from changes in the 'tools' of aggression which depend on bodily maturation and ego development. One line of development of tools tends to mitigate the results of aggression: for example, the shift from bodily expressions such as biting, soiling, kicking or hitting to verbal attacks; while another line leads to the amplification of aggression: the shift from bodily 'tools' such as fists and teeth, to the use of weapons. She recalled Sigmund Freud's statement: 'the man who first flung a word of abuse at his enemy instead of a spear was the founder of civilisation' (Freud S. 1893, p. 36), and added her own comment: 'the individual who first supplemented the action of his fist by the power of a mechanical device was the inventor of war' (Freud, A. 1972, p. 164).

She again noted the extra technical problems in childhood analysis raised by the greater proportion of aggressive material because of the child's physical activity, which may liberate aggression more easily than sexual strivings. She stressed the need (with adults as well as children) to clarify the motives for aggression: for example, anxiety, ego resistance to emerging material, superego reactions, denial of positive transference, defence against passivity. Such distinctions are essential for both clinical understanding and choice of technique (Freud, A. 1972).

The final steps from functioning in a moral and social way within the family to doing so within the community have their own difficulties. The normal family supports the child's development sympathetically, making allowances for his personal idiosyncracies. But the move to school and its rules is usually the child's first encounter with a more impersonal discipline, and in the adult community to be 'equal before the law' carries sacrifices as well as advantages. Even adults may find it difficult to accept their lack of exemption from laws, regardless of their needs or special circumstances. In any case, only the basic moral code and acceptance of the principle of a governing norm ever become part of the average individual's internal world, but not the content of specific laws (Freud, A. 1965a, pp. 181–184).

In *Normality and Pathology* there is a similar discussion of the series of developmental factors and external influences which may be involved in determining whether a person becomes homosexual or heterosexual as an adult. But none of these factors taken singly in childhood can predict the final sexual orientation, since most are variations of normal developmental experiences. The same applies to childhood 'cravings' for sweets or other foods, which do not have the same significance as adult addictions; and to children's enjoyment of dressing up, including cross-dressing, which rarely leads to adult transvestism (Freud, A. 1965a, pp. 184–212).

In Anna Freud's later work there was another shift of emphasis in which she no longer gave such a central place in development to the sexual and aggressive drives. For example, in 1978 she stated that in addition to success in work and sexual relations which '*used to be*' (my italics) taken as the sign of adult normality, we now recognise other capacities as equally characteristic of adulthood: self-reliance, control of the body, discharge via mental as well as phyical pathways; the shift to the reality principle; being objective rather than egocentric; the capacity for signal anxiety; adequate defence mechanisms; peer relationships. But the development of these functions is explored in adult analysis only when they have aetiological significance in the disturbance (Freud, A. 1978a, pp. 100–101). In this paper a developmental line 'From infantile to adult sex life' became only one example among many lines which she used to demonstrate the interaction of many factors in mental growth (ibid., p. 103).

In 1979 in a videotape address to the San Francisco Psychoanalytic Institute, not published in written form until 1981, Anna Freud made a further definitive contribution to the theory of developmental lines. Speaking of the lines already well known in the main body of psychoanalytic theory she listed the lines towards mature sexuality, towards mature forms of defence, and management of anxiety. But, she pointed out, there are many other characteristics expected from a mature adult, deriving from lines towards secondary process functioning, reality sense, impulse control, time sense, insight into one's own inner state, from somatic to mental discharge and from egocentricity to objectivity (1981e [1979b], pp. 123–130).

It was now her opinion that the really decisive lines are those towards secondary process functioning, reality sense, objectivity and insight, perhaps with some others which she did not name (ibid., pp. 130–131).

But, importantly, she suggested that individuals may be deemed adult without having achieved the end point on the lines towards adult sexuality; to verbal instead of physical aggression; from somatic to mental expression; towards mature peer relations (jealousy and rivalry remain common). In other words she seems to have reduced sexuality and drive control to a place of lesser importance compared to the development of some other crucial ego functions; and these are shown to depend on the child–parent relationship, and internalisation of aspects of this relationship (ibid., pp. 131–133).

In the same presentation she introduced for the first time a rough division of developmental lines according to the period of life during which they originate and the agencies interacting in them; also the beginnings of a hierarchy. Without the development of some of the earlier lines some of the later ones cannot develop normally. This account was extremely condensed and has to be read in the light of her previous pronouncements. Developmental lines not specifically mentioned can be allocated their beginning places. But she concentrated on those she regarded as most important for mature adult functioning.

### Developmental periods

1   In the first stage, lasting approximately for the first year, the interaction is between mother and child, the child contributes his potential id/ego functioning, the mother contributes her care for the child. [This is the beginning of the line from dependency to emotional self-reliance.] Out of this interaction develops the child's first moves from somatic to psychic functioning; the

early differentiations between his own and his mother's body, between self and object. These early developments within the attachment to the mother are crucial for the success of later lines. [Also having their early stages in this period are the lines towards bodily independence, from egocentricity to companionship, and from the body to toy and play to work. All continue through subsequent periods.]

2    In the second stage, roughly the rest of the pre-Oedipal period, when the child's own ego and id become more clearly differentiated, there are three 'agencies': the child's id and ego and the parents. During this period the lines towards motility and other physical functioning are developing, together with the lines towards impulse control and secondary process functioning; object constancy should be established, preparing the way for subsequent development of the capacity to relate to others.

3    In the final, Oedipal and post-Oedipal stage, when the superego has become internally established, there are four agencies interacting: the child's id, ego and superego, and the external world. The superego begins to take over much of the moral role previously played by the external world, which has, in the child's mind, gradually enlarged from mother to parents to a wider range of adults and peers.

(Freud, A. 1981e [1979b], pp. 133–135)

Anna Freud concluded that:

normality or pathology of development is seen to depend largely on four factors:

- on the constitutional and experiential element in the life of an individual not departing too far from what is average and expectable;
- on the internal agencies of the individual's personality maturing at approximately the same rate of speed, none of them being either precocious or delayed compared with the others;
- on external intervention being well-timed, coming neither too early nor too late;
- on the ego's mechanisms used to achieve the necessary compromises being age-adequate, i.e. neither too primitive nor too sophisticated.

She recommended investigating these points as 'a next rewarding trend for child analytic work' (ibid., pp. 135–136).

She thought that successes or failures on developmental lines shape the personality. At the same time, normal developmental conflicts create anxiety states, phobias, hysterical and obsessional manifestations. The two intertwine: conflicts interfere with progress on one or more lines; the nature and resolution of conflicts is influenced by levels of personality development which the child has reached. Thus, although deficit and neurotic disorders are two distinct types of pathology, they are intertwined in the clinical picture (Freud, A. 1974c, pp. 69–71).

The pathogenic impact of events such as the birth of a sibling, moving house or illness depends on the child's position on various lines. Choice of neurosis depends partly on levels reached on various lines, partly because the lines influence choice of defence. Repression depends on the id–ego division; the defensive use of projection and introjection depends on the capacity to distinguish self and object; somatisation is determined by arrests and regressions on the body–mind line; regression predominates in individuals whose development on all lines has been shaky; obsessional defence cannot be used before the lines from physical to mental discharge and irresponsibility to guilt have reached their climax (ibid., pp. 72–74).

Discussing multiple determination and the synthetic function, she noted the extreme importance of the synthetic function in integrating the various determining factors in each developmental line. But aberrant as well as normal features are integrated by this function of the ego, and may be detrimental to development (Freud, A. 1978a, pp. 105–106). Whether or not integration serves healthy development or contributes to psychopathology depends on the constitutional givens, the parental influence, and the rate of structuralisation of the personality (Freud, A. 1981e [1979b]).

Both neurotic and developmental disorders are based on disharmony: clashes between drive, ego, and internal or external interference leading to compromises. But neurotic symptoms begin with regression following drive frustration on higher levels, whereas developmental pathology is primarily due to imbalance in the unfolding of development.

Anna Freud proposed a further task: to devise methods for undoing the developmental damage, to identify developmental defects and pinpoint differences from neurotic symptomatology

(Freud, A. 1978a, pp. 108–109). This was, of course, a task she had already begun. Her work on matching techniques to forms of disturbance is discussed in Chapter 7.

A further task she undertook throughout her life was the application of psychoanalytic understanding of development to all forms of care and education of children.

## APPLICATIONS OF THE PSYCHOANALYTIC DEVELOPMENTAL POINT OF VIEW

The developmental point of view has value in any area of professional decision making concerned with children. Because it allows us to determine a child's readiness for and capacity to cope with various life experiences it can be applied to many areas outside psychoanalysis. *Normality and Pathology* summarised Anna Freud's views on a range of applications of the developmental point of view to various educational, psychosocial and legal issues, which were further extended in later works. Throughout the book runs her awareness of the caution with which analysts should approach questions and requests for advice whether from parents, other professionals or the general public. Since the early days in Vienna she had believed that the understanding of the unconscious mind was an important contribution that psychoanalysts could make to the upbringing and care of children. But she was aware that the success of such attempts depended on the extent of understanding of those unconscious processes, and that limitations of understandings had led to failures as well as successes. She also believed that actual psychoanalytic treatment was not the appropriate solution to all childhood difficulties. This was a major difference between herself and Melanie Klein, who believed that all children could benefit from prophylactic analysis. Anna Freud preferred to use psychoanalytic understanding to improve existing methods of upbringing, education, socialisation, medical care and legal decision making.

Throughout her professional life Anna Freud was interested in the application of psychoanalytic ideas to all aspects of the upbringing and management of children. In addition to her hands-on involvement in running the nurseries she had set up in Vienna, London and Essex, and the subsequent nursery schools, well baby clinic and toddler groups of the Hampstead Clinic, she was always willing to translate her psychoanalytic ideas into everyday language in talks and discussions with other professionals. She thought it important to spread as widely as possible what child analysts were learning about normal and pathological development, so as to influence decision making and policy at all levels in child care. For example, in 1946 she gave a paper at a symposium organised by Sir John Orr in connection with his World Food Plan. In this she succinctly outlined the child's needs for food and other physical care, showing the effects of bodily deprivation on mental development. But she also stressed the importance of providing for the intellectual, instinctual and emotional needs of the child, and warned of the serious results of deficiencies in providing for these areas (Freud, A. 1946a). In 1948 she gave an invited paper to UNESCO which offered a summary of psychoanalytic theory oriented to issues of social adaptation, conflicts and tensions between groups, projection of hatred on to strangers, and the difficulties of altering established hostile and suspicious attitudes in later life. This paper used the war nursery experience to demonstrate the role of stable relationships in promoting moral development and social adaptation, the role of sexual instincts and aggression and the defences used against them in determining human behaviour, and problems of dealing with ambivalence. She also made recommendations for revising educational methods, spreading knowledge of dynamic child psychology, and setting up further studies of the effects on later personality development and emotional development of early feeding situations, style of toilet training, handling of aggression in the child, loss of a parent and separation from family (Freud, A. 1953b).

Several of her papers sought to clarify the misconceptions that had arisen as new psychoanalytic ideas were taken over by other professionals. For example, she dissected the concept of the 'rejecting mother' in order to show that the importance placed on the mother–child relationship in all areas of development cannot be used to provide a simple explanation of all forms of childhood disturbance as due to a 'rejecting mother' – a concept in fashion in the 1950s. She described the many ways a mother may partially 'reject' a child due to her own difficulties or dislike of certain aspects of the child's behaviour. She considered that mothers who waver between acceptance and rejection may be more harmful than those who reject a child outright, since the latter leaves him free to form a substitute relationship. But most especially she stressed that what the child experiences as 'rejection' is often an inevitable aspect of development, for example, having to accept the Oedipal mother's preference for father, or a normal life event such as displacement by a younger sibling; or it is due to the child's misperception of unfortunate circumstances such as mother becoming ill, or externally imposed events such as wartime evacuation (Freud, A. 1955).

A substantial proportion of her papers between 1945 and 1965 (*Writings*, vols. 4 and 5), as well as a lesser number in the following decade, were devoted to such applications of psychoanalysis. These papers are sometimes derived from informal talks or discussions; some are introductions to the work of colleagues; they often contain illuminating brief examples. There is not space to cover them all here, but a few examples may indicate how she could explain the importance of the developmental point of view to colleagues in other professions. Many of her papers were originally addressed to parents, teachers, professionals in social services, psychiatrists, children's doctors and nurses, and family lawyers. For many years she ran a seminar for consultant paediatricians, and in her later years became part of a team which co-authored three books on children and the law.

She took the view, in many of her papers, that too much specialisation in services for children could be disadvantageous; and that all professionals needed a shared basic training because the differentiations between body and mind, self and object, intellect and emotion, normal and pathological, develop only slowly in children. Thus it is helpful to those who work with normal children to have some shared understanding of pathology and vice versa. Those who deal with physical illness need to understand the emotional side; teachers need to understand how emotions influence intellectual development, etc. (Freud, A. 1966a). She deplored the lack of opportunity for professionals to observe children in other professional and home settings (Freud, A. 1952b). This is one reason why her own trainees were required to observe and work with normal infants and children in various settings: home, school and hospital, as well as disturbed children.

In a 1953 paper based on a lecture to first year medical students in Cleveland, Ohio, whose course included infant observation, she gave a simple, clear explanation of what to look for and how to group the observed data. She described how to glimpse the infant's mental activity through his bodily activities, which indicate the alternating states of quietness and peace, and restless discomfort, unhappiness or pain due to rising need tension. The latter can only be relieved with outside help from a caretaker (Freud, A. 1953a, pp. 570–571). To develop the capacity to distinguish the baby's crying signals for different needs, the observer has to adopt something akin to the mother's emotional attachment to the infant, rather than scientific objectivity (ibid., pp. 572–573).

Having developed this capacity, the observer will be able to witness the 'birth of the mind out of the body' (ibid., p. 574). She went on to describe, for example, the development of inner imagery linking need with satisfaction and the person who provides it, and the infant's growing ability to distinguish the inner image from the real, external object, and the consequent growing purposefulness of his crying (ibid., pp. 575–576). She also described the observation of the infant's reactions to mother's presence and absence, his playing with her body as if it is part of his own, and how to see the gradual recognition of the limits of his own body. She described how to observe the gradual organisation of the infant's perceptions, sensations and responses and the gradual transformation of the infant's attachment to mother into a true love relationship on the child's side (ibid., pp. 577–582).

In a short paper which stressed the difference between the parents' bond to their child and the professional's more transient and less deeply rooted relationship, usually focused on a particular area of the child's needs, Anna Freud suggested that it is not to be expected that the professional worker will love the child in the same way as parents do. But as a substitute she suggested that all professionals need an insatiable curiosity about the problems of child development (Freud, A. 1977).

## Parenting

Those of Anna Freud's papers which were addressed to parents tended to focus on explaining how children develop, on demystifying apparently incomprehensible behaviour, and on clarifying the kind of support and guidance children need from parents. Throughout these papers runs an emphasis on the importance of stable relationships in promoting the child's healthy development. A paper given in 1949 but published only in 1968, 'Expert knowledge for the average mother', described succinctly the enormous demands made on mothers by child-rearing.

> Mothers . . . have to be clean, tidy, punctual, quiet and precise to fulfill the requirements necessary for baby nursing; at the same time they have to be flexible in their actions so as to adapt themselves to the varying needs of the child, and indulgent towards the noise, mess and disorder which are the inevitable accompaniments of an infant's life. They have to bear being imposed upon by their children without becoming resentful, and devoted to their task without expecting immediate returns. They have to safeguard the child from dangers without interfering too much with his love of adventure; and to assume authority without harming the child's growing sense of independence. They have to be warmhearted in their response to the child's feelings and cool-headed and objective in the emergencies which constantly arise in an infant's day. Where mothers bring up their children without domestic help their hours of work cover the whole day, with baby feeding and sick nursing extending into the night, at the expense of their own sleep and often of their health. Any moment of neglect on the part of the mother may involve the child in serious accidents which endanger his life. Any carelessness in watching out for the first signs of a childhood disease may cause either the spreading or the catching of infection. If a mother is too preoccupied with her own needs, her career, her ambitions, even with her married life, the infant will feel neglected, rejected, and respond with emotional upsets.
>
> . . . In return for these excessive claims on their time, strength, tolerance, devotion, and self-sacrifice, mothers used to hold a position of supreme and unquestioned authority over their children.
>
> (Freud, A. 1968a [1949], pp. 528–529)

She went on to discuss the dilemma of young mothers who are supposed to know everything 'by instinct', but often do not; the difficulties of those without help from her own mother, or moving from one culture to another, or those trying to use 'modern' instead of traditional child-rearing methods. She also considered the difficulties parents have in assimilating new knowledge about hygiene, nutrition and medical advances. She described how advances in psychoanalytic knowledge can equip parents with a more detailed understanding of mental development (ibid.).

She wrote relatively little, however, about techniques of working with parents. Erna Furman, one of the earliest graduates from the training, commented on Anna Freud's apparently conflicted attitudes to mothering. She reported Anna Freud's dictum: 'the child analyst has to keep in mind at all times three things: the child, the mother and the mother–child relationship.' Anna Freud was supportive and interested in Furman's later work with mothers of young children. But Furman contrasted this with the lack of specific teaching in the training course about ways of working with parents (Furman 1995).

I had a somewhat different impression, as a later trainee for whom supervised 'parent-guidance' cases were part of the training. I think that Anna Freud tended to believe that some parents, the relatively well-functioning ones, could be helped to change inappropriate handling of their children by giving them explanations of their children's developmental needs and how these affect behaviour. Such understanding could then be linked with discussion of alternative ways a parent might try approaching problems. But the more disturbed parents, with entrenched character problems or severely distorted views of their child, could not be influenced by such discussions, and would need analysis or therapy in their own right.

For many years the Clinic ran a research project using simultaneous analysis aimed at studying the interaction between parent and child (Burlingham *et al.* 1955; Freud, A. 1957–1960, pp. 18–19; Hellman *et al.* 1960; Levy 1960). Treatment of the parent, however, took a long time before it brought about changes which could benefit the relationship with the child. Further, many parents were neither willing nor able to undertake their own therapy. Consequently, the best that could be done with many parents was to prevent them from interfering with the child's treatment and schooling.

In a later paper, Anna Freud described various ways of influencing parents. They could receive therapy for themselves, or they could be guided through the child's analysis, i.e. helped to understand and cope with what is happening in the child's analysis. Special support and information would be needed, she believed, by mothers of handicapped children to deal with their own hurt and despair, as well as to equip them with the special understanding needed to help the child overcome the handicap. Treatment of the young child could be carried out by the mother: in this method the child's difficulties are discussed with the mother so that she can understand how they arise, and how to alter her approach so as to resolve them. Finally, Anna Freud thought that changing public opinion about child-rearing is a way of informing and helping mothers, and that the child guidance clinics have a role to play in setting up 'new traditions' to replace the waning religious, national and class traditions on which mothers can no longer rely (Freud, A. 1960c [1957]).

In diagnostic discussions using the profile, which resulted in analysis emerging as the treatment of choice for the child, there was often lengthy discussion about whether the parents could accept such a recommendation, what it would mean to them, how it could best be explained to them, and whether it would be possible to help them support the child's treatment. Often a period of work with the parents was decided on, to explore whether they might be helped to co-operate, before attempting to start work with the child.

Essentially, Anna Freud gave free rein to individuals under-taking work with parents so that those who wanted to try out different beliefs about who could be helped and how were free to do so and could, as Furman reported, elicit Anna Freud's interest and willingness to discuss issues that arose. A study group on work with parents, run in the early 1990s (after Anna Freud's death), attempted to formulate an 'Anna Freud Centre technique' for this work, but found it impossible to do more than describe the huge range of styles of working. All were based on two fundamental assumptions derived from the psychoanalytic developmental point of view:

> (1) that the parents have the central role in promoting the child's development and thus have an essential role to play in remedying psychological problems developed by their child; and (2) that when parents are experiencing difficulties in fulfilling this role they can best be helped by discussions about the child's emotional needs and development, and about their own experiences of being parents, with a worker specifically trained for this task.
>
> (Unpublished report 1995)

The members of the group were: E. Model, P. Radford, P.Cohen, A. Gavshon, M. Zaphiriou-Woods, T. Baradon, A. Gedulter-Trieman,

A. Pennington, S. Yabsley, M. Senez, K. Dearnley, C. Essenhigh, R. Edgcumbe.

Beyond that, these psychoanalytically informed discussions were extremely varied in nature, being the product of individual interactions between parent and professional worker. They might do no more than allow therapist and parent to exchange information about the child, or they might be aimed at improving the parent's understanding of the child, facilitating parenting skills, supporting the parent's confidence and self-esteem, helping them to see intergenerational patterns of relating. They might use verbalisation and clarification of emotional reactions in child and parent, interpretation of conflicts influencing the parent's perception of and behaviour towards the child, using the transference and countertransference to clarify issues influencing the parent–child relationship. In other words, the techniques used included a range of informative, educational and therapeutic approaches, but all focused on the parent's relationship with the child. Anna Freud herself tended to think that 'parent guidance' should not become therapy for the parent. But many of her trainees felt that they could make a good case for using a limited range of child-focused interpretative techniques, to free the parent–child relationship from some of its disturbances, in cases where parents could not use information about the child's needs and development because of interference from their own problems.

## Teaching

Many of Anna Freud's papers on education were aimed in a general way at parents, teachers, social services, child guidance clinics and all professionals who have care of children. Some of her earliest papers have already been mentioned in Chapter 3. She continued to use the war nursery experience in later papers, for example, in a discussion of uses and dangers of nursery school education (Freud, A. 1949e).

Some papers were more specifically addressed to teachers. A 1960 lecture to the Nursery School Association of Great Britain, another at a symposium of the American Educational Research Association in 1976, and one at a symposium in Vienna in 1979 all used simplified versions of some of the developmental lines to discuss the child's readiness for nursery school, and to explain some of the difficult behaviour teachers have to cope with (Freud, A. 1960b, 1981d [1976c], 1981f [1979c]).

A paper published in 1952 was derived from notes taken by students during an informal talk and question and answer session at Harvard Graduate School of Education. There, Anna Freud discussed how the teacher's role differs from that of the parent in relation to various needs of the child, and in responding to problems. She stressed the importance of being familiar with the development of children of all ages, of being able to keep an adult perspective, and of avoiding too great involvement with the individual child. She accepted that it is natural for teachers to develop strong feelings for children in their care; but they must avoid rivalry with the parents as well as remaining aware that the child will be with them for a relatively short time (Freud, A. 1952a).

Her 1949 paper on social maladjustment spelled out various ways in which a child's difficulties might become apparent in school. If pre-Oedipal and Oedipal attitudes remain too violent and unresolved, they may spill over into school which then becomes an extended battleground for fighting family conflicts. In this connection Anna Freud stressed the importance for the child of a different type of relationship, to help him discriminate between adults, and make new and different contacts instead of simply displacing feelings and conflicts from home.

But not all disturbed behaviour can be attributed to what is actually going on at home. Some of the child's anxieties, miseries, aggressiveness, excessive submissiveness and learning inhibitions may be manifestations of his own fantasy life. Sometimes these fantasies get enacted, for example, in bullying or being bullied; sometimes the child tries to curb them and suffers more silently (Freud, A. 1949d).

Applying her thinking to practical issues, she made recommendations that teachers have long agreed with but are rarely able to implement for lack of funding in the public education system. Since experiences in the early years are so important for future development, Anna Freud deplored the fact that teachers of younger children were less highly regarded and worse paid than teachers of older children, and that more financial resources were given to secondary than to primary schools. She believed that many later school problems could be ameliorated if nursery schooling was available, especially for disadvantaged children. She also stressed that primary school classes needed to be small, since in the early years the child's relationship with the teacher is especially important. She thought that twenty children was about the limit for forming good child–teacher relationships (Freud, A. 1964).

## Working with physically ill children

I have already mentioned Anna Freud's talk to medical students about what they could learn from infant observation (Freud, A. 1953a), and her paper on regression (Freud, A. 1963b) which was originally addressed to paediatricians. These papers, like many others, were also intended for wider professional audiences, since Anna Freud deplored the divisions between the professions which gave them little opportunity to observe in each other's settings. Parents, she commented, are the only people who see all aspects of a child's functioning, normal and abnormal, healthy and ill.

Her paper on the role of bodily illness in the mental life of children was similarly aimed at a wide audience of parents and professionals, but also specifically addressed the importance of distinguishing between the effects of separation anxiety caused by hospitalisation, the effects of nursing, medical and surgical procedures, external factors which are open to modification, and the internal factors in the child which derive from his own psychological reactions to and fantasies about his illness.

She pointed out that a child, especially a young one, cannot distinguish between the suffering caused by his disease, and the suffering imposed by the treatment for it. The loss of independence occasioned by 'being nursed' may be even more distressing for a child who is in the process of achieving independence in caring for his own body than it is for an adult. The child may also confuse it with the physical weakness caused by his illness. Enforced restriction of movement blocks the child's need for activity, especially for discharge of aggression, and may lead to symptoms ranging from irritability and tantrums to tics and serious inhibitions of other areas of functioning. Operations and medical procedures often arouse fantasies of castration and other attacks on the child's body. Anna Freud discussed the importance of offering the child enough reality information, help in expressing feelings, and enough time (but not too long) to prepare himself so as to minimise the buildup of frightening fantasy.

She suggested that children who are courageous in bearing pain are those who are not dominated by unconscious fantasy about it, whereas those who easily feel agonised are suffering from the augmentation of pain by anxiety and guilt deriving from their fantasies. Children also vary according to whether they withdraw into themselves to cope with illness, or whether they turn to objects and become extra demanding and clinging. She also discussed the problem of children who become hypochondriacal after an illness, linking it with their sense of being deprived of their mother's care; they identify with the lost mother and take over her role of caring for their body (Freud, A. 1952b).

She was cautious about recommending specific ways of handling particular medical procedures, always stressing that the individual child's perception and understanding of events is influenced by his developmental phase and particular fears and fantasies of the moment. For example, concerning the debate among paediatricians over the use of suppositories versus injections, she explained that for a child in the anal phase suppositories might feel like an attack, or might be found pleasurable and exciting, each reaction carrying its dangers for later development; whereas an injection might seem less significant. But for a child in the phallic phase, an injection might seem a frightening attack, with a suppository being some-what less alarming. In all cases a child's anxiety and resistance can be reduced if time can be taken for explanations and reassurance. Again, in each case the physical danger and urgency had to be weighed against the psychological dangers.

In considering questions about children who are not cuddly, crying babies, sleep disturbances and food refusals, each time she went into the question of individual constitutional differences, early handling by the mother, which might promote or interfere with good development, the passing developmental disruptions due to changes in the child's needs and urges, and what psychological factors might be involved in establishing more serious distur-bances. She believed that more study and experimentation was needed to find the best ways of managing the psychological side of physical treatment. Ideally, she wished that medical training could include a large element of developmental psychology from the beginning, not just an added-on bit, which she regarded as inadequate. In the meantime she recommended close co-operation between psychologically and medically trained workers (Freud, A. 1961, 1975a).

## Children and the law

Anna Freud's interest in the law in relation to the child has already been mentioned above in connection with the assessment of delinquent and antisocial tendencies in children. She believed that an accurate assessment required an understanding of the child's developmental status. In subsequent work she directly approached problems of the legal profession in decisions about custody and placement.

In the early 1960s she worked at Yale Law School with Professor Joseph Goldstein and Dr Jay Katz on problems of disposal of children (Freud, A. 1965b). At a conference at Yale in 1966 on residential versus foster care for children, she approached the issues, as always, from the point of view of which environment would best suit the needs of the individual child for continuity, stimulation, mutuality between mother and child, affection and help in working out conflicts and problems of development. She ended by wondering if authorities were doing enough to support the family, especially single mothers, in keeping the child. She stressed that this best fulfils the child's need for continuity, and that either the family could be helpled to meet the child's other needs more adequately, or some of these needs could be met by other educational or day care services (1967a [1953]).

The association with Yale developed into a collaboration with Professor Goldstein and Professor Albert Solnit, director of the Yale Child Study Centre, which produced three classic books (Goldstein *et al.* 1973, 1979, 1986), the last completed and published after her death. These have been influential, though probably more quickly in the United States than in the United Kingdom.

The first book, *Beyond the Best Interests of the Child*, challenged the notion of the child as a possession of the parents, and instead took the view that the law must regard the child as a person in his own right, whose developmental needs must be paramount in decisions about adoption, custody following divorce, and other placement decisions. Further, the authors defined some important concepts.

The psychological parent was defined as the person with whom the child has a continuous, unconditional and permanent relationship, who has raised and cared for the child, with whom the child has developed a loving and trusting relationship, and who has supported his emotional, intellectual and physical development.

The wanted child was defined in terms of his being loved and wanted because of the relationship that has developed between him and the psychological parent. Thus biological claims are excluded if the biological parent has not been the child's carer; and the authors warn against divorcing parents who 'want' the child mainly as part of a battle with the ex-spouse.

They wished to replace the concept of: the best interests of the child with: the least detrimental alternative. This recognises that if the child is having to be placed for adoption or in a custody decision during divorce, there has already occurred a serious disruption in the child's natural relationships, actual or potential. Priority must then be given to settling the child in a stable relationship as soon as possible. This implies that the duration of temporary fostering, or changes of foster-parents, must be minimised. They also emphasised that children can only maintain more than one primary relationship if the adults are in a good relationship with each other. Hence in cases of divorce, shared custody runs the danger of inducing loyalty conflicts in the child, so that visiting rights need very careful consideration and agreement.

Not only the psychoanalytic understanding of child development but the great practical experience of the authors is evident in their definitions and recommendations in the cases they discuss.

Special emphasis is placed on the child's sense of time (see Chapter 5, pp. 89–90), leading to the recommendation that legal processes must be speeded up to avoid lengthy uncertainty for the child. Similarly they recommend that decisions about placement should be final, in the sense that once the child is entrusted to a psychological parent, the relationship will be prevented from developing satisfactorily if there is uncertainty about its continuation. They take the view that the court cannot make long-range predictions or supervise interpersonal relationships. Thus once the legal decision about placement has been made, the court should withdraw and entrust further decision making to the psychological parent (Freud, A. 1975b; Goldstein et al. 1973).

In their second book, *Before the Best Interests of the Child* (1979), Goldstein et al. went further back in the disposal process, and examined the grounds for legal intervention in the child's existing relationships. They took as their starting point the concept of autonomous parents entitled to raise their child as they think best in the privacy of the family. They expressed a preference for minimising state intervention, and again stressed that the child's needs must be paramount; i.e. the intervention should aim to create or re-create a family for the child as soon as possible. This also implies the need to be very sure that intervention will not make matters worse for the child, bearing in mind his need for an uninterrupted relationship.

They also stressed the concept of fair warning, i.e. making very clear to parents the precise grounds on which the law would be required to intervene, so as to avoid unjustifiable violations of family integrity. Again, their emphasis was on the psychological family, and they stressed that long-term carers may have priority over the birth parents if a permanent, mutual relationship has developed between child and carer, so that the biological parents would seem like strangers to the child. The book went on to consider various grounds which constitute sufficient cause for state intervention: various gross failures of parental care, neglect and abuse (apart from cases where the parents request it, i.e. in adoption, divorce, and voluntarily placing the child in care).

The third book, *In the Best Interests of the Child: Professional Boundaries* (1986), discussed the difficulties faced by the professionals involved in decisions about child placement, and the limits of professional power, authority and expertise. All three books emphasise the difference between adults' views and children's needs. This one also explores the way personal views and fantasies can colour and confuse decision making.

## Summary: applications of the developmental point of view

Probably the best summary of Anna Freud's thinking on applications of psychoanalysis to children's services is to be found in a short paper given to a lay audience in New York in 1964. In it she succinctly described the difficulties of communication between professionals with insufficient knowledge of each others' areas of expertise. More importantly, she pointed out that professions founded long before the advent of psychoanalysis originally used assumptions about childhood that did not recognise the impact of emotions on other areas of development. Thus schools assumed that the intellect could be developed without regard for the child's fantasies, fears and emotions. Hospitals dealt with physical illness without taking into account the child's panics, loyalties to his family, and frightening fantasies of body damage. The courts tried to safeguard the child's religion, morality and financial security without considering his emotional needs. It was not surprising, she thought, that these services for children found it difficult to assimilate psychoanalytic thinking about the importance of children's emotional needs.

She also summarised the advances that were being made and what, in 1964, remained to be done. Schools had learned to make use of the child's natural curiosity and energy to make work more like play. But some progressive schools, she noted, had failed to understand the need to help the child make the shift on the developmental line from play to work, and to become more task oriented regardless of immediate pleasure. In particular she deplored the failure to recognise the importance of early learning and its close dependence on the relationship to the teacher, the lack of nursery school places, and the too large numbers in primary school classes.

In medicine, she noted the growing interest in psychosomatic illness and the understanding of psychological factors in physical illness, But she thought there was still too little account taken of the repercussions of bodily illness on the child's mind.

In family law, she thought that psychoanalytic findings were beginning to offer help in decisions about custody, visiting rights, adoption, foster placement, the child's reactions to mental illness in the parents, and the traumatic impact of criminal events in the family, as well as the effects of corporal punishment and other forms of discipline on social adaptation. She concluded that:

> The best interests of the child are served . . . by all measures which promote his smooth progression toward normal maturity. The latter . . . depends . . . on the coincidence of three factors: on the free interchange of affection between child and adult; on ample external stimulation of the child's inborn, internal potentialities; and on unbroken continuity of care.
>
> (Freud, A. 1964, p. 469)

Perhaps her final comment on the application of psychoanalytic understanding in other professions was made in 1981 on the occasion of the fiftieth anniversary of the Chicago Institute for Psychoanalysis, which coincided with the fiftieth anniversary of the publication in English of her 'Introduction to psychoanalysis for teachers' (Freud, A. 1930). She said that if she were to update these lectures,

I would attempt to engage the audience's interest in all the further steps of the humanising process which mark the child's path from immaturity to maturity.

It may be the fault of our earlier . . . emphasis on the battle with the drives if these [steps in the humanising process] are taken all too often for granted as mere consequences of growth and maturation . . . to correct [this myth] may be as much our task now as it was our task fifty years ago to familiarise educators with the emotional and instinctual side of the child's life.

(Freud, A. 1983, pp. 108–109)

## OVERVIEW OF CHANGES IN THEORY

Some of Anna Freud's later papers indicate how far she had moved since her early theoretical contributions. Her early work on ego functioning (1936) was set firmly within Sigmund Freud's then new structural theory. Her contribution at that time was to elaborate the role of the ego, giving it status equal in importance to drives. Her early interest in ego functioning led on to an interest in how the ego develops, its contribution to personality building, and how life experiences impact on this. From there she moved to studying the mother–child interaction, and the effects of separation. In the process of this study she abandoned her original belief (a common one at the time) that the first six months of an infant's life are largely a time of biological functioning, and moved to tracing from birth the emergence of psychological functioning and object attachment. This included her interest in the early somato-psychic functioning of the infant, and how it gradually differentiates as the capacity to mentalise instead of somatise grows. In the process of breaking down the interactions of drives, ego and object relations into their constituent parts she used the developmental lines which multiplied in these later years. Her view of the structures delineated by Sigmund Freud is that they are ever developing and changing dynamic systems. The profile stays close to Sigmund Freud's original conception of structure. But the developmental lines break down these systems into smaller units which allow us to see the details of the 'humanising process', both to understand the details of normal development and the minutiae of pathological development.

# Chapter 7

# Psychopathology and therapeutic technique

For many years psychoanalysts working with adult as well as with child patients had been discussing how to widen the scope of psychoanalysis to help patients with non-neurotic disturbances. The early discussions about technique had tended to focus around the broad issue of whether psychoanalysis was an appropriate form of treatment for any but neurotic illnesses in which current conflicts could be analysed. Patients needed a sufficiently strong ego and superego to contain impulses and feelings in thought, and a good enough capacity for object relationships to form a transference to the analyst which could be interpreted so as to give the patient an insight into conflicts. Patients with weak ego and superego functioning often could not contain their feelings and impulses in thought, but acted on them; and if they formed a transference it was often infantile and demanding, even delusional. Interpretation to such patients often seemed not to produce insight and greater control, but to provoke acting out because of their poor defences. Hence ego-supportive therapy was usually advocated for such patients. This helped them to manage themselves better but did not alter underlying defects. Increasing understanding of object relations and narcissistic development led to attempts to work with damage deriving from deficient or malignant aspects of early parent–child relationships, i.e. to find ways of reconstructing and interpreting these early experiences and their effects on the patient's expectations of himself and his objects, as well as on his internalised conflicts.

The improved understanding of development and the findings from child analysis contributed to the understanding of adults with borderline and narcissistic disorders in whom aspects of development had been delayed or distorted but who were not psychotic.

There were also implications for technique with these adults who, like children, often lacked the positive curative factors found in neurotic adults.

Anna Freud's way of exploring these areas was via the developmental lines which allowed the analyst to pinpoint specific deficits and distortions. Her own way of resolving the question of the suitability of analysis for non-neurotic disorders was to make a closer scrutiny of what analysts did in addition to interpretation of transference and resistance, and what patients made most use of. Verbalisation of affects and clarification of thinking play some part in any analysis, as does the presence of the analyst as a new object in the patient's life, with a new approach to the patient and his problems, and consequently offering a new model for identification. This happens whether or not the analyst intends it. Neurotic patients with a well-functioning ego and superego are relatively easily able to understand and make use of interpretations to work out new adaptations and compromises, without much need of help from the additional techniques. But it is these additional techniques which are most needed by patients with deficits who need to have the constituents of insight spelled out and built up for them via verbalisation, clarification, explanation, etc. These techniques help to make good missing experience and to get development moving again in areas that were stunted.

Anna Freud eventually arrived at the position of distinguishing not between analytic and non-analytic work, but between the primary analytic tasks: interpretation of resistance and transference, and the subsidiary techniques, classed as developmental help. Deficit illnesses require more developmental help before and alongside interpretation.

These issues were a major focus of Anna Freud's thinking in her later years. Her study of the role of psychoanalytic developmental help for children with developmental defects and distortions, and the ways in which this might be combined with interpretative work linked with her continuing interest in problems of symptomatology and psychopathology in children, and the implications for technique.


## DEVELOPMENTAL DISORDERS

In *Normality and Pathology* Anna Freud gave a summary of developmental psychopathology. Apart from the more obvious neurotic and psychotic states, children produce a range of pre-neurotic and non-conflictual disorders, which include non-organic disorders of eating and sleeping, as well as excessive delays in the acquisition of vital functions such as control of motility, speech, toilet training and learning; primary disturbances of narcissism and object relatedness, absence of control over destructive tendencies (towards themselves or others), and various other deficiencies of development. Anna Freud believed that some of these manifestations might turn out to be pre-stages of neurotic conflicts, but others were best categorised as developmental disturbances (Freud, A. 1965a, pp. 148–154). The summary she gives is a succinct but comprehensive guide to distinguishing between the conditions under which a child may be expected to grow out of his difficulties, and those in which he is more likely to develop a long-term disturbance.

## Developmental disturbances due to external stresses

Some disturbances are due to external stresses: for example, when the infant's natural sleeping and eating rhythms do not coincide with the demands of the environment; or when he is left alone too long because his need for company is not recognised; or when toilet training is begun too soon. Such babies then develop difficulties in falling asleep, food refusal, excessive crying, etc. If caught early these difficulties can be resolved or minimised by changes in handling. If not, they can leave a readiness to expect frustration and unpleasure; or through identification with the mother's handling he may develop a hostile attitude to his own needs and wishes, thus creating a readiness for internalised conflict (ibid., pp. 155–157).

## Developmental disturbances due to internal stresses

There are also disturbances due to internal stresses which are an inescapable part of maturation and development, though they can be made worse by external stresses. They include the toddler's difficulty in falling asleep which reflects his developing object ties and involvement in the happenings of the world around him. He may become reluctant to relinquish these interests and anxious about the kind of regression to a narcissistic state required for going to sleep, hence the calls for mother, drinks of water, wanting the door open or the light on. The child has his own ways of facilitating the process of falling asleep through autoerotic activities such as thumb sucking, rocking, masturbation, etc., or through cuddling a soft toy or transitional object. If the parents interfere with these activities an externally induced sleep disturbance can result. But an internally induced disturbance can occur in an older child if he is struggling to give up masturbation, or to abandon cuddly toys. Latency children often use compulsive reading, counting or thinking to cope with their difficulties (ibid., pp. 157–159).

## Development of eating disorders

There are eating disturbances linked with each stage on the developmental line towards independent eating. The earliest difficulties in breast-feeding may be a mixture of physical (difficulties in sucking, poor milk flow, etc.) and psychological (mother's anxiety or ambivalence and the baby's reaction to her feelings). With the introduction of solid foods refusals may begin, which can usually be prevented by considerate, gradual weaning; but if not they may result in dislike of new types of food and lack of adventurousness, as well as a more general lack of oral pleasure, or alternatively lead to greed and fears of hunger. Later battles about food, including table manners and some food fads, express the toddler's ambivalent relationship with mother, the provider. But some avoidance of particular shapes, colours and smells may come from purely internal conflicts over anality; refusal of meat may be a defence against cannibalistic fantasies; some refusals may express fantasy fears of oral impregnation. Phase-linked difficulties such as these will pass in due course provided nothing happens to fix them, but they may lay the ground for adult eating habits (ibid., pp. 159–161; Freud, A. 1947b).

## Behaviour disorders linked with drive phases

Toddlers show many behaviour disorders deriving from anal-sadistic drive impulses, such as destructiveness, messiness, restlessness, clinging, whining or temper tantrums, which can assume unmanageable proportions but which normally disappear as development gives the child other more controlled modes of expression, especially speech (Freud 1965a, pp. 161–162).

Moving out of the anal phase the child who is still struggling to overcome anal impulses and fantasies may pass through a phase of transitory obsessional manifestations. These are outgrown as development consolidates in the next phase, unless for some reason the child develops a fixation which leaves him vulnerable to regression (ibid., pp. 162–163).

The normal conflicts of the phallic Oedipal phase give rise to castration fears which may be expressed in many guises as fears of minor injuries, operations, injections, etc., and may lead to masculine overcompensation, or shifts to passivity, fears of death or inhibitions. Normally these disappear with the move into latency (ibid., p. 163).

Moving out of latency again, the pre-adolescent child may react to new drive pressures by temporary regression to oral or anal traits and symptoms, and may seem to lose social gains, sublimations and rationality. Apparently delinquent leanings may appear. In adolescence proper the emerging genital drive trends overcome the regressions to pre-genitality. But the age-appropriate restructuring of the internal world including object relations and the superego produces further transitory symptoms which may at times be quasi-psychotic, borderline or dissocial (ibid., pp. 163–164).

All this developmental symptomatology can be expected to pass as the child resolves the issues of each phase and moves on to the next. If resolution is not achieved then the child will be left with persisting difficulties which may eventually contribute to more major and permanent disturbance. (ibid., pp. 157–164). Dr H. Nagera, for some years director of research at the Hampstead Clinic, worked with Anna Freud on developmental disturbances and produced a book in which he distinguished between developmental interferences arising from external demands on the child which are not reasonable or age appropriate; developmental conflicts experienced by every child as the inevitable result of reaching certain levels of development and maturation, or having to cope with reasonable external demands; neurotic conflicts which indicate the internal operation of superego precursors opposing drive demands; and infantile neuroses which are the organised internal psychopathology of the child whose structural development has become autonomous and stable (Nagera 1966).

## Review of symptomatology

In a major paper on the symptomatology of childhood Anna Freud restored a measure of significance to symptoms and other signs of disturbance by examining them not from the phenomenological point of view but from the developmental point of view and by distinguishing underlying disturbances. She thought that by this time child analysts had reached a good enough understanding of the relation between surface and depth to be able to distinguish the different meanings of apparently similar manifestations. She discussed seven categories of symptoms starting from the underlying metapsychology and indicating what symptoms may result (Freud, A. 1970).

1  *Non-differentiation between somatic and psychic processes*: the normal somato-psychic unity of infancy gradually gives way to differentiation in the course of development, so that somatic responses to emotional experiences are normal in the early years of childhood, but become gradually less frequent as more mental pathways of expression are established. Where mind–body access remains more than usually open it may contribute to psychosomatic illnesses, such as asthma, eczema, ulcerative colitis and migraine. Individual preferences for bodily outlets may leave vulnerable areas in later life stresses, or may contribute the element of somatic compliance in the formation of hysterical symptoms, which are more complex neurotic formations with symbolic meaning.

2  *The id–ego compromises* the familiar hysterical, obsessional and phobic neurotic symptoms which can occur only in a personality that has achieved a degree of structuralisation.

3  *Irruptions from the id into the ego* indicate an insufficiently developed or fragile border between ego and id. The irruption of primary process functioning results in disturbances of thought and language, delusions, etc. Drive irruptions result in undefended enactments characteristic of some types of delinquency and criminality.

4  *Changes in libido economy* refer to various forms of narcissistic disorder, due to libidinal cathexis being shifted away from normal lines of development. Thus a shift from mind to body may result in hypochondriacal symptoms. The withdrawal of object libido on to the self results in self-centredness, or

overvaluation of self, with megalomania at the extreme. The shift of narcissistic libido on to the object may result in emotional surrender and overvaluation of the object. A decrease in narcissistic libido may result in bodily neglect, self-denigration, depression or depersonalisation.

5   *Changes in the quality or direction of aggression* are usually due to variations in the type of defence being used, which may result in swings of aggression from objects to self, and back again, or from mental to bodily attacks and vice versa. Symptoms which may result include inhibition, learning failure and self-injurious behaviour.

6   *Undefended regression* occurs in children who are avoiding conflicts of the phallic and Oedipal phases but do not go on to develop the usual neurotic conflicts about their regressive manifestations, i.e. the regression becomes ego-syntonic and manifests clinically as infantilism, with whining and clinging, incompetence, dependency, etc.

7   *Organic causes*, pre- or post-natal, may result in a range of delays in developmental milestones, difficulties with movement, speech, general intellectual functioning, concentration, management of affect, etc. Symptoms such as these can often be confused with inhibitions and other neurotic symptoms. In addition to the primary difficulties arising from handicaps, there are usually secondary difficulties arising from imbalances in development caused by the absence or defectiveness of some functions.

These seven categories of symptoms all belong to recognisable clinical pictures of psychopathology. There are other signs of disturbance and reasons for referring a child for help which are not always clearly pathological, but do represent interferences with normal processes of development. Anna Freud grouped these according to their surface manifestations, and then traced the range of possible meanings.

1   *Fears and anxieties* are extremely common; some forms are developmentally normal, while others play a role in clinical syndromes. To understand their specific significance for the individual child, Anna Freud believed, they must be viewed from the developmental, dynamic, economic and structural points of view.

Developmentally, the sequence begins with the archaic fears of early infancy, of noises, darkness, being alone; these may persist if the child does not receive the appropriate comfort and reassurance needed at this age, or if ego development is slow, so that he does not develop the reality orientation which permits mastery of such fears.

Next comes separation anxiety, i.e. fear of loss of the object in an infant still in the stage of unity with mother; this may take the form of fears of annihilation, starvation, helplessness, etc. and can be prolonged by actual separations, or by unreliability in the mother.

With separation–individuation and structuralisation of the personality comes the beginning of internalisation of objects as representatives of the demand for control of drives. Fear of rejection or loss of the object's love ensues; this anxiety is the beginning of moral development, manifest as fears of punishment, desertion, natural disasters or death. It marks the growing importance of inner conflicts, and its failure to emerge indicates developmental failure. These fears may become excessive if parental demands are too harsh, or if the internal conflicts are for any reason especially difficult to resolve.

The internal dynamics of conflicting forces within the child become increasingly important. In the phallic phase castration anxiety appears in the form of fear of operations, doctors and dentists, robbers, witches, ghosts, etc. and may be exacerbated by Oedipal conflicts.

When the child moves into a wider community of peers, social disgrace becomes a new fear due to dependency on the opinions of peers.

At whatever point the child's superego becomes fully internalised, i.e. when behaviour is no longer dependent on parental approval, anxiety turns into guilt.

The type of anxiety dominant in a particular child gives a clue to the phase of development in which the disturbance is rooted. But Anna Freud warns that symbolic fears are interchangeable, so the links with particular levels of anxiety are not completely correlated.

There is also a form of anxiety, fear of the id, which persists throughout life, and reflects the ego's concern for its own intactness and fear of being overwhelmed. It may appear whenever circumstances lead to a relative increase of drive strength or weakening of the ego, i.e. whenever the economic balance of forces is disturbed.

The fate of these forms of anxiety depends on the type of defences the child is able to use; for example, denial, projection, reaction formation all produce different adaptations. If the child cannot develop adequate defences, he may remain prone to panic states and anxiety attacks. The type of defence used, or lack of it, influences subsequent adaptation and character formation.

2   *Delays or failures in development* may appear in any of the major areas of development: drives, ego and superego functioning, and object relationships, and may be due to organic damage, poor endowment, inadequate care and stimulation from the environment, internal conflicts, inadequacies in the parents' personalitites, or traumatic experiences. It is essential to distinguish such failures and delays from inhibitions and regressions in which the achievements have been acquired and then lost again. This requires careful diagnostic examination of all relevant factors.

3   *School failures or learning disturbances* also have to be carefully differentiated, since apparently identical disorders may derive from quite different causes: arrested development, undefended ego regression, from the symbolic equating of particular subjects or the learning process as a whole with sexual or aggressive ideas, from defensive inhibition or ego restriction, or from symptom formation which has a crippling effect on ego functioning.

4   *Failures in social adaptation* may be the inevitable outcome of adverse environmental circumstances; or they may result from ego defects arising from developmental delays or neurotic regressions; or from imbalances between id and ego; from superego defects arising from various causes, or from faulty ego ideals due to deviant models for identification.

5   *Aches and pains* with no organic cause are frequent reasons for absences from school and visits to the doctor. They may be traced to three of the metapsychological symptom categories given earlier: Category 1 (psychosomatic) if they are direct somatic expressions of mental upsets; Category 2 (hysterical) if they symbolise mental conflict; Category 4 (hypochondriacal) if they arise from changes of cathexis.

Anna Freud ended this paper by stressing the importance of matching treatment with the underlying causes of disturbance, deploring the fact that what is offered too often depends on the resources of a particular department or clinic, rather than on the nature of the child's disturbance. She gives numerous examples of mismatching: for example, children may be placed in residential care when they need a one-to-one relationship; or adopted when they are not capable of forming the necessary attachment to an adult. They may get analysis when they need guidance, or educational help when they need analysis of internal conflicts. Reassurance will not work with a child whose anxiety is of internal origin: castration fear, guilt or fear of the strength of the id; these all need analysis. But analysis cannot help the separation anxiety of the very young child (Freud, A. 1970).

## THERAPEUTIC TECHNIQUES

Matching the form of treatment to the needs and capacities of the individual child became an important focus in the final years of Anna Freud's work.

The two major expositions of Anna Freud's later views on technique in child analysis are to be found in *Normality and Pathology*, and in the 1980 book based on discussions with Anna Freud in the Index Research Group (Sandler *et al.* 1980). The latter book, under headings used for indexing cases, contains summaries of discussions in the group, with many of Anna Freud's responses recorded verbatim. It is useful for clarifying details of technique and the understanding on which they are based. There was another series of discussions in which Anna Freud took part during 1970 and 1971. Ava Penman, then a senior student, chaired a clinical group at which cases were discussed at some length. In an unpublished paper Penman has drawn together a number of Anna Freud's comments linking choice of technique with specific aspects of a child's disturbance (Penman 1995). But Anna Freud's own book, together with some key later papers, gave the widest overview of her own thinking, and set out the overall framework within which, in her later years, she explored developmental psychopathology, and the problems of matching technique to type of disturbance.

## Therapeutic principles and curative tendencies

In *Normality and Pathology*, she reviewed all her thinking on psychopathology and technique as it stood at that time. Her basic ideas (described in Chapter 4) had changed relatively little, but had been refined and elaborated. She listed the therapeutic principles which govern both adult and child analysis, and distinguished these from the natural curative tendencies, which differ in children and adults (Freud, A. 1965a, pp. 25–28).

Translating Bibring's (1954) statement into terms of child analysis she listed four therapeutic principles for analysts:

1   not to make use of authority and to eliminate thereby as far as possible suggestion as an element of treatment;
2   to discard abreaction as a therapeutic tool;
3   to keep manipulation (management) of the patient to a minimum, i.e. to interfere with the child's life situation only where demonstrably harmful or potentially traumatic (seductive) influences were at work;
4   to consider the analysis of resistance and transference, and interpretations of unconscious material as the legitimate tools of therapy.

(Ibid., p. 26)

Using another paper by Bibring (1937) about curative tendencies in adults, she compared neurotic adults and children. The adult neurotic strives for normality which promises pleasure in sexual relationships and success in work; but the child may see getting well as having to give up immediate pleasures and secondary gains and having to adapt to unwelcome reality. The adult's tendency to repeat emotional experience is important in the creation of transference, a central tool of analysis, whereas the child's hunger for new experiences and objects interferes with transference. The adult tends to assimilate and integrate new experience, which assists in the analytic working through of material; the child still age-adequately tends to use mechanisms such as denial, projection, isolation and splitting, which oppose such integration. In adults the urge to obtain drive satisfaction serves to produce analytic material; but in children this urge can be so strong that it leads to enactments which can hinder rather than help the analytic process. The one area in which the child has the advantage over the adult is in the urge to complete development, which is stronger in the immature person than in later life. The child's personality is in a more fluid state than that of the adult, so that energies released by analysis can flow into new channels more easily than in the case of adults, in whom energies are constantly being drawn into the old symptomatology. Children often discard the symptoms developed in one phase as they move into the next (ibid., pp. 26–28).

## The different roles of drives and early object relations in the development of psychopathology

Anna Freud acknowledged the importance of understanding the contributions to psychopathology deriving from the child's experience from birth onwards. But she thought that we should differentiate between the parents' role in supporting, opposing or distorting the child's development, and the more direct effect of experiences of pain and pleasure, satisfaction and frustration on ego development. She thought that without the right experiences to form the nucleus of the 'pleasure-ego', the child did not have the base from which to move to a more reality-oriented ego. Without enough need satisfaction he did not have the base from which to move to object attachment and a more general capacity for object relationships.

She seems to have found direction in Sigmund Freud's 'Analysis terminable and interminable' (Freud, S. 1937) for going beyond the analysis of intrapsychic conflict 'into the darker area of interaction between innate endowment and environmental influence. The implied aim is to undo or counteract the impact of the very forces on which the rudiments of personality development are based' (Freud, A. 1969c). She doubted whether those very early states could be got into the transference. Research at this time was showing that many personality features were acquired which had previously been considered to be inherited. But she did not believe this meant that acquired features would necessariliy be reversible.

She took her views further in a paper on the infantile neurosis written in 1970 (Freud, A. 1971b [1970b]), and in an elaborated version, 'The widening scope of psychoanalytic child psychology' two years later but published only in 1981 (Freud, A. 1981b [1972]). In these papers she spelled out the different contributions made by early object relations and drive conflicts to psychopathology.

In the earlier paper she noted that we are now making an elaborate map of infantile mental difficulties, interferences with mental growth and development from birth onwards. Contributions to personality development are made by early somato-psychic reactions, interaction between the infant's potential and the mother's handling, and the infant's responses to the mother's moods, anxieties, preferences and avoidances. The satisfaction of early body needs opens the way for object attachment and the general capacity for object relationships. Imbalance in experiences of pleasure/unpleasure and frustration/satisfaction may prevent ego building and lead to ego distortion.

She believed, however, that the early mother–child relationship is not directly responsible for pathology; its primary effect is on personality development which may secondarily influence pathology. The development of basic trust in the object is important for the balance between narcissism and object love. Instincts, she thought, have a different contribution to pathology than object relationships: they provide the fixations to oral and anal phases which prepare the way for regression and form the basis for neurotic compromise formations. In this new context the infantile neurosis is a sign of positive progression to sophisticated reaction patterns, not reached by those with developmental failures which may result instead in borderline or more severe pathology. Therapeutic ambition now goes beyond dealing with conflict, to the basic faults and failure, defects and deprivations. But she saw significant differences between the two therapeutic tasks (Freud, A. 1971b [1970b]).

In the case discussions in Penman's group Anna Freud on a number of occasions stressed that techniques which had been used to address developmental deficiencies were attempting to influence aspects of basic personality development. Because personality factors contribute to psychopathology, there would be a secondary effect on this psychopathology. She stressed the difference between this approach and the direct interpretation of psychopathology.

Penman described some of her work with one of many children in a dysfunctional family. 'Alice' was a forlorn 4-year-old who wandered around the nursery school looking for a lap to sit on, but unable to develop relationships, take any initiative or join in group activities. Her mental activity seemed minimal and unfocused. She seemed constantly to be in a state of wanting, without knowing what it was that she wanted, or how to get it or keep it. At first all

Penman could do with Alice was to verbalise what she was doing, initiate drawings and games of asking and getting, letting Alice know that there might be a coherent story in what she was doing. She also put into words how Alice might be feeling, especially about wanting. At first Penman helped Alice get what she wanted. Only when a point was reached where she thought frustration might be useful in furthering understanding did Penman limit gratification and verbalise how that might make Alice feel. Gradually Alice became able to put words to her anger, hatred and fear of losing love. Concomitantly she became more organised and focused, and conflicts emerged which could be verbalised and eventually interpreted.

Anna Freud commented that Alice had not been helped by her depressed mother who could offer primitive comforting on her lap, but could not sort things out for Alice in a way that could support ego development. Alice had not been able to make the shift from receiving body care to her own mental functioning. In this case Penman had to begin by addressing the primary personality deficits which were contributing to the child's pathology before conflicts could emerge and be interpreted in a way that would be meaningful for Alice (Penman 1995).

In her 1972 paper, Anna Freud stated that analytic techniques can reverse misguided ego decisions in areas of internalised conflict. But it is not equally able to reverse the conditions which have affected ego development, and mother–infant interactions which have shaped the personality. The past cannot be undone, she thought, though we can help the ego to come to terms with its residues (Freud, A. 1981b [1972]).

## Insight and treatment alliance

In 1965 Anna Freud reiterated her view that children starting analysis lack insight into their abnormalities, have no wish for therapy and do not readily develop a treatment alliance (Freud, A. 1965a, pp. 28–29). She subsequently agreed with Hansi Kennedy whose paper suggested that insight cannot be expected from pre-latency children who have not yet developed the ego prerequisites for self-obervation and appraisal of what is going on in their inner world. They want to get rid of suffering, not to understand it. In normal development only advancing age and maturity helps unfold the capacity for insight which permits the use of a technique nearer to classical analysis and requiring fewer of the technical modifications forced on child analysts. Kennedy suggested that the analytic process may serve to develop insight precociously in young children, and formulated a developmental line for it (see Chapter 6, pp. 134–135), (Freud, A. 1979a, 1981a; Kennedy 1979).

In the Index discussions two definitions of treatment alliance were offered: a broad one encompassing all the factors that keep a patient in treatment in spite of resistance and hostile transference; and a narrower one specifying the patient's awareness of illness and of the need to do something about it, and the capacity to tolerate the pain of facing internal conflict. Anna Freud commented that the wish to be helped with inner difficulties is the most mature motive. Positive transference may initially help the alliance, but if it is too strong it runs the risk of the child wishing to live out the love for the analyst; and with the change to a negative transference cooperation may break down. She stressed that the child also forms a tie with the analyst as a new and different understanding object. Discussing the case of an adolescent boy who improved in spite of not forming a treatment alliance, she commented that his sense of masculinity had been improved by analytic work on his aggression and inhibitions, but his intense transference feelings were not helpful for the analytic work. He could only passively let himself be dragged through the analysis, probably on the basis of masochistic or homosexual elements. This was compliance rather than treatment alliance (Sandler et al. 1980, pp. 45–56).

Audrey Gavshon described a boy who was able to develop a treatment alliance because of his eagerness to be understood and to understand. 'Martin' suffered delayed development in many areas from infancy, probably of organic origin, compounded by intermittent hearing loss and delayed speech. His intelligence was above average, but when he began treatment at age 7, he was inarticulate, his speech often unintelligible, and he was unable to narrate a sequence of events. He was frustrated when Gavshon could not understand him and felt denigrated if she asked him to repeat something she could not understand. She was aware of his narcissistic vulnerability and shame about being incomprehensible. He was also physically rigid. In an inspired move, Gavshon showed him the finger game about the church, the steeple and the people inside. This led on to finger games in which they enacted movements and stories. He enjoyed these games and talking with fingers clearly felt safer for him than talking with words, perhaps recalling a pre-verbal time when he felt more at ease. Eventually, after his analyst's fingers enacted a story about a boy crying because he could not run as fast as his brother, he managed to say in words: 'Tell him why he is crying.' This permitted the beginning of interpretation of his fear of failure and ridicule if he could not understand and be understood, and his despair that he would never catch up with his clever brother. He dubbed Mrs Gavshon 'Queen of the people who don't get cross'. He taught her to speak slowly to him and in short sentences, for example, by responding to an interpretation with: 'Now say that again, but don't say so much.' This need for understanding carried him through the painful and difficult times in his analysis (Gavshon 1987).

## Acting out

Anna Freud still viewed the lack of free association as the major difficulty, since without it, however much children may talk and play, 'there is no reliable path from manifest to latent content'. The child's tendency to act rather than talk freely forces the analyst to set limits on behaviour (i.e. to 'manage' the child), whereas there need be no limits on talk. Free association tends to liberate sexual fantasy, but action tends to liberate aggression, increasing the management problem as well as biasing the content of the analytic material (Freud, A. 1965a, pp. 29–31).

In a 1968 paper on acting out, she discussed the history of the concept, and noted that with the shift in analytic interest to the very early months of life, much analytic material now belongs to a pre-thinking level, has never entered the ego organisation, and cannot be remembered, only relived in behaviour or attitudes in the transference. Analysts have consequently developed a greater tolerance for acting out, especially child analysts. The younger the child, the more blurred the distinction between remembering, reliving, repeating and acting out. She herself found it important to maintain these distinctions. She described the child analyst's aim as to facilitate the child's move from action and fantasy elaboration to verbalisation and secondary process thinking (Freud, A. 1968b).

It is a normal developmental task of the ego to master orientation in the external world and the organisation of internal emotional states. Putting impressions into thoughts and words is part of the process which achieves this. Young children, or older ones with developmental delays, bring a larger proportion than adults of material which has never yet been conscious because it has not yet been organised into secondary process thought. This disorganised, primary process material cannot be remembered, only relived within the transference. Thus, while verbalisation is part of the process of interpretation with patients of all ages, with children it also plays another vital role, that of promoting both reality-testing and control over inner feelings and impulses. The analyst of children has to spend relatively more time verbalising inner strivings and perceptions of the external world in order for interpretation of unconscious conflicts and anxieties to make sense to the child (Freud, A. 1965a, pp. 31–33).

Tessa Baradon described this type of work with 'Michael', a 7-year-old referred by his headmistress who found him 'the silliest boy in the school'. He had no friends and was constantly on the move, anxious and excited, rushing around impulsively, engaging in chaotic activity. He had no capacity to use thought, language or play in trial action, and lacked ego functions such as reality-testing and understanding of cause and effect. Therapy revealed an inhibition of mental processes of thinking, linking and explaining. His inability to give meaning to his feeling states and behaviour left him with a chaotic inner world. This developmental failure seemed derived from his confusing experiences of his mother, who was intensely but ambivalently involved with him, capable of being both adoring and raging towards him. His confusion had probably been compounded by his inability to cope with a separation from her at age 2, immediately after the birth of his brother, when he was taken abroad to visit his father's family for three weeks.

Baradon found that Michael experienced as attacks her attempts to interpret his anxiety and rage, which escalated his restless behaviour into attacks on his therapist. She realised that he lacked the mental capacity for reflection, and was confused and frightened by both the contents of his own mind and what he believed was in the analyst's mind. She therefore adopted a technique of carefully explaining her evidence for suggesting what he might be feeling and what he might think she was thinking; for example, he no longer wanted to play with his bricks, which made her think he might feel upset, and he might think that she thought him a silly boy when his bricks fell down.

As he came to feel more contained and understood, Michael began to use toys for symbolic play, and to want to understand the analyst's mind and identify with her perception of him. She kept track of changes in his feelings about her, and gradually introduced links with possible reasons for these feelings: cause and effect. Gradual improvements in his capacity to mentalise, and in his sense of self, at times allowed him to make use of a more interpretative analytic style to address his inner confusion and his conflicts in the transference (Baradon 1998).

## Resistance and basic unwillingness

Concerning resistances, Anna Freud stressed that in addition to true resistances to the analytic process, some children have a more basic unwillingness to come to therapy, since they have not chosen this for themselves. Such a child does not feel bound by analytic rules, and is not prepared to put up with the present discomfort of treatment for the sake of future gain; the tendency to externalise leads him to prefer environmental solutions to internal changes. There is often a mixture of basic unwillingness and resistance to the emergence of material: the child is ready to stay away from treatment whenever he is in resistance. Some resistances reflect the child's sense of being only insecurely in control of impulses and feelings, so that analysis seems a threat to his defences; the more primitive defences are age appropriately more used by the child than by the adult; the urge to outgrow the past makes the child reluctant to revive it in the transference especially during entry into latency and again in adolescence. Overall, the analyst has to manage without a therapeutic alliance for long stretches of the analysis (Freud, A. 1965a, pp. 33–36).

Anne Hurry gives the example of 'Paul', an 11-year-old boy who was extremely unwilling to come to treatment. This unwillingness was compounded of objections to being made to attend and fearful resistance to understanding his inner world. Several previous attempts at therapy had failed. His parents became willing to insist on his having analysis because of his alarming symptoms: crippling phobias, contamination fears, nightmares, food refusals, messiness, demanding, abusive and insulting behaviour, and especially his extreme hatred of his sister. For most of the analysis he was sadistic, degrading, mocking and insulting towards his analyst, attempting to force her to reject him. It was only Hurry's perseverance and skill in understanding the defensive nature of this behaviour that allowed the analysis to continue. He was especially afraid of the dangers of loving, and was abysmally convinced of his own badness, expecting his analyst to find him 'horrible' and 'inhuman'. Hurry had to tolerate outpourings of hatred and aggression while maintaining her commitment to him. She refers to Anna Freud's (1949a) linking of pathological aggressiveness with defects in emotional libidinal development, so that aggression cannot become fused with and controlled by libido. What Paul lacked was a loving relationship, partly because of his fears of the dangers of loving and losing. This made any development of positive transference frightening for him. Hurry had to be an object who would not reject Paul, but who set firm limits to his aggressive and destructive behaviour. She also had to be extremely honest in her appraisal of his behaviour because of his acute sensitivity to falsity in his objects. Hurry stated that interpretation would have been useless until Paul had some hope that he would not be rejected (Hurry 1998, pp. 100–123). Paul's extreme reluctance to undergo treatment contrasts with Martin's eagerness to be understood (see above).

## Transference

In 1965 Anna Freud clarified changes in some of her initial views on transference in child analysis, and also elaborated further developments in her thinking (Freud, A. 1965a, pp. 36–43). Her own later experience, together with Bornstein's (1949) demonstration that the use of defence analysis could serve as an introduction, had led her to eliminate the introductory phase. She was also more inclined to accept that children could develop a full transference neurosis, though still unconvinced that this was exactly the same as in adults.

Nor did she believe that transference manifestations occur from the very beginning of analysis, and that transference can supplant other sources of material. This view, she believed, was based on three assumptions:

1  that whatever happens in a patient's personality structure can be analysed in terms of his object relationship to the analyst;
2  that all levels of object relationship are equally open to interpretation and changed by it to the same extent;
3  that the only function of the figures in the environment is to be the recipients of libidinal and aggressive cathexis.

(Ibid., pp. 37–38)

She pointed out that the experience of child analysts does not confirm these assumptions. The hunger for new experience means that with the healthy part of their personality children treat the analyst as a new object, while using her for transference repetition of disturbed areas of development. 'To learn how to sort out the mixture and to move carefully between the two roles which are thrust on him are essential elements of every child analyst's training in technique' (ibid., pp. 38–39).

Anne Harrison describes such shifts in her work with a 4-year-old girl. 'Martha' was intelligent and gifted, but disabled by fears and phobias, rigidly controlling, and unable to form relationships outside her immediate family. Her relationship with her mother was stormy, she was close to her father, and persecuted her younger sister. She insisted on being treated like a baby. In her analysis she played many games, but in a ritualised way. She spoke only to ask for things, and ignored what the analyst said.

A character who came to be called 'messy pig' seemed to open up some possibility for her to hear the therapist talking about pig's wishes to splash, stamp and make a mess. Martha's play moved on a little in response to these verbalisations, though she made no direct response. Nor did she acknowledge the gap of the long Summer holiday, except for a game with dolls named 'big girl' and 'little girl' who moved towards and away from each other, though she seemed to listen to the transference interpretation about herself and her therapist. But for weeks she played an unvarying game of building uniform towers with single colours of Lego, always discarding irregular pieces she called 'the messy bits'. She ignored Harrison's attempts to find out what made them messy. Harrison, feeling stuck and hopeless, one day insisted on building her own house of mixed colours and using 'the messy bits'. Martha objected and looked worried, but the analyst simply said she did not think they were messy, just different, and went on to speak of the bricks feeling lonely and wanting to join the others. Martha tentatively added a 'messy bit' to one of her own towers, murmuring 'It's all right'. Harrison agreed it was all right. This intervention allowed the child to ease her controlling enough to have more of an exchange with the analyst in play about closeness and separation, and the fear of sadness and loss.

Harrison felt that her non-interpretative intervention had allowed Martha a chance to see that including the messy bits was safe, and that experiencing the therapist as separate and outside her control was bearable (Harrison 1998).

In the 'transference proper' the child regresses and repeats object relations from all levels of development. Anna Freud believed that pre-Oedipal and pre-genital elements usually need to be interpreted before Oedipal ones, since they tend to introduce negative, resistant attitudes into the transference, for example, regression to narcissistic self-sufficiency takes the form of withdrawal from the analyst; symbiotic attitudes appear as a wish to merge with the analyst; anaclitic dependence places the onus on the analyst to help the child without effort or sacrifice on the child's part; oral attitudes introduce demandingness; anal ones stubborn withholding, or hostile and sadistic attacks; the fear of object loss leads to compliance and misleading 'transference improvements'. Object constancy and Oedipal attitudes together with the co-ordinated ego achievements of self-observation, insight and secondary process functioning are the transference elements which contribute to the treatment alliance with the analyst. This, in Anna Freud's view, is what makes the analysis of very young children and those whose development has been arrested at early levels particularly difficult, since they have not reached the levels of development which contribute to the treatment alliance (ibid., pp. 39–41).

An example of one kind of pathology which makes any form of treatment alliance very fragile and dependent on the therapist's sensitivity to the child's needs is found in a paper by Agi Bene, on self-pathology in children. She described two cases (treated by Pat Radford and Peter Wilson) who both needed to make their therapists part of their own omnipotent fantasy existence. Both boys had established self–object boundaries and were aware of the object's separate existence, but for pathological narcissistic reasons each tried to force the object to be an 'adjunct' who would do exactly as told by the patient. Both had suffered from intrusive parents who often could not respond adequately to their children's needs. Bene recommended that in such cases the therapists had to begin by allowing themselves to be part of the child's grandiose, often destructive fantasies, because too early interpretation would be experienced as repetition of the parental intrusion. Only when the child began to internalise benign, tolerant aspects of the therapists could interpretation become useful to the child (Bene 1979).

Anna Freud also differentiated from 'transference proper' 'a sub-species of transference': the externalisation on to the analyst of parts of the patient's personality. Thus the analyst may be used to represent some aspect of the child's id, or used as an auxiliary ego, or as an external superego. In this way the child re-stages his internal conflicts as external battles with the analyst. But Anna Freud held that to interpret these battles in terms of object relationships within the transference is a mistake, because even though these conflicts have their origins in early relationships they now reveal what is going on in the child's inner world, and the conflicts need to be interpreted as within himself, not between himself and the analyst (Freud, A. 1965a, pp. 41–43).

Therapists frequently get called 'poohy' or 'yucky' by children who are in conflict over regressive anal wishes. An object-relationship interpretation would be something on the lines of: 'You'd rather I were the poohy one so you can be the clean one'; or 'Perhaps you're afraid I might think you are yucky'. But interpretation in terms of the child's own structural conflict would be on the lines of: 'Part of you wants to enjoy being little and poohy, but another bit of you thinks you should be big and clean'; or 'Part of you thinks it's safer to be little and poohy instead of doing big boy things, but you don't really like poohy things any more'.

## Dependency

The issue of infantile dependency is important in child analysis. The analytic technique was devised for use with fully developed adults, who could be taken as independent beings, however important their past dependency might have been. The environment was to be seen through the patient's eyes, and the transference re-enactments were private to the analyst and analysand. But in children dependency is still an ongoing process, and this raises the theoretical issue: at what point can the child be seen as a separate entity, no longer to be considered as the product and dependant of his family? It also raises the technical question of how far parents should be included in the child's analysis. From the child's side, the analyst can assess whether the way the child uses his parents is appropriate for his chronological age, and whether his dependency has therefore reached the appropriate stage. For example, the child may still lean on the parents' capacity to manipulate external conditions to suit the child; or he may have moved on to more constant relationships with them; he may use them to support his own ego's attempts at mastery of the id, or as models for identification in building up his own independent personality structures (ibid., pp. 43–53).

But the child analyst also has to consider the parents' role in the causation of the child's illness, which involves a careful distinction between the mother's pathogenic influence on the child, and the effects of the child's disturbance on the mother. Simultaneous analysis of parents and children (Burlingham *et al.* 1955; Hellman *et al.* 1960; Levy 1960; Sprince 1962) reveal various forms of pathogenic parent–child relations. The parent's attachment to the child may depend on the child's representing either an ideal, or a figure from the parent's past; this moulds the child into a pattern which may neglect or conflict with his own potential. Or the child may be assigned a role in the parent's pathology, in which the parent does not relate to the child's own needs; symptoms may be passed on from parent to child in the form of a *folie à deux*. Parents may also play a part in maintaining a child's disturbance, for example, by colluding with phobias or rituals.

Such factors as well as many others affect the extent to which the analyst can rely on the parents' support for the child's analysis. 'The analyst is helpless if they . . . side with the child's resistances' or with negative transference; or if they aggravate the child's loyalty conflicts at times of positive transference (Freud, A. 1965a, pp. 43–48).

For example, a 6-year-old boy with divorced parents suffered from a conflict of loyalties between them. As he developed a positive transference to his analyst he found himself caught in a similar conflict of loyalty between his mother and his analyst. This was manageable by interpretation until his mother's jealousy increased sharply after her own therapy was interrupted by her analyst's illness. By this time the boy's manifest symptoms had disappeared, and his mother determined to interrupt his analysis too, rationalising that her son was much improved and could no longer spare time for analysis from his many extra-curricular school activities. A 6-year-old child fearful of object loss cannot withstand such pressure from his mother, and he swung into a negative transference which took the common form of not wanting to come to sessions. His mother seized on this as reinforcement of her own arguments for ending treatment.

Whereas the analyst of adults can focus on the patient's psychic reality, the analyst of children is made aware of the powerful influence of the real environment. The child's material communicates not only his fantasies, but current events in his family which may be distressing or disturbing for him. The child analyst has to distinguish in his interpretations between the internal and the external world of the child. None the less, alterations in the environment are rarely sufficient to cure a disturbed child, except perhaps in early infancy, since the child's experiences soon become built into his inner world, whence they can be removed only by therapeutic measures which affect the structure of his personality (Freud, A. 1965a, pp. 48–53).

Marie Zaphiriou-Woods and Anat Gedulter-Trieman described a child whose developmental difficulties needed analysis because educational measures were insufficient to deal with her internal impasse. What at first sight looked liked developmental defects of constitutional or physical origin proved to be due to conflict and inhibition following trauma.

Maya, the child of Spanish immigrants, was a much-loved, healthy and happy baby who developed well in her first year. Both parents worked and they shared her care. Then her father had an accident and died after some weeks in hospital. During this time her mother divided her time between hospital and work, leaving Maya with unfamiliar carers. Mother and Maya then went to Spain to bury father. In this strange environment Maya was unsettled, and on the journey home became acutely ill and had to be hospitalised. Following this traumatic series of events she regressed in almost all areas of her development except toilet training.

She recovered spontaneously in many areas, and seemed to have re-established her relationship with her mother. At age 3 it seemed that attendance at the Centre's nursery school might be enough to help her overcome the remaining difficulties. The gradual separation from mother went smoothly and Maya could accept the teachers as substitute carers. But her socialisation and understanding were delayed. She was often clumsy, rough and aggressive to other children, and blank and uncomprehending when the teachers talked to her about such incidents. Her English was poor and her Spanish not much better. She became an 'outsider', disliked and excluded by the other children in spite of the teachers' attempts to mediate. Her own attempts to explain or to join in games were often misunderstood because of her speech which failed to improve. She seemed hungry for adult attention, but unable to use their help to verbalise feelings and wishes before acting on them. She was sometimes panic-stricken and dazed following minor accidents to herself or others. Her mother's attempts to keep father alive for Maya by showing her photographs and talking about him seemed only to prevent her from accepting his loss, until Zaphiriou-Woods helped mother to find ways of addressing father's death with Maya.

At home she was 'good', not aggressive. But Maya's clumsiness, and her problems with eyesight, speech and hearing caused mother to consult various specialists. Maya did need spectacles, and a learning disability was diagnosed by the speech therapist, but no hearing loss was found. The nursery school staff became increasingly convinced that emotional trauma rather than physical impairment lay behind her uneven development.

At age 4 she was taken into therapy where major conflicts over aggression soon emerged, revealing many fears of punishment for messiness and anger. Her mother was simultaneously helped to recognise the emotional elements in her 'defects' and to approach them differently.

In the countertransference the therapist (Gedulter-Trieman) was often made to experience Maya's helplessness, not knowing and not understanding. She sought out books with stories about danger and rescue. After the analyst repeatedly verbalised and linked the anger, fear and helplessness, Maya re-enacted her regression following the traumatic events, in a return to bottom-shuffling instead of walking as she left the session.

There followed much work on conflicts of loyalty between therapist and mother as analyst and child worked on Maya's ambivalence to her mother, and her fear of her own omnipotent thoughts. She could eventually verbalise her fear of losing mother as well as father.

The next focus was on her damaged body and mind, which she perceived as due to her own bad thoughts and feelings. A dramatic example of the interference of anxiety and conflict with learning was her continuing inability to count 1,2,3, though she could count 5,6,7,8. This improved after her therapist counted for her a family of 1,2,3 people.

Material about the experienced loss of mother around the time of father's illness and death was also enacted in losing and finding themes in the analysis. Eventually she understood that she and her analyst could keep each other in mind.

Her self-esteem improved and there were dramatic improvements in her peer relationships. She successfully made the transition to primary school where she made friends and was described by the teachers as kind and thoughtful, and keen to learn (Zaphiriou-Woods and Gedulter-Trieman 1998).

## Termination

In a paper on termination Anna Freud discussed some of the difficulties specific to child analysis. She distinguished negative transference, which can be handled in the analysis and which contributes useful material, from hostile reactions evoked by technical mistakes such as a too sudden interpretation of unconscious wishes which may arouse more anxiety than the child can tolerate. She noted that positive transference can be dangerous if it evokes in the child loyalty conflicts between analyst and parents, especially if the parents also become jealous of the analyst. Transferences of early demanding, need-satisfying types of relationship can make the child intolerant of the frustration inherent in the analytic situation. Adolescents frequently attempt to break the tie with the analyst at the same time as they are in rebellion against their internal ties to parents.

Parents who do not understand the child's underlying disturbance often wish to end analysis when the symptoms disappear or when the child ceases to present problems at home or in school. In cases of very disturbed autistic or borderline children, as analysis brings about improvement in internal functioning, it may disrupt the thin veneer of social adaptation which the parents have worked hard to produce, and they may be unable to tolerate this.

She also discussed the problem of how to determine when the child can safely be left to develop without the support of analysis, and whether the parents will be able to cope well enough with the child's future development. She did not agree with the view that analysis is a way of upbringing and should be continued throughout a child's development. She believed it should be used only preventively and therapeutically, and she emphasised the need to allow the child to reinstate his own defences which are to some extent suspended during the analytic work.

Viviane Green described her dilemma in ending therapy with a 5-year-old boy. Donald's mother died in an accident when he was 4, a traumatic loss which compounded his earlier experiences of her unreliability, and being shuttled between his parents who had separated in his first year. In nursery school he was appealing and intelligent, but aggressive to other children, and defiant and provocative to staff. He was overtly anxious and unhappy.

Therapy explored his confusion, grief and guilt over his mother's death. As a new object, Green recognised Donald's feelings, enabling him to be aware of them. In the transference they worked through his conflict over attachment, and his fear of rejection and abandonment especially for his anal aggression.

At a time when his conscious longing for a stepmother led to much rage and aggression towards his analyst for frustrating his wish that she and his father should marry, he began telling her and father how much he hated coming to therapy. In the treatment room Green had to set firm limits on his panicky rage and destructiveness while also interpreting his sense of helplessness. Outside therapy he was showing marked improvement as his difficulties were being contained and worked on. His father wondered how much longer Donald needed to attend, but was able to understand the importance of working towards a planned ending.

Donald became able to let his therapist know he would miss her during the next holiday break and, after it, returned without protest. He seemed to be managing his feelings much better, and to be feeling safer in the attachment to his therapist. Some defensive denigration of the analyst continued, together with a wish to stop attending. Since the overall balance seemed to be improving, the therapist agreed that he might be ready to stop, and they began to discuss a date for that, with Green stressing the need for a proper goodbye.

Perhaps feeling empowered by his therapist's acknowledgement of his wishes, Donald changed his mind, and they were able to discuss his more positive feelings. He told his father he wanted to continue, and father told the therapist that it might have been his, father's, wish to stop (there were many practical difficulties as well as emotional ones). Further discussion of death and loss followed in the therapy, and eventually Donald decided to reduce his sessions so as to have more time for other things after school. He seemed to be moving firmly into latency activities and interests, and Green felt he had sufficiently resolved his conflicts over trusting and relating to objects, and was making good enough developmental progress to manage without therapy, but with the possibility of a later return should he need it. It was now possible to reach an ending agreed between Donald, father and therapist (Green 1998).

Donald's case is an example of the difficulty which therapists experience in deciding whether they need to go on protecting and improving a vulnerable child's development, or whether the child is sufficiently restored to the path of normal development to need only his own ego strengths supported by the parent in order to cope with future difficulties.

Anna Freud thought that one reason for continuing analyses too long might be that analysts get caught up in attempts to reverse personality traits which are probably irreversible. She was referring to the effects of early, unfavourable environmental influences, comparable to physical deficiency illnesses. She doubted whether such deficiencies could be solved in a new, more age-adequate way as conflicts can, though they might be mitigated by later, more favourable influences (Freud, A. 1971a).

## Therapeutic factors in different forms of psychopathology

In her later work Anna Freud began to spell out what psycho-analysis can do for developmental disturbances, even though this is not the same as in the classical treatment of classical neuroses. Though she moved to acknowledge the importance of the first year of life in the causation of psychopathology, it was the mother–child interaction rather than the fantasy life of the infant on which she focused. And she thought it important to distinguish between the primary contribution of early environmental influences to personality development or distortion, and the secondary contribution they made to psychopathology.

As she came to place increasing emphasis on the importance of dissecting psychopathology according to the developmental lines which were affected, she also began to spell out to some extent what kind of help was needed for each form of developmental delay and distortion. Initially she distinguished this developmental help from analysis. In an earlier paper (Edgcumbe 1995) I have commented on the creative tension engendered not only in Anna Freud's own work, but in the clinical and therapeutic work of all the child analysts in the Hampstead Clinic. This tension arose, I think, from the conflict between a desire to remain loyal to Sigmund Freud's ideas, and the need to move beyond them in learning more about childhood development and psychopathology and the corresponding techniques needed for treating children.

Anna Freud seems to have resolved this conflict for herself when she described the need for child analysis to 'go it alone', instead of being a sub-speciality of adult analysis, and went on to view child analysis as a related but separate discipline whose special contribution was the developmental point of view (see Chapter 6, p. 132).

She continued to make a sharp distinction between analysis, the treatment of choice for primarily neurotic, conflict-based disturbances, and developmental help required for the developmental delays and distortions. Her insistence on this distinction was based on the fact that interpretation of conflict and resistance within the transference may not be among the techniques used in developmental help. In many papers, for example, in her study guide to Freud's writings, she wrote that he considered that every therapy based on interpretation of resistance and transference deserves to be called psychoanalysis (Freud, A. 1978b).

She had, however, moved away from her original position that educational work was not part of the child analyst's remit, to acknowledge that it takes analytic understanding and skills to select the right approach to the child's developmental disorder. Perhaps it was the fact that this work was still referred to as 'help' which created a sense that we were not doing 'proper analysis' with such children. There was at one time even doubt whether five-times weekly sessions consisting of developmental help could count as a training case for a student. However, what almost invariably happened with these children was that after a time, interpretable conflicts, transference and resistance began to emerge, and the developmental help would gradually transform into something closer to classical child analysis, at which point the relieved student could get it accepted as a training case.

In retrospect, it is not easy to know to what extent this attitude represented Anna Freud's own position or that of the analysts on the training committee; nor whether it was linked simply to a concern about the students not having the proper opportunity to learn the technique of interpretation, or to some deeper mistrust of techniques which might seem educational rather than analytic.

Ava Penman records a poignant moment at the beginning of the discussions she chaired, when Anna Freud, responding to Penman's wish for discussion of the details of developmental help, and viewing a room packed with qualified analysts and trainees, said:

> these are . . . questions which I have turned over in my mind for a number of years; but I could never find anybody in the Clinic who was really interested in them, and therefore I am quite surprised at the amount of interest there is shown today.
> (Penman 1995)

We may all join with Penman in wondering where the failure of communication occurred, since most of us working at the Clinic had struggled with borderline, autistic and other atypical children, and were aware of Anna Freud's interest and encouragement to go on exploring, even when she expressed doubts about the likelihood of success. Were we (and was it only some or all of us?) really being as unreceptive as Anna Freud experienced us? Or was it a projection of her own doubts on to us? Or was she reacting to analysts outside the Clinic? I do recall her saying with some concern after a presentation at an international meeting that she thought people had misunderstood what she meant by the concept of developmental lines, and seemed to think she might be abandoning metapsychology. We have been rather slow in publishing outside the Clinic papers on clinical work using developmental help, though these cases were certainly being discussed in Clinic meetings. Perhaps this reflects a hesitation on all our parts to formulate clinical theory in a way that gave a legitimate place to developmental therapy, rescuing it from relegation to being a mere making good of things which parents had failed to do for the child. Perhaps we had not kept pace with Anna Freud's shift to recognising that it takes analytic skills to belatedly make good things not done by parents at the appropriate time.

About a decade after Anna Freud's death a research study by Jill Miller elicited the repertoire of concepts that child analysts of the Anna Freud Centre were using to think about psychoanalytic methods and processes, and also compared what therapists were actually doing with their theoretical formulations about technique. In spite of a good deal of individual variation a consensus emerged on two main dimensions: the concepts and techniques defining so-called classical analysis, and those defining developmental help. What also emerged was that in addition to the recognised 'ego-supportive' and 'ego-auxiliary' techniques of developmental help, analysts were also compensating for patients' defects by adapting their techniques to the patients' capacities in many unlabelled and often unrecognised ways (Miller 1993).

In the psychoanalytic world at large, developmental therapy has slowly been achieving respectability. Greenspan's recent book, for example, sets out a clear framework for identifying the developmental processes missing or stunted in a patient's functioning, and matching appropriate techniques for mobilising these processes (Greenspan 1997). In the Anna Freud Centre Miller's study was part of a widening range of research, as a result of which developmental help has been firmly promoted to the status of developmental therapy in papers by Fonagy and co-workers (1993; Fonagy and Target 1996a) and in Anne Hurry's recent book. Hurry comments that child therapists have always intuitively done the work which children needed to help them to be able to play, name feelings and control instead of enacting wishes and impulses, to relate to others and to understand that other people think and feel. But this work has been undervalued and unrecorded, partly because of the lack of a theoretical framework for it (Hurry 1998, p. 37).

Anna Freud had begun to create such a framework in 1965, when she ended *Normality and Pathology* with a brilliant summary of the different forms of psychopathology and the therapeutic factors which influence each (Freud, A. 1965a, pp. 213–235). She stressed that in child analysis the work alternates between therapy and fact finding, in varying proportions and at different times. Cases range from those where the therapist feels analysis would not have been necessary had preventive work been done earlier to help parents and others give the child the right opportunities for development and avoid harmful influences, to those dominated by internalised conflicts where analysis is clearly the treatment of choice. But in between are many where the genetic, dynamic and libido-economic factors have to be clarified before the correct treatment can be identified (ibid., pp. 213–214).

Since the early days when psychoanalysis was considered best suited to the neuroses, the scope of adult analysis has widened to include many other forms of disturbance, such as the psychoses, borderline states, perversions, addictions and delinquencies. In cases where intrapsychic conflict is the main pathogenic agent, the main therapeutic effect of psychoanalysis comes from the changes in strength of id, ego and superego, increase in their tolerance for each other's aims and increased harmony between them. In child analysis this also holds true for children whose development has reached the point where id, ego and superego are sufficiently differentiated to have different aims and therefore come into conflict. In normal development such conflicts are dealt with by the child's own ego, supported by the parents' guidance. Where the parents are unable to do this, and the ego gets overwhelmed, child analysis can help since verbalisation, clarification and interpretation help to reduce anxieties as they arise, prevent defences from becoming too crippling, and open up outlets for drive activity. This helps the child maintain equilibrium and accounts for the claim that all children can benefit from analysis. But here the child analyst is simply performing a task that belongs to the child's own ego and to the parents (ibid., pp. 215–218).

In cases where the internal balance is seriously upset by uneven progression between drives and ego/superego, it can be more difficult to predict whether the balance will right itself in the course of development, or whether analysis is needed to prevent a permanent imbalance which will result in pathological conflict solutions (ibid., pp. 218–219).

The infantile neurosis deriving from the conflicts of the oedipus complex is the form of child psychopathology nearest to the adult form of neurosis; both follow the classical sequence: danger – anxiety – permanent regression to fixation point – rejection of reactivated pre-genital impulse – defence – compromise formation; and it offers the analyst a role nearest to that with adults: working with the patient's ego to change maladaptive conflict solutions. Such neurotic children come nearest to a willingness to undertake analysis because they are aware of suffering from their symptoms in the sense of being prevented by phobias or compulsions from getting on with ordinary things they would like to do, or of feeling bad compared with their friends. But children have not yet developed the self-observing capacity which is important in maintaining the ability to overcome resistances and to withstand periods of negative transference. The natural inquisitiveness of the child is directed to the outer world rather than the inner world. It is only in adolescence that the natural shift to introspection occurs. It is the child's tendency to explore outer rather than inner factors which promotes the use of externalisation, i.e. seeing the problems in external terms, to be solved by external solutions. Children commonly deal with their own guilt by provoking punishment from parents or teachers; or they displace anxieties into phobias, seeking to avoid an external situation rather than resolving an internal conflict. They may often want the therapist to help bring about such solutions: for example, removing the child from a school where he is bullied, rather than analysing his own passive–masochistic inclinations; organising a change of class to avoid a dreaded teacher, rather than understanding the child's own guilt; helping him get away from the 'bad' influence of a companion, rather than exploring the projection of his own impulses. This form of lack of insight is not the same as a resistance; it is a normal feature of childhood (ibid., pp. 219–224).

As mentioned earlier, in later papers Kennedy (1979) and Anna Freud (1979a) agreed that child analysis can induce a precocious capacity for self-observation in child patients which assists the therapeutic alliance.

When the child resolves conflicts by lowering his ego/superego standards, as in some forms of atypical, dissocial or apparently retarded development, he ceases to suffer anxiety or guilt, and feels content with his state. Analytic intervention then has first to create the conditions for conflict to re-arise in order to alert the child to his inner disharmonies again, and prompt a wish for change. This was the purpose of Anna Freud's introductory phase, and Aichhorn's fostering in his delinquent patients an identification with himself and his value system in order to create conflict which can then be clarified, verbalised and interpreted (Freud, A. 1965a, pp. 224–227).

The nature of the therapeutic process changes in cases where arrests, defects and deficiencies of development are more important than the conflict-based aspects of the disturbance, 'even though child analysis is still applicable and effects improvements' (ibid., p. 227).

In addition to interpretation, widening of consciousness, verbalisation and clarification, which form the mainstay of the psychoanalytic process, there are other elements which may not be intended by the analyst but which are inevitable. Suggestion operates because of the analyst's temporary position of emotional importance to the patient, which gives rise to the educational side-effects of analysis. The patient may misuse the transference for a corrective emotional experience, and this tendency becomes stronger in a child who uses the analyst as a new object (ibid., pp. 227–228). In the Index discussions Anna Freud distinguished the *patient's* use of experiences within the transference and relationship to the analyst as a new object for correcting earlier experience, from the original idea of 'corrective experience'. The latter was a deliberate choice by the analyst to provide a new experience rather than interpreting past experience (Sandler *et al.* 1980, p. 113). The child also derives reassurance from his intimacy with a trusted adult which the therapist sooner or later becomes. Anna Freud (aligning herself with Sigmund Freud, Ferenczi and Eissler) points out that even when the analyst tries to guard against these non-analytic elements, it is the child who selects which therapeutic elements he needs from all the possibilities contained within child analysis.

Suggestion, reassurance, corrective experience and management play little part in the analysis of a basically neurotic child. If the child himself seeks them it is usually an expression of resistance. But they have little therapeutic effect, since they do not change the balance of internal forces.

But non-neurotic cases may need more of the non-interpretive elements. A borderline child, for example, may respond badly to interpretation of fantasy content, using it not to alter the balance between ego and drive functioning, and to gain control over his fantasy world, but to weave it into his fantasy, thereby increasing his anxiety. Such a child gains more relief from verbalisation and clarification of internal and external dangers, and of the frightening affects which his ego is not strong enough to integrate and bring under secondary process dominance.

Children with libido defects relate to the analyst on immature levels of object relationship at which they are arrested, for example, they may seek only need-satisfaction and lack object constancy. Transference interpretation only helps such children if their arrest is based initially on conflict or traumatic events, but not where it is due to severe early deprivation in object relationships. In such cases the child may respond to the close relationship with the analyst which favours the development of a libidinal attachment because of the frequency of meetings, and the analyst's undivided attention. This may indeed provide a corrective emotional experience which allows the child to move to higher levels of libidinal object relationship.

Intellectually retarded children are often beset by archaic fears, unable to master internal or external dangers because of their ego immaturity, and caught in a vicious circle because their anxiety further impedes ego growth. Here the reassuring role of the analyst is important in helping the child to master each level of anxiety and move on to gradually higher levels.

Even in cases of organic damage, if the defect lies mainly in the drives, analysis can help by opening up possibilities for fantasy or new outlets for drive activity, to counterbalance the relatively normal ego pressures which are too strong for the relatively weak drives to withstand. Or if it is ego functioning which is damaged so that drive control is weak, the analyst's role as auxiliary ego can help to strengthen the child's own ego (Freud, A. 1965a, pp. 227–232).

Anna Freud remarked on the role parents themselves can play in remedying or increasing imbalances in a child's development. The mother's involvement serves to 'libidinise' lines in which she takes a special interest. This involvement can be used to help the child catch up on lines in which he lags behind. But it is a common mistake to promote the areas in which he is already ahead, for example, by talking a lot to a verbal child, giving the bodily active child yet more opportunities for action, or giving the highly intelligent child yet more food for intelligence (ibid., pp. 232–233).

Audrey Gavshon's patient, 'Martin' (see above, p. 174) was a case in which the analyst had to do much of the work normally done by parents. Martin's parents were loving and well intentioned towards him. But they were highly intelligent people who expected all their children to develop intellectual interests and capabilities similar to their own, and who especially valued verbal ability and thinking capacity. Neither had experienced close relationships in their childhoods, but they worked hard to achieve a warm marital relationship. However, they had little idea how to help children cope with feelings or make sense of experiences. Thus they were not well suited to providing the extra-sensitive support their developmentally delayed child needed. They tended to reinforce his 'clever' achievements which he used defensively, such as learning lists of French words, endless calculations of mileage to and from home, the Clinic and various other places, complicated working out of the timing of events, accumulating knowledge about the sizes of planets, the time it would take to get to them and so on.

Martin was acutely sensitive to their disappointment in him, and especially distressed by his failure to be articulate and clever. Gavshon described many things which most children acquire naturally that Martin needed to be taught in his therapy, ranging from how to pronounce difficult sounds, to understanding cause and effect, working out how to explain the sequence of his thoughts to others, or figuring out what people were thinking of him. This work was essential alongside the more interpretive aspects of the analysis (Gavshon 1987).

Anna Freud noted that some therapists have advocated focused therapy which matches specific types of intervention to specific types of disturbance (Alpert 1959; Mahler and Gosliner 1955). But in Anna Freud's view, while such specialisation might seem rational and economical, there are objections: few child patients present a pure clinical picture; most are mixed and therefore require a range of therapeutic procedures such as are available in child analysis. Our diagnostic skills are not yet good enough to predict with certainty exactly what is wrong with the child and what form of therapy is needed. Child analysis allows the fact finding to continue and leaves open the therapeutic possibilities for the child to select from (Freud, A. 1965a, pp. 232–235).

She suggested that it takes more than the usual analytic courage to work with children whose essential development is incomplete, but she believed that only such attempts held the promise of filling gaps in our understanding of developmental problems (Freud, A. 1974b [1954]).

In a number of papers Anna Freud had taken the common view that in psychoanalysis the method of enquiry is identical to the method of treatment, but in a 1976 symposium on psychoanalytic practice and experience she acknowledged that the method of enquiry is no longer identical to the method of therapy. Our understanding now reaches further, to the harm inflicted on the ego by the environment. Reconstruction of this damage does not cure it. Analysts, she believed, now had to accept this humiliating fact. She wrote that we were still struggling to convert the new understanding into effective therapy (Freud, A. 1976a).

Elsewhere she wrote that the analytic method is essential for clarifying the clinical picture and revealing causation, but that by itself the method cannot undo early damage. She believed that the child analyst's next task was to devise methods for this. In the meantime they can help the child patient to cope with the consequences of developmental defects. This, she thought, may be a step towards a more basic therapy (Freud, A. 1978a). The steps we are taking are clear from the papers by clinicians discussed in this chapter and in Anna Hurry's book (Hurry 1998).

## Chapter 8

# Conclusions

## The legacy

### Can the questions be answered?

Rather than trying to summarise Anna Freud's contributions to psychoanalytic theory and practice, and to the welfare of children, I return to the questions posed in Chapter 1.

#### Why did she not accept developmental help as a legitimate psychoanalytic technique?

The answer to this seems to be that she was moving towards doing so, once she could see how the historical development of psychoanalysis had led to its widening its scope to explore and then attempt to treat the non-neurotic disturbances, as she accepted the necessity to find analytic rather than educational ways of helping the developmental deficiency illnesses. But these ideas appeared in her late papers, while what was still being taught were in her earlier ones. Her ideas were put forward less as findings and definite techniques, more as the future task of child analysis to work out. She was always cautious about testing out new ideas with clinical research before proclaiming them as facts. She was no longer treating children herself by the time she wrote these papers, and relied on the reports and discussions of Clinic cases for her material. Those of us who discussed cases with her were aware both of her openness to helping us explore new problems, as well as her caution in making sure we had not encountered the problem simply because of our own technical mistakes. Wallerstein (1984) aptly recognised both the 'staunch conservative and radical innovator' in her. He points out the great technical innovation she introduced in 1936 in *The Ego and the Mechanisms of Defence*, which shifted the balance of interpretation, establishing analysis of the ego as of equal importance to analysis of the id. Now an established part of 'classical' technique, at that time it was revolutionary. When forced to choose, however, she perhaps tended to see her role, or her duty, as to hold the conservative line in a situation in which new ideas were pouring out in a sometimes undisciplined way. She felt these ideas required more research before they should be accepted. Just as her own psychoanalytic theories of personality development and psychic functioning developed slowly, on the basis of experience and examination of observational and clinical data, so did her theory of technique gradually mature in parallel.

## Why is she still thought of as a drive theorist only, in spite of her excellent object relations theory?

Insofar as she did not abandon drive theory for object relations theory, she perhaps cannot be considered an object relations theorist. Greenberg and Mitchell (1983) maintain that drive and object relations theories are incompatible theories of motivation. But they do cite Joseph Sandler as one of the people who attempted to bridge the two by attributing motivation to object relations as well as drives. They place Anna Freud among those who use the strategy of accommodation: finding a place for object relations within the drive/structural theory. Certainly this is where Anna Freud would put herself, because she viewed early need-satisfaction experiences as essential for the development of object relationships. This is the concept of the anaclitic relationship: love for the object is built on early satisfaction of self-preservative needs. But insofar as she worked out a theory of object relations within the drive-structural theory she certainly deserves credit for a very detailed developmental theory of object relations. One of her developmental lines conveys a very clear view of the development of relationships, external and internal, and she showed how many other lines depend heavily on the mother–child relationship for their optimal progression. Indeed, she demonstrated again and again how important is the context of a stable, loving relationship for the optimal development of both sexuality and aggression. So in that sense she saw drives as being organised and expressed within the context of an object relationship.

The controversial discussions drove her into a position in which both politically and theoretically she avoided alignment with Melanie Klein, who became thought of as the developer of object relations theory. Evidentially her willingness to consider and assess Klein's clinical ideas continued. Her writings demonstrate that she was, perhaps, more willing than many of her followers to separate the theory from the politics and continue trying out the theory against the clinical evidence. The Kleinians, however, seemed at that time unwilling to consider Anna Freud's ideas at all. Over the years a very slow *rapprochement* has taken place. But it is a great pity that the projected meetings between Anna Freud and Melanie Klein never took place, as this might have permitted a more fruitful argument and mutual recognition.

The Kleinians were, in any case, not the only group in Britain working out object relations theories at that time. The Independents were also doing so, notably Fairbairn, Winnicott and Balint. Fairbairn explicitly substituted object relations for drives as motivators of behaviour, and Anna Freud would not agree on that. But she found more congenial the ideas of Balint and Winnicott about the effects of experiences in early relationships. Anna Freud certainly did not agree with a good deal of Kleinian theory, especially those formulations which appeared to be destroying Freudian drive theory. She also avoided formulations which might align her with Bowlby, though with less determination. She continued to cite Bowlby's findings as similar to her own, and to argue only over the way to interpret them. She did not like his use of ethological theory if it was to replace psychoanalytic theory, but their mutual interest in the effects of early separation of child and mother remained strong, as evidenced in Anna Freud's reviews of the Robertsons' films (Freud, A. 1953c, 1969d). The personal link with the Robertsons endured, since James continued to teach in the Hampstead Clinic, and Joyce was on the staff in the Well Baby Clinic. In 1975 Anna Freud and Dorothy Burlingham were founder members of the Robertson Centre, whose aim is to promote understanding of the emotional needs of young children.

What emerges from Anna Freud's writings over the years is that she came to place more and more importance on the early years, eventually abandoning even her initial idea that the first six months have to be viewed largely as a period in which biological functioning predominates and does no more than lay the groundwork for later psychological growth. She conceded that important psychological experiences happen from birth. The form of object relations she favoured was, however, very different from the Kleinian emphasis on the child's fantasy world. Anna Freud aligned herself more with those who emphasised the infant–mother interaction, and became increasingly interested in tracing the effects of early experiences within this relationship on personality development. In some of her late writings she seems to put these effects on a par with the effects of drive development, as she writes that they contribute different things to the development and potential psychopathology of the individual.

### Why is she not better known?

She herself offers some explanations. Discussing changes in public attitudes to psychoanalysis (1969c, p. 130) she commented that though psychoanalytic ideas were initially met with indignation and incredulity, today it is not regarded as mystic, eccentric, revolutionary or unduly progressive to believe in the importance of the unconscious mind, sex and aggression, or dreams. In an Introduction to a book on Aichhorn she made a comment which might also be applied to herself: that people no longer remember who led the way in the methods they now use (1976b, pp. 344–345). In a comment she made in 1981 about the fate of her own work after half a century, she said: 'Assuming its message to have been successful at all, it becomes superfluous, obsolete, and loses its readership. In order simply to survive, it needs to be changed, updated' (Freud, A. 1983, p. 107). She did update her work constantly. But as Peter Neubauer put it:

> In the changing emphasis on issues and topics, those who stay close to the central body of analytic theory and clinical practice may lose visibility. Those who set themselves apart or who add knowledge which cannot easily be integrated into the main body of psychoanalysis usually are conspicuous.
>
> (Neubauer 1984, p. 15)

It is certainly true that her 1936 book *The Ego and the Mechanisms of Defence*, though revolutionary at the time, eventually became so influential as to be absorbed into the mainstream of psychoanalytic theory and clinical technique with both adults and children. Perhaps with this absorption she lost visibility.

It may also be relevant that most of her later published work was about child analysis and child development. In the British Psychoanalytic Society the majority of analysts prefer to restrict themselves to work with adults. Only a relatively small minority also train in child analysis, in spite of the encouragement of Anna Freud, Melanie Klein and Winnicott and their associates and successors. This is also true of other associations for pychoanalytic psychotherapy with the exception of the Association of Child Psychotherapists. Inevitably, then, there is more interest in the work of those who write about problems of working with adults. In fact Anna Freud continued to work with adult patients until almost the end of her life. She wrote relatively little herself about work with adults, but much of her thinking was absorbed into the work of Hampstead Clinic Groups studying problems of adult patients, and can be discerned in publications by her colleagues. Her developmental lines and thinking about developmental disharmony were particularly pertinent to understanding details in the clinical picture of psychotic and borderline patients (see e.g. Freeman 1983; Yorke 1983).

Her preference for working in discussion groups with colleagues rather than alone meant that some of her ideas were disseminated through the writings of others. They acknowledged her authorship of ideas, but perhaps their readers would not have registered this as fully as if she had written the books or papers herself. She was more concerned to get the ideas right than to publicise her own role in creating them.

Anna Freud was a rather private person, not readily making herself conspicuous by crusading for her own ideas. She preferred to allow the evidence she presented to speak for itself. Some of her talks and seminars were given in Britain, but these were mainly in applied fields. Her major papers and seminars were given at various psychoanalytic centres in America. Thus people in Britain may not be aware of her share in shaping not only the theory and practice of child analysis, but also its applications to many other services for children. A major institution for the analytic treatment of adolescents and research into adolescent disturbances, the Brent Consultation Centre, was founded in London by Moses Laufer, an analyst in the British Society who trained as a child and adolescent analyst at the Hampstead Clinic. This Centre not only received Anna Freud's support, but many Hampstead trained analysts were also attracted to work there, and the Centre produced a flow of research into adolescent developmental problems (e.g. Laufer and Laufer 1984, 1989). Anna Freud's theories and methods are alive and well in many child mental health clinics where Hampstead graduates work in Britain and in the United States.

This brings in another point: that many of the students at the Hampstead Clinic came from the US and returned there after training. Many British students also emigrated to the US at a time when the climate there was more favourable to psychoanalysis than in Britain. They were welcomed by the existing analysts, many of whom were colleagues of the Freuds who had fled from Europe as the Nazis rose to power. The list Anna Freud gave, in a history of child analysis (1966c), of clinics similar to Hampstead is heavily biased towards the US; and many of those she lists as colleagues with whom she had worked before the Second World War emigrated to the US. Several of them were among the major supporters in fund-raising for the Hampstead Clinic in the US (Helen Ross, Peter Neubauer, Kurt Eissler, Albert Solnit and others). It was US foundations which provided most of the funding. This flow of colleagues and students to the United States meant that her ideas were more widely disseminated there than in the UK.

A final point is that her later writings are not easily understood by those without a good basic knowledge of psychoanalytic theory and clinical experience. Whereas her earlier writings contain many case examples to demonstrate clinically what she means in her theoretical statements, her later ones contain few examples. For these one has to turn to the writings of her colleagues and students, but the work of putting them together falls on the reader. In her applied papers she does write simply and with examples. But many of these papers were not published at the time she wrote them, or appeared in journals not readily available to the average British reader looking for work on psychotherapy. She did try to make her theorising clear and simple, and she is certainly much more easily readable than some theoretical writers. She herself bemoaned the fact that clinical practice and theory had become split, so that many people no longer saw the relevance of metapsychology for their clinical work, and clinicians and theoreticians worked separately.

Those who are unaware of the origins of developmental lines may misinterpret them as rigid sequences on which a child is to be 'judged' and 'placed'. This is similar to the mistake many people make with the profile, i.e. trying to use it as a questionnaire they can fill in. Both are actually intended to be ways of helping the child analyst to use theory to think about the intricacies of development in order to be as specific as possible about what underlies a child's symptoms.

In Anna Freud's innovative thinking the lines were a natural development out of her interest in ego functioning, and her wish to explore the importance of interpretation of defence as well as wishes and impulses. Via exploring the role of the ego in shaping drive expressions, and the role of the object in shaping ego functioning, she moved into a finer dissection of the id–ego–object interactions. She was breaking down the macrostructures into microstructures. But they are not rigid structures, they are ever changing and developing. Not only are there interactions within each line, but the lines have repercussions on each other. This is a complex way of thinking about development and psychological functioning. Perhaps not everyone is willing to master the complexity.

## The legacy

Her legacy can be seen on many levels. It is in the institution which she founded, the Hampstead Clinic, as well as in similar institutions influenced by her ideas. After her death in 1982 the Clinic was renamed the Anna Freud Centre in her honour. Though undergoing changes, the Centre still carries out the three functions she envisaged for it: training, treatment and research.

### Training

The training now has degree status, through its link with University College, London. The first (pre-clinical) year has for several years been accredited as an M.Sc. in psychoanalytic developmental psychology. More recently the following years of clinical training have been accredited with Psy.D. status, and the first group of students are currently pursuing their doctorates. This development was for many years advocated and pursued by Joseph Sandler, who held the first Chair of Psychoanalysis in the Psychology Department of UC; and it was finally brought to fruition by Peter Fonagy, Sandler's successor.

The increasing difficulty in finding charitable funding for training, together with the provision of training posts in the NHS, have meant that more students now work in the NHS rather than full time in the Centre. This has the disadvantage of limiting their time available for clinical study groups, as well as reducing the number of cases in treatment at the Centre. But it has the advantage of giving the students wider experiences of the many facets of work they nowadays need to do in educational, social and legal services. In addition, they bring new ideas into the Centre.

The content of the training has changed somewhat to accommodate the different research requirements of the degrees, as well as the new findings and theories at the interface between psychoanalysis and other disciplines, and the new demands on therapists in the health, educational and social services, but it remains solidly psychoanalytic.

### *Treatment*

The patient population in the Centre has changed over the years. Among the children in intensive treatment there is now a greater emphasis on the more severe disturbances with fewer primarily neurotic children. This change is based partly on sound clinical assessment of the child's treatment needs, especially on our greater capacity for differential diagnosis of developmental delays and deficits. But it also reflects parental difficulties in supporting the burden of bringing a child for intensive therapy.

In other child and family clinics there is a greater availability of other, briefer forms of therapy, including family therapy and non-intensive forms of individual psychoanalytic therapy. In most clinics these are the only forms of therapy on offer because of the restrictions on funding. Anna Freud would doubtless be greatly distressed that clinics still fit children into whatever treatment they have available or can afford rather than being able to offer what the child most needs. Family therapy is often appropriate for families of young children whose difficulties are based mainly in the child–parent interaction. Developments in therapeutic skills also permit therapists to achieve results with co-operative neurotic children or those with less severe developmental delays relatively easily in non-intensive individual therapy. But the more seriously disturbed children and families still require more intensive work on their internal worlds as well as external interactions in relationships. At the Anna Freud Centre it is now often the children whose disturbance is not primarily neurotic but those in the more severe borderline and atyptical categories who are deemed most in need of intensive treatment. The children with conflict-based pathology originating in later developmental levels, though still agreed to be the children who would respond most quickly and successfully to analysis, are also deemed able to respond well to less intensive psychoanalytic therapy. Parents, especially single parents struggling to bring up several children, often cannot cope with daily treatment, some for practical reasons, others for emotional ones.

The work which used to be done informally by the social worker or therapist who initially interviewed a parent – to get a first idea of the problem, to determine whether a full diagnostic assessment is appropriate and whether the parent could support assessment and therapy if recommended – has now been formalised into a Family Support Programme, which processes most referrals. As the name implies, a good deal of initial clarificatory and supportive work is done with parents and children in whatever combinations seem appropriate, as well as undertaking whatever work is needed with the parents to support individual treatment for the child if that is recommended. The Well Baby Clinic has been replaced by the Parent–Infant Project, specifically aimed at addressing the early emotional difficulties in the parent–infant relationship. The toddler groups and nursery school are finding that their numbers contain an increasing proportion of disturbed families and children. The nursery school, at the time of writing, is considering whether to formalise its increasingly therapeutic role. These changes partly reflect the improvements in statutory provision of infant health care, day care and nursery schools, partly the difficulty in obtaining charitable funding for services for normal children when these are available in the statutory sector.

### Research

In research over the last decade or more there has been a gradual reduction in the number of clinical study groups, with more academic style controlled studies. This is due partly to limitations on the clinical staff's time, but also to the changing demands for 'proof' in research. The accumulation of clinical experience, comparison of cases and exchange of ideas and findings among colleagues has for many years provided a solid base from which to explore each new difficulty and problem. But fund-raising nowadays increasingly requires controlled studies producing results in a limited amount of time.

The massive amount of data recorded in the Clinic's case files continues to be the subject of research. Most recently a retrospective study has been able to comment on the outcome of various intensities of treatment in different types of disorder. (Fonagy and

Target 1996b; Target and Kennedy 1991). The sheer volume of cases means that even in the absence of controlled conditions, certain comparisons between groups can be made and clinical conclusions drawn. The advent of computers has meant that the vast and complex amount of data generated by every analytic case becomes more manageable. Peter Fonagy and Mary Target initially examined 763 case files, using the Hampstead Child Adaptation Measure to measure clinically significant overall adaptation before and after treatment. Among their many findings were the following: the greatest improvement occurred in younger children (under 6) regardless of severity of disturbance. Younger children did better in intensive (four to five times per week) therapy, but adolescents did better in non-intensive (one to three times per week) therapy. Mental illness in the mother was associated with poorer outcome in children under 6, but with better outcome in latency children. Children with emotional disorders were more likely to improve than those with disruptive behaviour disorders; but children with disruptive behaviour disorders who also experienced high anxiety did well. There was a high drop-out rate among the disruptive behaviour disorders, but those who could be kept in therapy for three years or more did improve. In general, for the more severe disorders extent of improvement was associated with length of treatment.

Fonagy and Target suggest that these and other findings reflect the correlation between severity of disruption of developmental processes and the intensity and length of work required to bring about improvements. They specify some of the types of developmental help needed to cope with defects in ego functioning and in self and object representations (Fonagy and Target 1996b). Their examples of the effectiveness of this kind of approach versus the more classical interpretation of conflicts raise the historical point that during the period covered by these case reports (late 1950s to about 1990), changes in technique will have reflected the shift from focusing primarily on interpretation of phallic-Oedipal issues, to also exploring early difficulties in in the mother–child relationship and in ego development. It would be interesting to have a time dimension built into the analysis of the data.

Following on this research, a prospective study led by Karen Ensink is now in its pilot phase. This will use latency children with severe behaviour disorders from a number of clinics whose usual therapeutic resources are limited. The children will be randomly assigned to four forms of treatment. The study will compare the results of intensive psychoanalytic therapy, non-intensive psycho-analytic therapy, behaviour therapy and 'the usual treatment', i.e. whatever is normally on offer at the clinic concerned. In most cases this will be a minimal amount of parent guidance or family therapy (unpublished report).

A follow-up study on past clinic patients has also begun, led by Mary Target. Results so far indicate that children whose outcome was rated positive in the retrospective outcome study are showing good adult outcome as compared to siblings who were not treated. Those who showed no improvement in the retrospective study continue to be as impaired as those referred but not treated (unpublished report).

There have been many other research projects since Anna Freud died, of which there is space to mention only a few of the recent and present ones.

Moran and Fonagy used the single case study method to track the effect of psychoanalytic treatment in improving control of diabetes in young adolescents whose previously poor control had been life-threatening (Moran and Fonagy 1987).

One study which combines the old form of clinical discussion group with statistical evaluation of results is the young adult study group, whose work began in 1990 and is now drawing to a close. This group is also close to Anna Freud's developmental views, since one of its aims is to study the particular difficulties of young adults just emerging or failing to emerge from adolescence. It also compares frequency of treatment and techniques. Each analyst treated a five-times-a-week patient and a once-a-week patient.

Some clinical papers have already emerged from the weekly discussions of patients' progress. At a one-day conference in 1992 to commemorate the tenth anniversary of Anna Freud's death, several papers were given. Peter Fonagy and Maria Tallandini-Shallice dis-cussed problems of psychoanalytic research (Fonagy and Tallindini-Shallice 1993); Duncan McLean gave a sample profile modified for young adults (McLean 1993); Julia Fabricius compared manifes-tations and precipitants of developmental breakdown in twelve patients (Fabricius 1993); Joan Schachter gave a clinical paper on one young man's search for identity (Schachter 1993); and Brian Martindale gave an account of a young woman's difficulty in separating from her mother (Martindale 1993). Further case studies were included in Rosini Perelberg's book on the psychoanalytic treatment of patients who have committed serious acts of violence against themselves or others (Perelberg 1999).

But in addition to the psychoanalytic diagnostic assessments and profiles, and written treatment reports, analysts also filled in lengthy weekly questionnaires, and the patients endured formal psychiatric interviews at the beginning of treatment and at approximately eighteen-month intervals thereafter. All these computerised data are in the process of being analysed.

A current study group led by Duncan McLean, consultant psychiatrist, is working on further modifications of the profile. Among other things they are reformulating the role of object relations in the child's psychopathology.

An ongoing study of attachment uses controlled situations and interviews to study intergenerational patterns of relating. This study does not use analytic material, but it does use analytic ideas in the experimental exploration of the influence of parental expectations and early parent–child relationships on the child's later development. The studies have so far found that the security of the infant's attachment can be predicted from qualitative aspects of parental accounts of their own childhoods, and the child can form different types of attachment to each parent (Fonagy *et al.* 1993).

A study of adoption also links up with Anna Freud's interest in problems of separation and remaking or replacing relationships. This study is run, in conjunction with the Thomas Coram Foundation and Great Ormond Street Hospital, by Miriam Steele and Jill Hodges. It uses Adult Attachment interviews and story stem techniques to predict outcome of adoptive placements of maltreated childen (Steele *et al.* 1999a, 1999b).

It was preceded by a study of internal representations of parents and self in abused children, run by Jill Hodges and Miriam Steele. This used story stems to provide a systematic and sensitive assessment of the child's feelings and expectations where there were placement decisions to be made (Hodges, forthcoming).

That the most enduring legacy from Anna Freud is her psychoanalytic thinking about development seems evident from the present research at the Anna Freud Centre, as well as from publications by present and former students and co-workers in other countries. Many of the commemorative papers written after Anna Freud's death refer to this (e.g. Abrams 1996; Colonna 1996; Elliot-Neely 1996; Flashman 1996; Mayes and Cohen 1996; Miller 1996; Neubauer 1984, 1996; Sandler 1996; Yorke 1996). Phyllis and

Robert Tyson have written an integrated account of psychoanalytic theories of development (Tyson and Tyson 1990). Others have also focused on Anna Freud's applications of psychoanalysis to other disciplines (Goldstein 1984; Solnit and Newman 1984) or have themselves taken the application of psychoanalytic ideas into new fields, such as policing (Marans 1996).

Anna Freud's elaboration of the important areas involved in development was a major contribution to understanding the effects of early experience on later functioning, the distinctions between the two basic forms of psychopathology: conflict based and deficit based, with the different forms of psychoanalytic intervention appropriate for each. She used her own lifetime of experience and work with colleagues to create an extensive and detailed framework for the psychoanalytic study of development which remains immensely useful to all who care to use it, whether in treatment, research or in applications of psychoanalytic thinking to other professional services for children.

# Glossary

I have given here only terms introduced by Anna Freud, or having a particular usage in her work which may differ from that of some other psychoanalysts. Readers who require definitions of a wider range of psychoanalytic terms are referred to Rycroft (1968) or Laplanche and Pontalis (1973).

**Attachment**   The infant's earliest relationship with the mother (or mother-substitute). It develops in the early months of life out of the baby's experience of having needs satisfied and being nurtured by a particular person, so that the infant comes to prefer this person to others. This early attachment leads on to love for the object. If there is no object available to the child, or if the available object is inadequate in some way, or if the relationship is disrupted, there will follow serious disturbances in many areas of development which depend on the child's love for, wish to please and fear of losing the object. Anna Freud and John Bowlby agreed on the importance of early attachment, and on the psychopathological consequences of its disruption or failure to develop, but they propounded different theories of its development.

**Defences**   One of the major functions of the ego, conceptualised by Sigmund Freud in terms of mental forces which prevent us from becoming conscious of our instincts, wishes and feelings in their more primitive and raw forms. Only acceptable derivatives are allowed through to consciousness. In analysis, defences become evident in the form of resistance to free association. Anna Freud's contribution to the conceptualisation of defence was to enumerate in more detail both the methods of defence, and a developmental sequence showing the gradual shift from primitive to more mature forms of defence. The failure to develop age-adequate defences forms one of the important areas of deficit psychopathology. Her major contribution to psycho-analytic technique was her emphasis on the need to analyse the defences as well as the unconscious impulses, wishes and feelings.

**Developmental deficit**   Failure to develop normally in one or more areas. Specific areas of deficit can be pinpointed by using the developmental lines.

**Developmental delay**   The individual lags behind his expected level in some or all developmental lines.

**Developmental disharmony**   The individual is not developing evenly on all developmental lines. A certain amount of dis-harmony falls within normal bounds, but serious or persistent disharmony indicates psychopathology.

**Developmental help**   Techniques used by therapists for remedy-ing delays and deficits in development. They may make use of interpretation, but more often use verbalisation of feelings, clarification of cause and effect, demonstrations of how to think, how to make sense of the behaviour of other people and of one's own behaviour, how to manage one's own behaviour, etc. Individual therapists develop a multitude of ways to help individual patients to express themselves, to find meaning in their experience of themselves and others, and to develop inter-nal ways of controlling themselves. Anna Freud originally saw these techniques as educational rather than as part of psycho-analytic treatment, since they do not focus on interpretation of transference and resistance, and since they seek to rememdy not conflicts so much as defects which are either constitutional or due to environmental inadequacies in the child's upbringing. But eventually she moved towards the view that they do form part of psychoanalytic technique, since it takes the detailed understanding of the development of the internal world and of mental functioning to perceive precisely what is lacking in the child. She also reached the conclusion that most childhood disturbances are a mixture of deficit and conflict pathology.

**Developmental lines**   Areas of the personality in which progress occurs through the interaction of internal and external factors. In Sigmund Freud's structural theory three major areas of the personality are conceptualised. The id comprises the constitu-tional forces in the personality, especially the instinctual drives;

these operate largely outside consciousness. The ego develops out of the id and becomes that part of the personality most in touch with the demands of external reality; it exerts control over drives and affects, mediating between id, superego and external world; it is the part of the personality most easily recognised by the individual as himself. The superego is a further development out of the id, essentially the individual's conscience; it develops partly through identification with the demands and prohibitions of the child's parents or other important objects, partly through the ego's recognition of the dangers of uncontrolled instinctual behaviour. Anna Freud examined many areas in which aspects of these inner agencies – id, ego and superego – interact with external forces, especially the child's objects, to produce gradual progress in specific areas. The best known line, already described by Sigmund Freud and Abraham, was that from infantile to adult sexuality. Anna Freud added many more. In the paper which first introduced her concept of developmental lines she gave a central place to the line from dependency on the object, through the various stages of object relationships to adult self-reliance. She also described a line leading from egocentricity to the capacity for companionship with peers, several lines leading towards independence in areas of body management and care, and a line leading through various forms of play to the capacity for work. These lines were described in some detail. Later other lines were sketched out in less detail, for example, from somatic to mental pathways of discharge, from irresponsibility to the capacity for guilt, from primitive to mature forms of defence, lines towards mature forms of thinking, impulse control, reality sense, time sense, etc. Other lines were described by colleagues, for example, for insight, anxiety management and language.

**Developmental profile** (aka the diagnostic profile)   Anna Freud's schema for assessing a child's disturbance against the background of normal development, rather than in terms only of symptoms, which can be misleading in children. It is based on Sigmund Freud's structural theory, and breaks down information about an individual under headings which describe his developmental history, important environmental influences, the status of his drives, relationships, ego and superego functioning, affective states, conflicts and general personality characteristics. Its aim is to ensure that all aspects of the individual's functioning are considered, and thus to avoid partial or biased diagnoses. Once all areas of a person's development have been examined, the findings can be put together to give an overall diagnosis. Anna Freud originally devised the profile for assessing children, but it has subsequently been modified for babies, adolescents and adults, as well as for some forms of pathology which require special sections.

**Diagnostic profile**   *See* Developmental profile.

**Ego**   One of the agencies of the mind, consisting of functions which subserve the individual's comprehension of the realities of the external world, his awareness of his own internal world, and his ability to adapt to and manage both. It develops through the interaction of constitutional endowment and the influences of the environment, especially the stimulation, reinforcement and opportunities for identification provided by the adults who nurture the child. In Sigmund Freud's writings the concept of the ego often overlapped with the concept of self, being contrasted with the object; or it referred to the individual's conscious sense of himself. But Anna Freud followed Hartmann in differentiating between the concepts of self and ego, and she used the concept of the ego to refer to a collection of functions which are vital for the individual's control of his internal world and for his adaptation to the environment. She was aware that the concepts of id, ego and superego often get personified in describing internal conflict; but she believed this could be useful as long as we remain aware that we are talking about different aspects of one personality.

**Ego-dystonic**   Behaviour, feelings or symptoms which are unacceptable to the ego because they risk superego condemnation, disapproval of the object, or reality danger of some kind.

**Ego-syntonic**   Behaviour, feelings or symptoms which are acceptable to the ego. Anna Freud employs the term less often in its looser usage of fitting in with the individual's view of himself.

**Synthetic function of the ego**   The tendency to integrate all mental contents and processes. Anna Freud regarded this as a particularly important ego function, because it is the one which builds both normal and pathological aspects of mental functioning into the overall personality.

# Chronology

*3 December 1895*   Birth of Anna Freud in Vienna, youngest of Sigmund and Martha Freud's six children.

*1913*   Anna Freud began reading psychoanalysis.

*1915*   Anna Freud began work as an apprentice teacher.

*1917*   She became a certified teacher.

*1915–1918*   She attended ward rounds at the Psychiatric Clinic of the Vienna General Hospital.

*1918*   She began her psychoanalytic training.

*1922*   Elected to membership of the Vienna Psychoanalytic Society.

*1923*   She began accepting child patients for analysis.

*1927*   Publication of 'Four lectures on child analysis'.

*1930*   Publication of 'Four lectures on psychoanalysis for teachers and parents'.

*1936*   Publication of *The Ego and the Mechanisms of Defence*.

*1938*   Emigration to Britain.

*1939*   Death of Sigmund Freud.

*1941–1945*   The war nurseries.

*1943*   The controversial discussions.

*1948*   Anna Freud organises training in child analysis for former workers in the war nurseries.

*1952*   Opening of the Hampstead Clinic.

*1965*   Publication of *Normality and Pathology in Childhood: Assessments of Development*.

*9 October 1982*   Death of Anna Freud, following which the Hampstead Clinic was renamed The Anna Freud Centre.

# Bibliography

Abraham, K. (1924) 'A short study of the development of the libido: viewed in the light of mental disorders', in *Selected Papers on Psychoanalysis*, London: Maresfield Reprints.

Abrams, S. (1996) 'Differentiation and integration', *Psychoanalytic Study of the Child*, 25–34.

Aichhorn, A. (1925) *Wayward Youth*, London: Imago 1951.

Alexander, F. (1948) *Fundamentals of Psychoanalysis*, New York: International Universities Press.

Alpert, A. (1959) 'Reversibility of pathological fixations associated with maternal deprivation in infancy', *Psychoanalytic Study of the Child*, 14: 169–185.

Balint, M. (1968) *The Basic Fault*, London: Tavistock Publications Ltd.

Baradon, T. (1998) 'Michael: a journey from the physical to the mental realm', in Hurry, A. (ed.) *Psychoanalysis and Developmental Therapy*, London: Karnac, pp. 153–164.

Bene, A. (1979) 'The question of narcissistic personality disorders: self pathology in children', *Bulletin of the Hampstead Clinic*, 2: 209–218.

Bennett, I. and Hellman, I. (1951) 'Psychoanalytic material related to observations in early development', *Psychoanalytic Study of the Child*, 6: 307–324.

Berger, M. and Kennedy, H. (1975) 'Pseudobackwardness in children: maternal attitudes as an etiological factor', *Psychoanalytic Study of the Child*, 30: 279–306.

Bibring, E. (1937) 'On the theory of the therapeutic results of psychoanalysis', *International Journal of Psycho-analysis*, 18: 170–189.

—— (1954) 'Psychoanalysis and the dynamic psychotherapies', *Journal of the American Psychoanalytic Association*, 2: 745–770.

Bolland, J. and Sandler, J. (1965) *The Hampstead Psychoanalytic Index: A Study of the Psychoanalytic Case Material of a two-and-a-half-year-old child* [Monograph series of the Psychoanalytic Study of the Child, No. 1], New York: International Universities Press.

Bornstein, B. (1949) 'The analysis of a phobic child', *Psychoanalytic Study of the Child*, 3/4: 181–226.

Bowlby, J. (1958) 'The nature of the child's tie to his mother', *International Journal of Psycho-analysis*, 39: 350–373.

—— (1960a) 'Separation anxiety', *International Journal of Psycho-analysis*, 41: 89–113.

—— (1960b) 'Grief and mourning in infancy and early childhood', *Psychoanalytic Study of the Child*, 15: 9–52.

—— (1961) ' Note on Dr. Max Schur's comments on "Grief and mourning in infancy and early childhood", *Psychoanalytic Study of the Child*, 16: 206–208.

Bowlby, J., Robertson, J. and Rosenbluth, D. (1952) 'A two year old goes to Hospital', *Psychoanalytic Study of the Child*, 7: 82–94.

Brenner, C. (1982) *The Mind in Conflict*, New York: International Universities Press.

Brinich, P.M. (1981) 'Application of the metapsychological profile to the assessment of deaf children', *Psychoanalytic Study of the Child*, 36: 3–32.

Burgner, M. and Edgcumbe, R. (1973) 'Some problems in the conceptualisation of early object relationships; Part II: The concept of object constancy', *Psychoanalytic Study of the Child*, 27: 315–333.

Burlingham, D. (1952) *Twins: A Study of Three Pairs of Identical Twins*, New York: International Universities Press.

—— (1975) 'Special problems of blind infants: blind baby profile', *Psychoanalytic Study of the Child*, 30: 3–13.

Burlingham, D. and Barron, A.T. (1963) 'A study of identical twins: their analytic material compared with existing observation data of their early childhood', *Psychoanalytic Study of the Child*, 18: 367–423.

Burlingham, D., Goldberger, A. and Lussier, A. (1955) 'Simultaneous analysis of mother and child', *Psychoanaltyic Study of the Child*, 10: 165–186.

Colonna, A. (1996) 'Anna Freud: observation and development', *Psychoanalytic Study of the Child*, 51: 217–234.

Cooper, S.M. (1989) 'Recent contributions to the theory of defence mechanisms: a comparative view', *Journal of the American Psychoanalytic Society*, 37: 865–891.

Dyer, R. (1983) *Her Father's Daughter: The Work of Anna Freud*, New York: Jason Aronson.

Earle, E. (1979) 'The diagnostic profile: V. A latency boy', *Bulletin of the Hampstead Clinic*, 2: 77–95.

Edgcumbe, R. (1980) 'The diagnostic profile: VIII. A terminal profile on a latency boy', *Bulletin of the Hampstead Clinic*, 3: 5–20.

—— (1981) 'Towards a developmental line for the acquisition of language', *Psychoanalytic Study of the Child*, 36: 71–103.

—— (1983) 'Anna Freud – child analyst', *International Journal of Psychoanalysis*, 64: 427–433.

—— (1995) 'The history of Anna Freud's thinking on developmental disturbances', *Bulletin of the Anna Freud Centre*, 18, 1: 21–34.

Edgcumbe, R. and Burgner, M. (1973) 'Some problems in the conceptualisation of early object relationships; Part I: The concepts of need-satisfaction and need-satisfying relationships', *Psychoanalytic Study of the Child*, 27: 283–314.

—— (1975) 'The phallic-narcissistic phase: a differentiation between pre-oedipal and oedipal aspects of phallic development', *Psychoanalytic Study of the Child*, 30: 161–180.

Edgcumbe, R., Lundberg, S., Markowitz, R. and Salo, F. (1976) 'Some comments on the concept of the negative oedipal phase in girls', *Psychoanalytic Study of the Child*, 31: 35–62.

Eissler, K. (1950) 'Ego-psychological implications of the psychoanalytic treatment of delinquents', *Psychoanalytic Study of the Child*, 5: 97–121.

Eissler, K., Freud, A., Kris E. and Solnit, A. (eds) (1977) *Psychoanalytic Assessments: The Diagnostic Profile*, New Haven and London: Yale University Press.

Ekins, R. and Freeman, R. (1998) *Selected Writings by Anna Freud*, Harmondsworth: Penguin Books.

Elliott-Neely, C. (1996) 'The analytic resolution of a developmental imbalance', *Psychoanalytic Study of the Child*, 51: 235–254.

Fabricius, J. (1993) 'Developmental breakdown in young adulthood: some manifestations and precipitants', *Bulletin of the Anna Freud Centre*, 16: 41–55.

Fairbairn, W.R.D. (1952) *Psychoanalytic Studies of the Personality*, London: Routledge & Kegan Paul.

Ferenczi, S. (1909) 'Introjection and transference', in *Sex in Psychoanalysis*, New York: Basic Books (1950), pp. 35–93.

Flashman, A.J. (1996) 'Developing developmental lines', *Psychoanalytic Study of the Child*, 51: 255–269.

Fonagy, P. and Tallandini-Shallice, M. (1993) 'Problems of psychoanalytic research in practice', *Bulletin of the Anna Freud Centre*, 16: 5–22.

Fonagy, P. and Target, M. (1996a) 'A contemporary psychoanalytic perspective: psychodynamic developmental therapy', in Hibbs, E. and Jensen, P. (eds) *Psychosocial Treatments for Child and Adolescent Disorders*, Washington, DC: American Psychological Association.

—— —— (1996b) 'Predictors of outcome in child psychoanalysis: a retrospective study of 763 cases at the Anna Freud Centre', *Journal of American Psychoanalytic Association*, 44: 27–73.

Fonagy, P., Moran, G.S., Edgcumbe, R., Kennedy, H. and Target, M. (1993a) 'The roles of mental representation and mental processes in therapeutic action', *Psychoanalytic Study of the Child*, 48: 9–48.

Fonagy, P., Steele, M., Moran, G., Steele, H. and Higgitt, A. (1993b) 'Measuring the ghost in the nursery: an empirical study of the relation between parents' mental representations of childhood experiences and their infants' security of attachment', *Journal of American Psychoanalytic Association*, 41: 957–989.

Freeman, T. (1973) *A Psychoanalytic Study of the Psychoses*, New York: International Universities Press.

—— (1975) 'The use of the profile schema for the psychotic patient', in *Studies in Child Psychoanalysis: Pure and Applied*, New Haven and London, Yale University Press.

—— (1976) *Childhood Psychopathology and Adult Psychoses*, New York: International Universities Press.

—— (1983) 'Anna Freud – psychiatrist', *International Journal of Psychoanalysis*, 64: 441–444.

Freud, A. (1927) 'Four lectures on child analysis', *The Writings of Anna Freud*, 1, pp. 3–69, New York: International Universities Press (1974).

—— (1928) 'The theory of child analysis', *The Writings of Anna Freud*, 1, pp. 162–175, New York: International Universities Press (1974).

—— (1930) 'Four lectures on psycho-analysis for teachers and parents', *The Writings of Anna Freud*, 1, pp. 73–133, New York: International Universities Press (1974).

—— (1934 [1932]) 'Psychoanalysis and the upbringing of the young child', *The Writings of Anna Freud*, 1, pp. 176–188, New York: International Universities Press (1974).

—— (1936) *The Ego and the Mechanisms of Defence*, London: Karnac (revised 1993).

—— (1945) 'Indications for child analysis', *The Writings of Anna Freud*, 4, pp. 3–38, New York: International Universities Press (1968).

—— (1946a) 'Freedom from want in early education', *The Writings of Anna Freud*, 4, pp. 425–441, New York: International Universities Press (1968).

—— (1946b) 'The psychoanalytic study of infantile feeding disturbances', *The Writings of Anna Freud*, 4, pp. 39–59, New York: International Universities Press (1968).

—— (1947) 'The establishment of feeding habits', *The Writings of Anna Freud*, 4, pp. 442–457, New York: International Universities Press (1968).

—— (1949a) 'Aggression in relation to emotional development: normal and pathological', *The Writings of Anna Freud*, 4, pp. 489–497, New York: International Universities Press (1968).

—— (1949b) 'On certain difficulties in the pre-adolescent's relation to his parents', *The Writings of Anna Freud*, 4, pp. 95–106, New York: International Universities Press (1968).

—— (1949c) 'Notes on aggression', *The Writings of Anna Freud*, 4, pp. 60–74, New York: International Universities Press (1968).

—— (1949d) 'Certain types and stages of social maladjustment', *The Writings of Anna Freud*, 4, pp. 75–94, New York: International Universities Press (1968).

—— (1949e) 'Nursery school education: its uses and dangers', *The Writings of Anna Freud*, 4, pp. 545–559, New York: International Universities Press (1968).

—— (1950) 'The significance of the evolution of psychoanalytic child psychology', *The Writings of Anna Freud*, 4, pp. 614–624, New York: International Universities Press (1968).

—— (1951a) 'Observations on child development', *The Writings of Anna Freud*, 4, pp. 143–162, New York: International Universities Press (1968).

—— (1951b) 'An experiment in group upbringing', *The Writings of Anna Freud*, 4, pp. 163–229, New York: International Universities Press (1968).

—— (1952a) 'Answering teachers' questions', *The Writings of Anna Freud*, 4, pp. 560–568, New York: International Universities Press (1968).

—— (1952b) 'The role of bodily illness in the mental life of children', *The Writings of Anna Freud*, 4, pp. 260–279, New York: International Universities Press (1968).

—— (1952c) 'The mutual influences in the development of ego and id: introduction to the discussion', *The Writings of Anna Freud*, 4, pp. 230–244, New York: International Universities Press (1968).

—— (1953a) 'Some remarks on infant observation', *The Writings of Anna Freud*, 4, pp. 569–585, New York: International Universities Press (1968).

—— (1953b) 'Instinctual drives and their bearing on human behaviour', *The Writings of Anna Freud*, 4, pp. 498–527, New York: International Universities Press (1968).

—— (1953c) 'James Robertson's *A Two-year-old Goes to Hospital*: Film review', *The Writings of Anna Freud*, 4, pp. 280–292, New York: International Universities Press (1968).

—— (1955) 'The concept of the rejecting mother', *The Writings of Anna Freud*, 4, pp. 586–602, New York: International Universities Press (1968).

—— (1957) 'The Hampstead Child-Therapy Course and Clinic', *The Writings of Anna Freud*, 5, pp. 3–8, New York: International Universities Press (1969).

—— (1957–1960) 'Research projects of the Hampstead Child-Therapy Clinic', *The Writings of Anna Freud*, 5, pp. 9–25, New York: International Universities Press (1969).

—— (1958a) 'Child observation and prediction of development: a memorial lecture in honor of Ernst Kris', *The Writings of Anna Freud*, 5, pp. 102–135, New York: International Universities Press (1969).

—— (1958b) 'Adolescence', *The Writings of Anna Freud*, 5, pp. 136–166, New York: International Universities Press (1969).

—— (1960a) 'Discussion of Dr. John Bowlby's paper', *Psychoanalytic Study of the Child*, 15: 53–62.

—— (1960b) 'Entry into nursery school: the psychological pre-requisites', *The Writings of Anna Freud*, 5, pp. 315–335, New York: International Universities Press (1968).

—— (1960c [1957]) 'The child guidance clinic as a centre of prophylaxis and enlightenment', *The Writings of Anna Freud*, 5, pp. 281–300, New York: International Universities Press (1969).

—— (1961) 'Answering paediatricians' questions', *The Writings of Anna Freud*, 5, pp. 379–406, New York: International Universities Press (1969).

—— (1962a) 'Assessment of childhood disturbances', *Psychoanalytic Study of the Child* 17: 149–158.

—— (1962b) 'The emotional and social development of young children', *The Writings of Anna Freud*, 5, pp. 336–351, New York: International Universities Press (1969).

—— (1963a) 'The concept of developmental lines', *Psychoanalytic Study of the Child*, 18: 245–265.

—— (1963b) 'The role of regression in human development', *The Writings of Anna Freud*, 5, pp. 407–418, New York: International Universities Press (1969).

—— (1964) 'Psychoanalytic knowledge and its application to children's services', *The Writings of Anna Freud*, 5, pp. 460–469, New York: International Universities Press (1969).

—— (1965a) *Normality and Pathology in Childhood: Assessments of Development*, London: Karnac 1989.

—— (1965b) 'Three contributions to a seminar on family law', *The Writings of Anna Freud*, 5, pp. 436–459, New York: International Universities Press (1969).

—— (1966a) 'Interactions between nursery school and child guidance clinic', *The Writings of Anna Freud*, 5, pp. 369–378, New York: International Universities Press (1969).

—— (1966b) 'Links between Hartmann's ego psychology and the child analyst's thinking', *The Writings of Anna Freud*, 5, pp. 204–220, New York: International Universities Press (1969).

—— (1966c) 'A short history of child analysis', *The Writings of Anna Freud*, 7, pp. 48–58, New York: International Universities Press (1971).

—— (1967a [1953]) 'About losing and being lost', *The Writings of Anna Freud*, 4, pp. 302–316, New York: International Universities Press (1968).

—— (1967b) 'Residential vs. foster care', *The Writings of Anna Freud*, 7, pp. 223–239, New York: International Universities Press (1971).

—— (1968a [1949]) 'Expert knowledge for the average mother', *The Writings of Anna Freud*, 4, pp. 528–544, New York: International Universities Press (1968).

—— (1968b) 'Acting out', *The Writings of Anna Freud*, 7, pp. 94–109, New York: International Universities Press (1971).

—— (1968c) 'Indications and contraindications for child analysis', *The Writings of Anna Freud*, 7, pp. 110–123, New York: International Universities Press (1971).

—— (1969a) 'Discussion of John Bowlby's work on separation, grief and mourning', *The Writings of Anna Freud*, 5, pp. 167–186, New York: International Universities Press (1969).

—— (1969b [1962–1966]) 'Assessment of pathology in childhood', *The Writings of Anna Freud*, 5, pp. 26–59, New York: International Universities Press (1969).

—— (1969c) 'Difficulties in the path of psychoanalysis: a confrontation of past with present viewpoints', *The Writings of Anna Freud*, 7, pp. 124–156, New York: International Universities Press (1971).

—— (1969d) 'Film review: *John, Seventeen Months: Nine Days in a Residential Nursery* by James and Joyce Robertson, *The Writings of Anna Freud*, 7, pp. 240–246, New York: International Universities Press (1971).

—— (1969e [1964]) 'Comments on psychic trauma', *The Writings of Anna Freud*, 5, pp. 221–241, New York: International Universities Press (1969).

—— (1969f [1956]) 'The assessment of borerline cases', *The Writings of Anna Freud*, 5, pp. 301–314, New York: International Universities Press (1969).

—— (1969g) 'Adolescence as a developmental disturbance', *The Writings of Anna Freud*, 7, pp. 39–47, New York: International Universities Press (1971).

—— (1970) 'The symptomatology of childhood: a preliminary attempt at classification', *The Writings of Anna Freud*, 7, pp. 157–188, New York: International Universities Press (1971).

—— (1971a) 'Problems of termination in child analysis', *The Writings of Anna Freud*, 7, pp. 3–21, New York: International Universities Press (1971).

—— (1971b [1970b]) 'The infantile neurosis: genetic and dynamic considerations', *The Writings of Anna Freud*, 7, pp. 189–203, New York: International Universities Press (1971).

—— (1971c [1970c] 'Child analysis as a sub-speciality of psychoanalysis', *The Writings of Anna Freud*, 7, pp. 204–219, New York: International Universities Press (1971).

—— (1972) 'Comments on aggression', *The Writings of Anna Freud*, 8, pp. 151–175, New York: International Universities Press (1981).

—— (1974a) 'Introduction to psychoanalysis', *The Writings of Anna Freud*, 1, New York: International Universities Press (1974).

—— (1974b [1954]) 'Diagnosis and assessment of childhood disturbances', *The Writings of Anna Freud*, 8, pp. 34–56, New York: International Universities Press (1981).

—— (1974c) 'A psychoanalytic view of developmental psychopathology', *The Writings of Anna Freud*, 8, pp. 57–74, New York: International Universities Press (1981).

—— (1975a) 'On the interaction between paediatrics and child psychology', *The Writings of Anna Freud*, 8, pp. 285–299, New York: International Universities Press (1981).

—— (1975b) 'Children possessed: Anna Freud looks at a central concern of the children's bill: the psychological needs of adopted children', *The Writings of Anna Freud*, 8, pp. 300–306, New York: International Universities Press (1981).

—— (1976a) 'Changes in psychoanalytic practice and experience', *The Writings of Anna Freud*, 8, pp. 176–185, New York: International Universities Press (1981).

—— (1976b) 'August Aichhorn', *The Writings of Anna Freud*, 8, pp. 344–345, New York: International Universities Press (1981).

—— (1977) 'Concerning the relationship with children', *The Writings of Anna Freud*, 8, pp. 96–109, New York: International Universities Press (1981).

—— (1978a) 'The principal task of child analysis', *The Writings of Anna Freud*, 8, pp. 96–109, New York: International Universities Press (1981).

—— (1978b) 'A study guide to Freud's writings', *The Writings of Anna Freud*, 8, pp. 209–276, New York: International Universities Press (1981).

—— (1979a) 'The role of insight in psychoanalysis and psychotherapy: introduction', *The Writings of Anna Freud*, 8, pp. 201–205, New York: International Universities Press (1981).

—— (1979b) 'Personal memories of Ernest Jones', *The Writings of Anna Freud*, 8, pp. 346–353, New York: International Universities Press (1981).

—— (1981a) 'Insight: its presence and absence as a factor in normal development', *The Writings of Anna Freud*, 8, pp. 137–148, New York: International Universities Press (1981).

—— (1981b [1972]) 'The widening scope of psychoanalytic child psychology, normal and abnormal', *The Writings of Anna Freud*, 8, pp. 8–33, New York: International Universities Press (1981).

—— (1981c [1974b]) 'Beyond the infantile neurosis', *The Writings of Anna Freud*, 8, pp. 75–81, New York: International Universities Press (1981).

—— (1981d [1976c]) 'Dynamic psychology and education', *The Writings of*

*Anna Freud*, 8, pp. 307–314, New York: International Universities Press (1981).

—— (1981e [1979b]) 'Child analysis as the study of mental growth, normal and abnormal', *The Writings of Anna Freud*, 8, pp. 119–136, New York: International Universities Press (1981).

—— (1981f [1979c]) 'The nursery school from the psychoanalytic point of view', *The Writings of Anna Freud*, 8, pp. 315–330, New York: International Universities Press (1981).

—— (1983) 'The past revisited', *Bulletin of the Hampstead Clinic*, 6: 107–113.

Freud A. and Burlingham, D. (1944) 'Infants without families: the case for and against residential nurseries', in *Infants without Families and Reports on the Hampstead Nurseries 1939–1945*, London: Hogarth (1974), pp. 543–664.

—— —— (1974 [1940–1945]) 'Reports on the Hampstead nurseries', in *Infants without Families and Reports on the Hampstead Nurseries 1939–1945*, London: Hogarth, pp. 3–540.

Freud, A., Nagera, H. and Freud, W.E. (1965) 'Metapsychological assessment of the adult personality: the adult profile', *Psychoanalytic Study of the Child*, 20: 9–41.

Freud, S. (1893) 'On the psychical mechanism of hysterical phenomena: a lecture', *Standard Edition of the Complete Psychological Works of Sigmund Freud (S.E.)*, 3, pp. 27–39.

—— (1905) 'Three essays on the theory of sexuality', *S.E.*, 7, pp. 130–243.

—— (1909) 'Analysis of a phobia in a five year old boy', *S.E.*, 10, pp. 5–149.

—— (1911) 'Formulations on the two principles of mental functioning', *S.E.*, 12, pp. 218–226.

—— (1914) 'On narcissism: an introduction', *S.E.*, 14, pp. 73-102.

—— (1915) 'Instincts and their vicissitudes', *S.E.*, 14, pp. 109–140.

—— (1920) 'Beyond the pleasure principle', *S.E.*, 18, pp. 7–64.

—— (1923) 'The ego and the id', *S.E.*, 19, pp. 3–66.

—— (1926) 'Inhibitions, symptoms and anxiety', *S.E.*, 20, pp. 75–175.

—— (1930) 'Civilisation and its discontents', *S.E.*, 21, pp. 64–145.

—— (1937) 'Analysis terminable and interminable', *S.E.*, 23, pp. 209–253.

Freud, W.E. (1967) 'Assessments of early infancy: problems and considerations', *Psychoanalytic Study of the Child*, 22: 216–238.

—— (1971) 'The Baby Profile: Part II', *Psychoanalytic Study of the Child*, 26: 172–194.

Furman, E. (1992) *Toddlers and their Mothers: A Study in early Personality Development*, Madison, CT: International Universities Press, Inc.

—— (1995) 'Memories of a "qualified student"', *Journal of Child Psychotherapy*, 21: 309–312.

Gavshon, A. (1987) 'Treatment of an atypical boy', *Psychoanalytic Study of the Child*, 42: 145–171.

Geissman, C. and Geissman, P. (1998) *A History of Child Psychoanalysis*, London: Routledge.

Goldstein, J. (1984) 'Anna Freud in law', *Psychoanalytic Study of the Child*, 39: 3–13.

Goldstein, J., Freud, A. and Solnit, A.J. (1973) *Beyond the Best Interests of the Child*, New York: Free Press/Macmillan.

—— (1979) *Before the Best Interests of the Child*, New York: Free Press/ Macmillan.

—— (1986) *In the Best Interests of the Child: Professional Boundaries*, New York: Free Press/Macmillan.

Green, V. (1998) 'Donald: the treatment of a 5-year-old boy with experience of early loss', in Hurry, A. (ed.) *Psychoanalysis and Developmental Therapy*, London: Karnac, pp. 136–52.

Greenberg, J.R. and Mitchell, S.A. (1983) *Object Relations in Psychoanalytic Theory*, Cambridge, MA, and London: Harvard University Press.

Greenspan, S.I. (1997) *Developmentally Based Psychotherapy*, Madison, CT: International Universities Press.

Grosskurth, P. (1986) *Melanie Klein*, London: Hodder and Stoughton.

Harrison, A. (1998) 'Martha: establishing analytic treatment with a 4-year-old girl', in Hurry, A. (ed.) *Psychoanalysis and Developmental Therapy*, London: Karnac, pp. 124–135.

Hartmann, H. (1939) *Ego Psychology and the Problem of Adaptation*, London: Imago (1958).

—— (1950a) 'Psychoanalysis and developmental psychology', *Psychoanalytic Study of the Child*, 5: 7–17.

—— (1950b) 'Comments on the psychoanalytic theory of the ego', *Psychoanalytic Study of the Child*, 5: 74–96.

—— (1952) 'The mutual influences in the development of ego and id', *Psychoanalytic Study of the Child*, 7: 9–30.

Hayman, A. (1994) 'Some remarks about the "Controversial discussions"', *International Journal of Psycho-analysis*, 75: 343–358.

Heinicke, C.M. (1965) 'Frequency of psychotherapeutic session as a factor affecting the child's developmental status', *Psychoanalytic Study of the Child*, 20: 42–98.

Heller, P. (1990) *A Child Analysis with Anna Freud*, Madison, CT: International Universities Press.

Hellman, I. (1962) 'Hampstead nursery follow-up studies: I. Sudden separation', *Psychoanalytic Study of the Child*, 17: 159–174.

Hellman, I., Friedmann, O. and Shepheard, E. (1960) 'Simultaneous analysis of mother and child', *Psychoanalytic Study of the Child*, 15: 359–377.

Hodges, J. (in preparation) 'Self, others and defensive processes as represented in the narratives of severely abused and neglected children removed from their parents'.

Hoffer, W. (1952) 'The mutual influences in the development of ego and id: earliest stages', *Psychoanalytic Study of the Child*, 7: 31–41.

Holder, A. (1975) 'Theoretical and clinical aspects of ambivalence', *Psychoanalytic Study of the Child*, 30: 197–220.

Holmes, J. (1993) *John Bowlby and Attachment Theory*, London & New York: Routledge.

Hurry, A. (ed.) (1998) *Psychoanalysis and Developmental Therapy*, London: Karnac.

Jacobson, E. (1946) 'The effect of disappointment on ego and superego formation in normal and depressive development', *Psychoanalytic Review*, 33: 129–147.

James, M. (1960) 'Premature ego development: some observations upon disturbances in the first three years of life', *International Journal of Psycho-analysis*, 41: 288–294.

Joffe, W.G. and Sandler, J. (1965) 'Notes on pain, depression and individuation', *Psychoanalytic Study of the Child*, 20: 394–424.

Kennedy, H.E. (1950) 'Cover memories in formation', *Psychoanalytic Study of the Child*, 5: 275–284.

—— (1979) 'The role of insight in child analysis', *Journal of American Psychoanalytic Association*, Supplement 27: 9–28.

King, P. (1994) 'The evolution of controversial issues', *International Journal of Psycho-analysis*, 75: 335–342.

King, P. and Steiner, R. (eds) (1991) *The Freud–Klein Controversies 1941–45*, London and New York: Tavistock/Routledge.

Klein, M. (1932) *The Psychoanalysis of Children, The Writings of Melanie Klein*, 2. Hogarth and Institute of Psychoanalysis (1980).

—— (1935) 'A contribution to the psychogenesis of manic-depressive states', *The Writings of Melanie Klein*, 1: 262–289. Hogarth and Institute of Psychoanalysis (1981).

—— (1946) 'Notes on some schizoid mechanisms', *The Writings of Melanie Klein*, 3: 1–24. Hogarth and Institute of Psychoanalysis (1981).

—— (1957) 'Envy and gratitude', *The Writings of Melanie Klein*, 3: 176–235. Hogarth and Institute of Psychoanalysis (1981).

Lament, C. (1983) 'The diagnostic profile: XIV. A latency girl', *Bulletin of the Hampstead Clinic*, 6: 351–383.

Laplanche, J. and Pontalis, J.B. (1973) *The Language of Psychoanalysis*, London: Hogarth.

Laufer, M. (1965) 'Assessment of adolescent disturbances: the application of Anna Freud's diagnostic profile', *Psychoanalytic Study of the Child*, 20: 99–123.

Laufer, M. and Laufer, M.E. (1984) *Adolescence and Developmental*

*Breakdown: A Psychoanalytic View*, New Haven and London: Yale University Press.

—— — (eds) (1989) *Developmental Breakdown and Psychoanalytic Treatment in Adolescence: Clinical Studies*, New Haven and London: Yale University Press.

Levy, K. (1960) 'Simultaneous analysis of a mother and her adolescent daughter: the mother's contribution to the loosening of the infantile object tie', *Psychoanalytic Study of the Child*, 15: 378–391.

Likierman, M. (1995) 'The debate between Anna Freud and Melanie Klein: an historical survey', *Journal of Child Psychotherapy*, 21: 313–325.

McLean, D. (1993) 'Provisional diagnostic profile on a young adult', *Bulletin of the Anna Freud Centre*, 16: 27–40.

Mahler, M. (1968) *On Human Symbiosis and the Vicissitudes of Individuation*, New York: International Universities Press.

Mahler, M. and Gosliner, B.J. (1955) 'On symbiotic child psychosis: genetic, dynamic and restitutive aspects', *Psychoanalytic Study of the Child*, 10: 195–212.

Mahler, M., Pine, F. and Bergman, A. (1975) *The Psychological Birth of the Human Infant*, New York: Basic Books.

Marans, S. (1996) 'Psychoanalysis on the beat: children, police and urban trauma', *Psychoanalytic Study of the Child*, 51: 522–541.

Martindale, B. (1993) 'To stay – or not stay – at home with mother', *Bulletin of the Anna Freud Centre*, 16: 77–89.

Mayes, L.C. and Cohen, D.J. (1996) 'Anna Freud and developmental psychoanalytic psychology', *Psychoanalytic Study of the Child*, 51: 117–141.

Miller, J. (1993) 'The development and validation of a manual of child psychoanalysis', Doctoral thesis, University of London.

—— (1996) 'Anna Freud: a historical look at her theory and technique of child analysis', *Psychoanalytic Study of the Child*, 51: 142–171.

Moran, G.S. and Fonagy, P. (1987) 'Psychoanalysis and diabetic control: a single case study', *British Journal of Medical Psychology*, 60: 357–372.

Nagera, H. (1966) *Early Childhood Disturbances, the Infantile Neurosis and the Adulthood Disturbances*, New York: International Universities Press.

Nagera, H. and Colonna, A. (1965) 'Aspects of the contribution of sight to ego and drive development: a comparison of the development of some blind and sighted children', *Psychoanalytic Study of the Child*, 20: 267–287.

Neubauer, P.B. (1984) 'Anna Freud's concept of developmental lines', *Psychoanalytic Study of the Child*, 39: 15–27.

—— (1996) 'Current issues in psychoanalytic child development', *Psychoanalytic Study of the Child*, 51: 35–45.

Novick, J. and Novick, K.K. (1972) 'Beating fantasies in children'. *International Journal of Psycho-analysis*, 53: 237–242.

Penman, A. (1995) 'There has never been anything like a classical child analysis': Clinical discussions with Anna Freud: 1970–1971. Unpublished paper.

Perelberg, R. (1999) *The Psychoanalytic Understanding of Violence and Suicide*, London: Routledge.

Peters, U.H. (1985) *Anna Freud: A Life dedicated to Children*, London: Weidenfeld & Nicolson.

Radford, P. (1980) 'The diagnostic profile: IX. A comparison of two sections from the profiles of two deaf boys', *Bulletin of the Hampstead Clinic*, 6: 351–383.

Radford, P., Wiseberg, S. and Yorke, C. (1972) 'A study of main-line heroin addiction: a preliminary report', *Psychoanalytic Study of the Child*, 27: 156–180.

Robertson, J. (1952) *Film: A Two Year Old Goes to Hospital*, London: Tavistock.

Roberston, J. and Robertson, J. (1971) 'Young children in brief separation: a fresh look', *Psychoanalytic Study of the Child*, 26: 264–315.

Rycroft, C. (1968) *A Critical Dictionary of Psychoanalysis*, Harmondsworth: Penguin Books (1972).

Sandler, A-M. (1996) 'The psychoanalytic legacy of Anna Freud', *Psychoanalytic Study of the Child*, 51: 270–284.

Sandler, J. (1960) 'On the concept of superego', *Psychoanalytic Study of the Child*, 15: 128–162.

Sandler, J. and Freud, A. (1985) *The Analysis of Defence: The Ego and the Mechanisms of Defence Revisited*, New York: International Universities Press.

Sandler, J. and Joffe, W.G. (1965) 'Notes on obsessional manifestations in children', *Psychoanalytic Study of the Child*, 20: 425–438.

Sandler, J. and Nagera, H. (1963) 'Aspects of the metapsychology of fantasy', *Psychoanalytic Study of the Child*, 18: 159–194.

Sandler, J. and Rosenblatt, B. (1962) 'The concept of the representational world', *Psychoanalytic Study of the Child*, 17: 128–145.

Sandler, J. and Sandler, A-M. (1994) 'Phantasy and its transformations: a contemporary Freudian view', *International Journal of Psycho-analysis*, 75: 387–394.

Sandler, J. Holder, A. and Meers, D. (1963) 'The ego ideal and the ideal self', *Psychoanalytic Study of the Child*, 18: 139–158.

Sandler, J., Kennedy, H. and Tyson, R.L. (1980) *The Technique of Child Psychoanalysis*, London: Karnac (1990).

Sandler, J., Kawenoka, M., Neurath, L., Rosenblatt, B., Schnurmann, A. and Sigal, J. (1962) 'The classification of superego material in the Hampstead index', *Psychoanalytic Study of the Child*, 17: 107–127.

Schachter, J. (1993) 'A young man's search for a masculine identity', *Bulletin of the Anna Freud Centre*, 16: 61–72.

Schafer, R. (1994) 'One perspective on the Freud–Klein controversies 1941–5', *International Journal of Psycho-analysis*, 75: 359–366.

Schur, M. (1960) 'Discussion of Dr. John Bowlby's paper', *Psychoanalytic Study of the Child*, 15: 63–84.

Segal, H. (1964) *Introduction to the Work of Melanie Klein*, London: Hogarth (1978).

—— (1979) *Klein*, London: Fontana/Collins.

—— (1994) 'Phantasy and reality', *International Journal of Psychoanalysis*, 75: 395–401.

Solnit, A.J. and Newman, L.M. (1984) 'Anna Freud: the child expert', *Psychoanalytic Study of the Child*, 39: 45–63.

Spitz, R. (1946) 'Anaclitic depression', *Psychoanalytic Study of the Child*, 2: 313–342.

—— (1960) 'Discussion of Dr. Bowlby's paper', *Psychoanalytic Study of the Child*, 15: 85–94.

—— (1965) *The First Year of Life*, New York: International Universities Press.

Sprince, M.P. (1962) 'The development of a pre-Oedipal partnership between an adolescent girl and her mother', *Psychoanalytic Study of the Child*, 17: 418–450.

Steele, M., Kaniuk, J., Hodges, J. and Hayworth, C. (1999a) 'The use of the adult attachment interview: implications for adoption and foster care', in Byrne, S. (ed.) *Assessment, Preparation and Support: Implications from Research*, London: British Agencies for Adoption and Fostering Publications.

Steele, M., Hodges, J., Kaniuk, J., Henderson, S., Hillman, S. and Bennett, P. (1999b) 'The use of story stem narratives in assessing the inner world of the child: implications for adoptive placements', in Byrne, S. (ed.) *Assessment, Preparation and Support: Implications from Research*, London: British Agencies for Adoption and Fostering Publications.

Target, M. and Kennedy, H. (1991) 'Psychoanalytic work with under-fives: forty years experience', *Bulletin of the Anna Freud Centre*, 14: 5–29.

Thomas, R. in collaboration with Edgcumbe, R., Kennedy, J., Kawenoka, M. and Weitzner, L. (1966) 'Comments on some aspects of self and object representation in a group of psychotic children: an application of Anna Freud's diagnostic profile', *Psychoanalytic Study of the Child*, 21: 527–580.

Tyson, P. and Tyson, R.L. (1990) *Psychoanalytic Theories of Development: An Integration*, New Haven, CT: Yale University Press.

Wallerstein, R.S. (1984) 'Anna Freud: radical innovator and staunch conservative', *Psychoanalytic Study of the Child*, 39: 65–80.

—— (1988) 'Final summing up: international colloquium on playing: its role in child and adult psychoanalysis', *Bulletin of the Anna Freud Centre*, 11: 168–182.

Winnicott, D.W. (1949) *The Ordinary Devoted Mother and her Baby*, London: Tavistock Publications.

—— (1951) 'Transitional objects and transitional phenomena: a study of the first not-me possession', in *Through Paediatrics to Psycho-analysis*, London: Hogarth (1958).

—— (1960a) 'The theory of the parent–infant relationship', *International Journal of Psycho-analysis*, 41: 585–595.

—— (1960b) 'Ego distortion in terms of true and false self', in *The Maturational Processes and the Facilitating Environment*, London: Hogarth.

Wiseberg, S., Yorke, C. and Radford, P. (1975) 'Aspects of self cathexis in mainline heroin addiction', in *Studies in Child Psychoanalysis: Pure and Applied*, New Haven, CT, and London: Yale University Press.

Yorke, C. (1983) 'Anna Freud and the psychoanalytic study and treatment of adults', *International Journal of Psycho-analysis*, 64: 391–400.

—— (1996) 'Anna Freud's contributions to our knowledge of child development: an overview', *Psychoanalytic Study of the Child*, 51: 7–24.

—— (1997) *Anna Freud*, Paris: Presses Universitaires de France.

Yorke, C., Wiseberg, S. and Freeman, T. (1989) *Development and Psychopathology*, New Haven, CT, and London: Yale University Press.

Young-Bruehl, E. (1988) *Anna Freud*, London: Macmillan.

Zaphiriou-Woods, M. and Gedulter-Trieman, A. (1998) 'Maya: the interplay of nursery education and analysis in restoring a child to the path of normal development', in Hurry, A. (ed.) *Psychoanalysis and Developmental Therapy*, London: Karnac.

# Index